NEW ENGLAND
PROSPECTS

FUTURES OF NEW ENGLAND

NEW ENGLAND PROSPECTS
Critical Choices in a Time of Change
CARL H. REIDEL, *EDITOR*, 1982

WILDLANDS AND WOODLOTS
The Story of New England's Forests
LLOYD C. IRLAND, 1982

THE NEW ENGLAND REGIONAL PLAN
An Economic Development Strategy
NEW ENGLAND REGIONAL COMMISSION, 1981

BUSINESS AND ACADEMIA
Partners in New England's Economic Renewal
JOHN C. HOY AND MELVIN BERNSTEIN, *EDITORS*, 1981

NEW ENGLAND PROSPECTS

Critical Choices in a Time of Change

CARL H. REIDEL, editor

UNIVERSITY PRESS OF NEW ENGLAND

Hanover and London, 1982

Library of Congress Catalogue Card Number 81-51604
International Standard Book Number 0-87451-213-1 (cloth)
0-87451-220-4 (paper)
Library of Congress Cataloging in Publication Data will be found on the last printed page of this book.

CONTENTS

PREFACE

THE SIX ESSAYS that follow, commissioned for this book by the University Press of New England, offer a wide-ranging and provocative look at some of the major forces that will shape the future of New England. The writers have chosen to focus on several especially critical problems and policy issues rather than attempt an all-inclusive examination of the region's future prospects. And though they do not share a common style or shared vision of the future, they do illustrate the importance of drawing on scholars with diverse backgrounds and experiences who can speak convincingly about the options and alternatives before the people of New England.

These writers present compelling evidence that New England in the years immediately ahead will be confronted with critical choices of ways to manage its resources, provide essential human services, preserve the region's heritage, and adapt to new technology and rapidly changing economic, social, and political conditions. The argument is persuasive that decisions made in the decade of the 1980s, in response to changes taking place in the region and to national and global forces, will shape the character of life in New England for decades into the future. Their evidence is set forth objectively and comprehensively, and they explore the implications of their findings without being doctrinaire. They warn us of the hazards of simply allowing the future to overtake us, and offer new insights into the possibilities for shaping the future through conscious choice.

Although each of the essays addresses a discrete set of issues, reflecting the disciplinary perspectives of the individual authors, all are concerned with two interrelated themes. First, although the essays focus specifically on the six states of New England, and the potential for the region to make meaningful choices among future options present and future, they also speak to the nation at large by asserting the relevance of all regions as appropriate units of landscape and society to make these choices, even though forces influencing the choices are national and global in origin. The essayists share with René Dubos the notion that an environmentally sound future will rest on our ability to "think global and act local."

Secondly, the authors insist that the process of weighing and choosing future alternatives must include careful consideration of vital human and ecological values—ones that define our "quality of life" now and in the future. These important values, they point out, are often ignored or undervalued in such usual measures of the conditions of life in America as Gross National Product, productivity indexes, and similar indicators of material achievement. Here again they speak not only to people of New England but to those across the nation.

In the introductory essay, Thomas Jorling confronts directly the need for defining new decision-making criteria which encompass the quality-of-life concerns expressed by the other writers in this volume. Such criteria, he insists, must be sensitive to the essential interrelationships between fundamental natural systems and social choice. Linking the impacts of our technological and geographic "distance" from essential resources to the ideals of freedom, liberty, and independence, he turns to the basic laws of thermodynamics and the life-supporting processes of ecological systems for principles to guide policy decisions. He explores the power of megasystems, corporate and technological, to increase our vulnerability to forces from outside the region and thus foreclose future options which may be essential to maintaining qualities of life most valued by the people of New England.

Jorling examines the alternatives of centralized and decentralized levels of decision-making in his search for criteria, insisting that people must be able to conceptualize alternatives and understand how each option affects the values most important to them. Although he admits that not all the necessary elements of change are under the control of a region, he finds enough to believe that we must begin to control our destiny there. In this he has considerable support in the essays of his fellow authors. We must have sound information, a comprehensive understanding of the interrelationships of the relevant factors, and the wisdom to make decisions at a scale of landscape and society where those essential relationships are in focus. With such knowledge and capabilities, Jorling is convinced that the people of New England will be able to define the quality-of-life they seek, and employ those criteria "most effectively at a regional level."

In his essay "An Historical Perspective," Benjamin Labaree examines the control and use of land as major factors in shaping New England's distinct identity. Though often neglected by historians, he finds the history of land policy an important source for gaining a better understanding of communities and their value structures. For Labaree, "A shared past is at the heart of regionalism." Without a common history, he insists, "no degree of similar physical conditions can unite an area." He provides a vivid description of the changing uses of the region's land resources, and the patterns of settlement and ownership that developed over the past three centuries. He probes the meanings which land has for New Englanders, concluding that this "distribution of resources and their subsequent use by succeeding generations have greatly influenced the development of the entire region."

Labaree's historical insights into the nature and values of New England are the prologue for examining future options, reminding us of our land-use heritage, a cultural and natural heritage that will exert a powerful influence on the future. In a region where "the possession of land was above all else the only way to find a home and get ahead in the first three hundred years," he suggests that land and resource policy-makers will need a good sense of history to gain popular support for their decisions.

Mark Lapping's "Toward a Working Rural Landscape" offers another view of the New England landscape, this time from the perspective of the region's agricultural sector. In a review of past policies relating to land use, economics, and energy, he provides a synthesis of the influences that have shaped the history of agriculture in New England. He criticizes current policies that preserve farmland on the grounds that they fail to address the full range of economic pressures facing farmers. "A warmed-over Jeffersonianism is not enough," he argues, nor are incremental changes in tax systems and public regulatory programs.

Lapping calls for a comprehensive rural-development strategy that addresses the need to "extend private credit back into the region's rural areas," reduces the agricultural sector's "energy vulnerability," and promotes a more diversified agriculture. This, he believes, will require new efforts in "extension" education, strengthening of marketing systems, and a "land rationalization program" that will consolidate prime farmland under the control of working farmers. In addition to these socioeconomic programs, he believes, with Herbert Bormann, that there is a pressing need to come to grips with the serious environmental problems of soil erosion and air pollution. The objective of such a comprehensive rural development strategy, he insists, must be an "economically viable and sustainable agricultural economy capable of meeting many—though not all—of the region's needs." For Lapping, "The reestablishment of a working rural landscape" is critical for New England's future.

F. H. Bormann also looks to the landscapes of New England for evaluating resource policies in his essay—"The Landscape: Air Pollution Stress and Energy Policy." He synthesizes a wide range of research findings which he believes "indicates that the New England landscape may be endangered." Current levels of air pollution, he states, are probably causing "large-scale genetic, biological, and ecosystem changes" which are decreasing both plant and animal diversity and substantially reducing plant productivity. He warns that any weakening of air quality standards nationally will have especially serious implications for New England. "We are at the end of the pollution pipeline, in effect the garbage can of the United States, and we have a vulnerable landscape of great importance to us."

Although the immediate significance of his essay is to reveal the enormous hazards of current energy policies for this region, he also presents a forceful demonstration of the power of ecology as an integrative science. Using the ecosystem as the guiding concept, he leads the reader through a complex array of ecological facts and systems without losing track of essential interrelationships. Drawing on research from a broad spectrum of sources, Bormann has written the primer on the effects of air pollution on the natural ecosystems of New England. He explains clearly the critical role that these living landscapes play in maintaining the quality of our lives—landscapes that he believes are "at the heart of the concept we call New England." He warns that current energy policies are "shortsighted" and calls for major reforms in those policies to prevent further degradation of the New England landscape.

The role of energy policy in New England's economic future is examined in "The Future of Energy," by Henry Lee. In tracing the region's energy past, he identifies four significant themes which have characterized changes in energy use and which will continue to shape policy in the future. First, in contrast to popular wisdom, Lee believes that "New England has consistently responded to change by taking those actions which were in its economic self-interest." Also, he finds that these responses were gradual and continual, that they were "inextricably tied" to the economic and energy patterns of the nation, and, finally, that the impacts of past energy crises were not as severe as they seemed at the time when understood in the context of wider economic changes under way in the region.

Lee examines the various ways in which the region uses energy, identifying problems that are unique to New England and will have the most significant influence on future energy policy alternatives. "The first and foremost is the price of oil," which is reflected in the high cost of heating homes and the competitive disadvantage of the region's industries as a result of federal energy-pricing policies. Solving these problems will be difficult, he concludes, "in a period of financial austerity, an unhealthy utility industry, and continuing difficulties in meeting air pollution standards."

Lee looks to New England's "imagination and entrepreneurial leadership" as important resources for the future—resources that historically have made this a self-reliant region.

In "Reformulation of the Cities," Kenneth Geiser "explores the current conditions of cities and city life in New England, examines probable changes in the future, and suggests choices that could favorably or adversely affect that future." His view of the New England city is expansive, presenting a vision of urban life which he claims "is true of life throughout the region." Although he finds "an unforgiving rigidness" in the formal aspects of the region's urban areas, he believes that New England cities have major advantages over cities in more rapidly developing regions because of the "infrastructure and traditional structure in place." The region's cities can therefore serve as models for more rapidly developing cities elsewhere as they mature and slow in growth.

He examines a variety of trends and public policies which have shaped New England's cities, but warns that observing trends is not the only means to predicting the future. "Extrapolations tell nothing of surprises or willful efforts to alter courses of events. New Englanders are shaped by the quality of their life, but they also have the capacity to take hold of that quality of life and shape its development," he states.

Geiser explores several options for the future, stressing that the quality of life in our cities will be decided by the balance between the decisions of private investors and public policy-makers. Regardless of the paths chosen, however, he believes that living "in urban New England requires valuing its heritage more, its varied environments, and its ultimate community and family orientation more" than conventional goals of material accomplishment. It is these special qualities of life which make New England's cities special places.

This volume of essays seeks to inform the people of New England in ways consistent with this view, as will the books to follow in this series on The Futures of New England. If we begin, as René Dubos suggests, to think globally and act locally—as a region—the pursuit of happiness may not prove to be as elusive as we think. With wisdom, our decisions now can make all the difference.

Burlington, Vermont   C. H. R.
September 1981

NEW ENGLAND
PROSPECTS

ALTERNATIVES
IN A TIME OF CHANGE

Thomas Jorling

THROUGHOUT HISTORY public figures have always maintained that the era or period during which they hold power is, if not a historical turning point, something very close to its rhetorical equivalent. In retrospect we can see that the correspondence is not so pat; yet it is clear that within relatively short time frames the durability and character of entire societies and cultures have changed. Today our political and academic language is filled with the words of crisis and challenge. Although history should make us cautious about thinking of them as turning points, it seems clear that we have entered a period of compression, or what Gerald Piel has described as the "acceleration," of history.

This acceleration is an unappreciated phenomenon of modern technological civilization. We are experiencing a spread of change in society, culture, and the environment, in an ever-decreasing time period. The evidence points to further acceleration. In fact, many of the underlying principles on which our present socioeconomic dynamics rest generate such acceleration. For instance, we measure and value the performance of most elements of society in terms of percentage increases. Whether the subject is income, production, or profit, the headlines generally refer to how many percentage points the index being reported has moved up or down. The percentage of growth has, in fact, become an objective of our society and has thereby become itself a cause of further acceleration.

This acceleration is most graphically represented by the curve of exponential growth. This curve, with its implications, although portraying almost every important dimension of human society—

whether population, production of chemicals, loss of agricultural land, consumption of resources, or whatever—is not widely understood. Yet comprehending and interpreting the underlying dynamics of such patterns is a necessary background for any consideration of the future, whether New England or the globe. Any positive percentage increment of growth has a doubling time. Thus a one percent increase will cause a doubling of the original amount or base in seventy years. A 7 percent rate of growth will bring about a doubling in ten years. In understanding implications for the future, the rate or percentage of increase must be considered in the context of the base or quantity subject to that rate. For instance, the world population is growing on the order of 2.3 percent, which means a doubling time of approximately thirty years. If the world's population were low, the annual increase would be low, but with a population in excess of 4 billion it means that we are adding more than 100 million people a year, and a billion in a decade. When the base is large, even a relatively small percentage of increase produces a huge change. Another manifestation: the annual production of synthetic organic chemicals in the United States is now some 330 billion pounds. It has been growing since before World War II at a rate in excess of 10 percent. If it grew at a rate of 7 percent, in 150 years the annual production of such chemicals would equal the biomass of the earth.

The significance of these patterns of change is difficult to assess, and for several reasons. First, there is sheer complexity, with many elements of change interacting cybernetically, primarily positively, but generally in ways that cannot be predicted. Second, while certain features can be measured in objective terms, assessment of change is value-laden and the sources of these values are less and less dependable and are themselves changing. Third, the historically operative norms measuring the ends of society—provided in the western world primarily by Judeo-Christian traditions—are being challenged by a newer self-oriented materialism and are no longer providing the consensus once shared.

One of the characteristics that distinguish humans from other species inhabiting the biosphere is consciousness of the future, providing, at least in theory, an ability to plan for and to control the future; yet, paradoxically, even efforts at prediction have been notorious failures, and efforts to control the future are often derided.

Questions nevertheless emerge—among individuals, among groups, among nations, and, within our context, among regions.

—What (or who) is controlling change?
—What (or who) is controlling the rate of change?
—What (or who) is controlling the direction—much less the purpose—of change?
—What are the criteria that might be used to evaluate, even to understand, change?

The last question is the focus of this chapter and should take precedence over any effort to answer the others. If such criteria cannot be generated, the other questions become moot. If we cannot evaluate or understand change, questions about the direction and rate of change, much less what or who is controlling it, can be answered only by resort to such intellectual crutches as a Prime Mover—God in some accounts, the invisible hand in others. If there is resort to such crutches, man cannot, in fact, control present or future conditions, a view that is not shared by the author.

Implicit also in the notion that meaningful criteria can be developed is the view that humans have choices—that there are alternatives and that between and among such alternatives conscious choice can be exercised. Criteria in this sense are the benchmarks against which choices are made. They should provide common references enabling and clarifying what, in contemporary jargon, are called "trade-offs," a hybridized word that basically means choice.

Generating such benchmarks is presumptuous, always incomplete, yet necessary. Advocates of all courses of action have a special obligation to articulate criteria, so that the proposals they urge can be evaluated. Only with such evaluation is choice informed and thereby made real.

Life Support

The ever-increasing mechanization of our culture often causes us to gloss over the fact that humans are biological creatures and as such are part of the biosphere. Humans can therefore be investigated and analyzed by using concepts and methods developed in the synthesizing science of ecology. Specifically, these methods can be applied to the structure and function of humans, their communities, and the underlying life-support system. Notwithstanding the massive intervention of technology, humans cannot escape this biological character.

There should be no doubt that my assumption in what follows is that individuals, persons, are the primary reference point, rather than collective measures. Human individuals, as do all biological organisms, have a spectrum of life-support needs, at one end of which is biological necessity and at the other end those which are culturally derived. No list of needs is adequate, but a partial one should include *water, food, air, housing, waste, clothing, energy, transportation, communication,* and *materials.*

For purposes of evaluating the relationship of individuals to those needs (but without advocating a return to the period used in reference), it may be useful to look at two dimensions of this relationship: the geographical and the technological distance of the individual/community served from the source of the need in, say, the years 1850 and 1975. Of these two parameters, geographical distance is the easier to conceptualize. For instance, in 1850 people/communities were proximate to their food supplies, and therefore were a zero or minimal distance from them. In contrast, a CIA report declassified in 1970 estimates that in this country the average molecule of food now travels more than 1300 miles from the point of production to the point of consumption.

It is possible to hazard rough estimates of *geographical distance* in miles for life-support needs:*

	1850	1975
Food	0–5	1300
Water	0–5	50
Housing	20	750
Clothing	20	1000
Sewer/Waste	0	200
Materials	30	1000
Transport	10	500
Energy	30	500

*These estimates were developed by taking Albany, New York, as a representative community and evaluating the geographical distance of various needs in that context. For instance, for housing, the distance was derived by taking the basic materials—

Food and water are easier to measure than are most other needs. One has merely to calculate the distance between where the resource is harvested to where it is consumed. Other needs, such as housing and clothing, require a more complicated measurement, especially since they are often an assemblage of resources. Houses, for instance, are made of a wide diversity of materials: wood, gypsum, vinyl or metallic pipes, wiring, and the like, which require an assessment of each and averages to be taken. Plywood, for instance, includes foreign wood fiber—especially African and Latin American—as well as domestic. Although the distance traveled for housing components varies from region to region, something on the order of 750 to 1000 seems a fair average.

Technological distance, which might also be called distance created by complexity, is harder to describe, but common sense or intuition does inform. It might be best described somewhat rhetorically. If the technologically based system fails, for whatever reason, can the individual provide the life-support need personally or is it available within the local community? Technological distance is a concept we can appreciate from examples. Can a person fix his or her own heating plant or water supply? Can it *be* fixed? Or is the system so dependent on complicated technology, machinery, tools, or specialized skill that its maintenance lies beyond the individual/community?

Technological distance is a concept that is itself a function of the changed circumstances of what we call modern life. In earlier days people generally knew how to produce or obtain and maintain the various requirements necessary to support life. To the extent that they did not have either of these two forms of knowledge, they knew, in a personal sense, the individuals who did know how to produce it and maintain it. And they knew that through those persons, in essentially a human interaction, they could gain access to these life-support needs. Essential to this, of course, is personal knowledge. Even more important is the confidence in that knowledge which enables a sense of security that is essential, and precedent, to freedom.

---

concrete, lumber, wallboard, pipe, wiring, roofing, and the like—and then calculating from retail sources an overall average distance from place of origin of the material to the place of use.

That relationship is in marked contrast to the relationship people now have to their life-support needs. Even where the need may be purchased geographically proximate to the individual or group that is dependent upon the resource, industrial systems have complicated the production, distribution, and use of the life-support requirement. It is this complication which in fact represents technological distance between the persons dependent on the resource and the resource itself. People do not know what it takes to produce the resource, what it takes to distribute it, what it takes to utilize, maintain, or replace it.

Dependency Relationships

We cannot ignore the way in which the two aspects of distance, technological and geographical, reinforce each other to affect drastically the sense of security people have in the availability of, and access to, support needs—a lack of security that can produce great anxiety. We see these symptoms in each crisis that arises—in energy, food, water, or whatever. As our life-support needs are made more distant in both dimensions, it will deprive people of a sense of independence from a megasystem on which they must depend but over which they have no control.

These growing dependency relationships are extremely vulnerable to disruption and failure, for causes intentional or benign (including the ever-present laws of thermodynamics). Thus, since larger and larger populations are hostage to remote, complex, centralized systems, a response from government or other power centers becomes necessary. We create methods of regulation, of protection, of assurance in order to make sure that the life-support resources will continue to be available through such a system to the people who require it. It is possible that the growing exhortation of joint government-industry cooperation, as represented by the Chrysler bailout, or by the Energy Security Corporation, or by deregulation, are only current symptoms of the need for absolute control over those systems.

In such a situation it becomes clear that production and delivery systems are more important than persons who are served by the systems; the general good—the great expanse of population dependent upon the system—overrides the interests of any individual or group of individuals within it. Individuals in such systems have no control or influence over the production and distribution of these life-support requirements; they are puppets on the end of a very long and elaborate network of strings.

This analogy is not solely applicable to the consumer who utilizes the life-support requirements; it extends, in fact, to those within the system who are supposedly in control of it, like political officials and those in charge of the so-called private systems whch produce and distribute the support requirements. This is why there have been few suggestions for alternatives to the present way of doing things. Everyone is dependent upon the systems. As long as we assume the validity of growing geographical and technological distance between people and life-support requirements, the system will grow larger, more centralized, and more vulnerable, and increasing intervention by authority and conformity by citizens will be necessary.

It should be obvious that since most people depend on a weekly or monthly paycheck to bridge the increasing gaps, any interruption of the paycheck is an interruption of life support and explains why no large employer like Chrysler, Lockheed, or Ford Motor can be allowed to fail. It also explains why the labor movement is no longer independent of management in basic objectives. Workers simply must go along to get along.

The base question, then, is whether these trends are inexorable. The answer is that they are becoming so rapidly.

Is Trend Destiny?

It is appropriate to ask why our society, and all industrial societies of whatever political structure have followed the path toward bigness and centralization. Was choice exercised or is it our destiny to expand until expansion causes collapse? Choice, even the theoretical possibility of choice, requires that we focus on values. It requires that we ask what objectives we seek in the future. It may be that people, even if they had freedom to make the choice, would select the course revealed by present trends. And merely a negative posture toward such a future is futile and somewhat escapist. Frequently those concerned, often environmentalists, say "It can't work that way," "It will fail," or other variants on the theme. This negative posture does two things, neither of which are persuasive. First, it smacks of being against everything. Any alternative view of the future must, if it is to be successful, advocate being for something. A view of the future that is only negative leaves no freedom to choose.

Second, a negative posture sells science and technology short when experience, knowledge, and capability are growing rapidly. It is nonsense to argue that technology cannot be made to achieve something—whether nuclear energy, artificial intelligence, behavioral modification, creation or synthesis of living material, or almost anything else. It is escapist, because it suggests that there is an easy answer to our choices of the future: one of them cannot happen. But it can. We *can* create a society in which individuals through massive technologically based systems will fully satisfy the material and sensate needs of man. That it will be a system substituting for and far removed from the biosphere does not mean it cannot happen. That it will be a system in which individuals will have to conform to both the management and value imperatives of the system does not mean it cannot happen. That it will be a system in which individual autonomy and freedom will be subordinate to the fabric of the larger collective system does not mean it can't happen. It can.

Can New England Control Its Future?

If a collective homogeneous megasystem is not created, that will be because a different future is portrayed, one that successfully appeals to a different set of imperatives and values, one that people support. We must ask, as New Englanders and as members of the global community, whether it is possible to develop policies and programs in the 1980s and beyond which will reverse the trend toward greater and greater geographic and technological distance from life support. One imperative, implicit in such an alternative, is the subdivision of geography and human settlements, the globe and nations, into more environmentally integrated units, with more secure life-support systems. In the context of the United States, individual states are not appropriate units, and neither are most regions. It is possible, however, that New England is such a unit; that possibility is the premise of this volume. It is consistent with the Yankee tradition.

Students of biological evolution describe as a distinguishing characteristic of our species the ability to foresee and to act on that basis, in short, to control our destiny. In the words of George Gaylord Simpson, "It is another unique quality of man that he, for the first time in the history of life, has increasing power to choose his course and to influence his future evolution." If the people of a region such as New England are to consider their future meaningfully, to evaluate alternatives, to understand historical trends, to measure the present, to test the future, and, ultimately, to make choices, they must have criteria in addition to the parameters of distance.

Ideally, criteria in the sense used here should have several characteristics if they are to inform peoples' choice. First, they should admit to commonsense application—that is, they should not require specialized jargon or training or sophisticated methodology before a person derives meaning from applying them to facts or circumstance. Second, they should operate so that citizens can see implications and relationships, understand consequences. Third, if criteria are to be useful, they should allow citizens to relate to and draw upon common experience. In this sense they should foster common reference and discussion among individuals who disagree about their importance, significance, or outcome.

In short, criteria, to be effective, should not be dependent on experts, nor create a sense that no valid judgments can be made about the future. Jefferson said, "I know no safe depository of the ultimate powers of the society but the people themselves; and if we think them not enlightened enough to exercise their control with a wholesome discretion, the remedy is not to take it from them, but to inform their discretion." Identifying and describing criteria which satisfy these tests is risky, and difficult if not presumptuous. But it is essential. It disciplines debate. It forces disclosure of assumptions, presumptions, and special interests on all sides in regard to public policy questions. Too often dialogue on public issues focuses on surrogate measures, such as GNP, inflation, productivity, and percentage of growth, as if solving those problems somehow achieves progress in the human condition. We need more direct consideration of how alternative pathways to the future affect our goals, objectives, and values. We cannot rely on surrogates that mask actual effects. New criteria are essential.

Criteria to Assess Technology

Ours is the age of technology. If there is a phenomenon that is universal in modern life, it is the seeming quest to apply technology to existing circumstances in order to create new circumstances. H. G. Wells in *Mind at the End of Its Tether* provides us with what might be called a description of this phenomenon: "everything is driving anyhow to anywhere at a steadily increasing velocity."

But the character of technology varies, and can change the relationship of individuals to each other and to the biosphere. Technology and systems of its use and management can be large and complicated and when applied, such technology can make individuals or communities dependent on supporting institutional structures—for example, in relation to energy from oil, think of government (for licensing or regulation), manufacture (for making the technology available), and service (for distributing, operating, and maintaining the technology). Or technology can be liberating, as in the case of a solar collector.

As a result of the oil crisis, most Americans now recognize their dependency on Middle Eastern oil and the consequences of that dependence. A political consensus that something must be done has been created. On the other hand, Americans, and especially New Englanders, are no less dependent on remotely produced food, materials, and other forms of energy; yet the awareness of such dependencies has not spread beyond certain small groups. No widespread political consensus exists.

It would be possible to apply criteria that would address the character of technology so that, for instance, to the maximum extent technology would be developed in scale with individuals or communities and serviceable by them. But some technologies—for instance, air travel and communications—simply don't admit to such scale, and to the extent that they don't the institutions administering such technology should be evaluated by other criteria, that relate to the control of such power and that operate to establish accountability in the exercise of such power. An explicit criterion for the value of technology would allow some focus on the current trend or drift, which simply stated is toward more centralized and more complex technology.

Vulnerability

Scale and complexity are two elements by which to measure and evaluate technology. These two considerations, by themselves, do not address the fact that technology is incorporated increasingly into the systems which provide the essential life-support needs of people. The secure availability of such life-support needs suggests another important consideration: the vulnerability of the providing system or technology. Vulnerability is a concept with many dimensions. It results from cumulative or aggregate characteristics, of which distance and complexity are important components. There are others, including the basic design of the system. For instance, does the system depend on the performance of a long chain or sequence of events or conditions, or does it produce its benefit only after a small number of steps or linkages?

Compare the ideal (nonexistent) self-sufficient farm, producing adequate nutrition for a household, with the present agribusiness system. Inherent in the latter is (1) high technology agriculture, including such elements as irrigation, fertilizers, pesticides, migrant labor, and complex machinery for the production and harvesting of food; (2) high technology food-processing, including chemical additives, refrigeration, packaging; (3) high technology transportation over great distances; and (4) high technology marketing. On a global scale we could add the crucial dimension of shipment across national boundaries. The more dependent on technology a life-support system becomes—and in the case of food it is noteworthy that current trends will amplify this dependency—the more vulnerable that system will be. Of course, it is possible to overcome such inherent vulnerability with redundancy—such as that included in the space program—but rarely can redundancy be built into a system: we do not have two Alaska pipelines, nor could we have two Imperial Valleys. It is also possible, at least theoretically, to avoid vulnerability by police power. We could put an armed trooper and repairman every fifty yards along the Alaska pipeline or on every agribusiness site.

Another example of two systems varying immensely in respect to design vulnerability is a hydroelectric plant and a nuclear electric generating facility. Comparatively, the hydro plant requires little except water flow to keep it operating. A fission plant requires an astonishing number of subsystems to function properly, and because the consequences of failure are so significant, more systems must be operating within extreme limits if disruption of even greater magnitude is to be avoided.

Scale does make enormous difference in determining the degree of vulnerability: the greater the population dependent on a given life support system or service, the more significant the vulnerability and need for forms of expertise and regimentation to protect the system. If experience is a guide, this control or protection will often be under the guise of analysis based on "predictive" models, which models, of course, are valid—that is, will protect the system—only if there is assurance that people will behave as the models assume. Thus it will become increasingly important to control persons so that they live according to the assumptions of such models. Nor is it altogether too futuristic to remember the tremendous strides in this direction in biological, behavioral, and psychological engineering techniques.

The rapid shift to large centralized systems of life support raises serious questions centering on the individual and his or her relation to sources of such collective power as the state and other large institutions, especially those which make available life support needs, whether they are multinational corporations or international labor unions. So again we ask: Are there alternatives, or is the present system inexorable and beyond human control?

Neither the character of technology, nor its direction toward bigness, centralization, and uniformity with their attendant risks for the human community is inevitable. Humans can exert control over the technology they develop. My thesis is that there are choices, and selection among alternative technological choice can be based on whether any particular technology or system of technology makes the life support of human communities more or less vulnerable, more or less resilient, more or less dependent on remote and complex sources.

Individual Freedom

Freedom, liberty, independence—they are all concepts around which high passion is generated. They are inescapably involved when we consider individual autonomy. One definition of freedom is the ability to avoid coercive control of political, religious, or other views (thought control), rather than the modern perversion: "freedom" to experience sensate pleasure on demand (i.e., consumer freedom). Simply put, we must ask whether dependency relations for life support needs are so great as to cause persons in need of life support to change political or other views in order to obtain or retain it. In a regional context we must ask further if any policies or programs can be adopted which will provide life support and at the same time run counter to the trend of increasing dependency.

Often subordinated to the 1973 oil embargo in terms of public attention, the interstate truckers' strike that occurred at the same time is more instructive to New Englanders of the nearly total dependency on remote areas for one of their basic life-support needs—food supply. The truckers' strike forced government, especially state officials, to focus on the system that now brings food to the population of the Northeast. What they found was alarming and has led most New England states, especially Vermont and Massachusetts, to adopt policies to encourage more locally based food production. A recent report prepared by a special Commission for the Governor of Massachusetts is instructive:

Today this state imports fully 85% of its food—97% of the meat and poultry it consumes, 70% of the eggs, 80% of the milk, and 90% of the potatoes. As population increases in states and nations from which Massachusetts imports food, the supply for Massachusetts to import will become increasingly scarce and costly.

The forces of the last several decades within Massachusetts and nationally have led this state to an excessive reliance on imported food that is unnecessarily expensive, to a situation where consumers have little choice but to pay high food prices, and where farmers lack the means of reversing the decline in the agricultural base of the Commonwealth. Massachusetts has been viewed as an "industrial state" and the erosion of farming inevitable. Left unchecked, these trends will continue to make food more expensive than need be. In the long term the prospect is that within a few decades the supply of food available for import from many areas may be so reduced as to cause exorbitant prices or even food shortages. None of this, however, is inevitable. We have time to meet this challenge if we recognize it and begin to act now.

The strike in 1973 revealed that in the Northeast at any one time there is on the order of ten days of food supply with no present capability within the region to expand it. Any interruption is, therefore, potentially devastating in its impact. Without changing the meaning of the terms, it is possible to state that New Englanders are hostage to the truckers, to the railroads, to the large conglomerate food producers and processors. We are dependent on them for our survival. If survival is at stake, freedom is an issue.

Resource Consumption

The immediately past era of readily available and consequently cheap resources, from aluminum to oil to zinc, is the basic cause of the mushrooming of the material-based standard of living in the industrialized world, and especially in the United States. The transition to the era of scarce and expensive resources is occurring at the same time as a technologically based worldwide revolution in communications. Among other consequences is everyone's awareness, around the globe, of the standard of living, the consumption of resources, the circumstances of luxury in the United States. This situation is in stark contrast to the conditions ranging from hardship to nearly total deprivation in much of the rest of the world.

The data that describe this disparity are often couched in the abstract jargon of the analyst; although the numbers are staggering they tend not to arouse passion or compassion. To state that a citizen of the United States. with 5 percent of the global population consumes 35 percent of the resources, or that a citizen of the United States has twenty-five times the adverse impact on the biosphere of a citizen in a developing country, seems to generate no greater impact on people's behavior than to state that it is hundreds of light years to the nearest galaxy. Some data, however, though no match for actual observation, come closer to the mark. In low-income countries with a 1980 population of 1.2 billion, life expectancy is still less than fifty years, compared to 73.5 years in the industrialized countries. In low-income countries only 38 percent of the adult population is literate, compared to 99 percent in the industrialized countries. In the lowest-income countries, where some 400 million live, the average annual death rate of children aged one to four was more than 20 per 1000—twenty times that in the industrialized countries.

By putting ourselves in the shoes of a bright, idealistic patriot of a low-income country who is observing only the basic living standards of the industrial West, we can gain some respect for the increasingly exercised claim for justice, for sharing, for equity. And we in New England are not immune to it. We must examine our circumstances against this background. To obtain needed resources is not going to get easier. Even if New Englanders are not persuaded by the equity or the ethical argument, the intense competition for resources should cause New Englanders to look within their own geographical boundaries to satisfy as many resource needs as possible. Even a selfish motivation, if the result is a move toward regionally generated resources, will help the global picture.

If we return for a moment to the outlook of our third world patriot, we can anticipate a claim that even the most elementary notion of justice extends to all citizens of the globe a right to the basic needs of life support and access to the resources of the biosphere which fulfill those needs. The interconnectedness of the globe makes the implications of that basic notion of justice inescapable, to all Americans but especially to New Englanders.

Exercising Power

Criteria or measures of the consequences of power are most effectively applied and understood at the time of the exercise of power. Yet it is precisely at this time when the norms or standards applied in our society are mostly surrogate or obscure. For instance we measure the exercise or power by its effect on "profit" or "rate of return" or "productivity." Very little attention is given to the effect directly on people or on the biosphere, now or in the future. Such surrogate measures especially when coupled to large collective institutions like corporations and government also dilute, if not avoid, accountability in the exercise of power. Whenever power (to hire, to fire, to relocate an employment cell, to use a biospheric resource, etc.) is exercised—and whenever those who are affected by the exercise of such power personally know and are known by the exerciser of the power—accountability can result from that human interaction, with the exception of decisions on the use of public trust resources, air, water, and biota. However, if power is exercised without that inter-

action, as the Constitution wisely recognized in the federal exercise
of power, enforceable measures can be defined, such as due process
and standards of public interest, in order to discipline or control that
power. The most appropriate time to consider the scale or complexity of technological system is at or prior to the time power is exercised, rather than after such decisions have added their increment
to the overall drift toward larger and more centralized systems.

Any amendment to the present standards governing the exercise
of power necessarily raises questions of corporate governance. Deep
concern over accountability in the exercise of power, especially as it
affects individuals, has been a hallmark of American society.

At the time the Constitution was being adopted, many provisions
were introduced to constrain and make accountable that principal
agent of power the federal government, which was presumed to be
larger and therefore independent of personal mechanisms protecting against abuse of power. During the past 200 years, new aggre-
gates of such power have come into being, especially the large,
often multinational corporation. Brought into existence by state
charter, these institutions were once constrained by limits on size
and power, limits that were rapidly made obsolete by interstate
competition. Justice Brandeis, in a dissent in *Liggett v. Lee* (1932),
described the history of the business corporation concisely:

Although the value of this instrumentality in commerce and industry was
fully recognized, incorporation for business was commonly denied long
after it had been freely granted for religious, educational, and charitable
purposes. It was denied because of fear. Fear of encroachment upon the
liberties and opportunities of the individual. Fear of the subjection of labor
to capital. Fear of monopoly. Fear that the absorption of capital by corporations, and their perpetual life, might bring evils similar to those which at-
tended mortmain. There was a sense of some insidious menace inherent to
large aggregations of capital, particularly when held by corporations. So at
first the corporate privilege was granted sparingly; and only when the grant
seemed necessary in order to procure for the community some specific benefit otherwise unattainable . . . The removal by the leading industrial states
of the limitations upon the size and powers of business corporations appears
to have been due, not to their conviction that maintenance of the restrictions was undesirable in itself, but to the conviction that it was futile to insist upon them; because local restriction would be circumvented by foreign

incorporation. Indeed, local restriction seemed worse than futile; Lesser States eager for the revenue derived from the traffic in charters, had removed safeguards from their own incorporation laws.

(288 US 517, 518, 557)

Nothing took the place of the limits—limits designed to control power—once imposed by states. Subsequently, corporations continued to expand in size and power, until now they exercise more power in national and global society than any other source. This power has many dimensions; it has the ability to distribute new chemicals, to provide or withhold food, to determine income differentials, to make us dependent on technology—in short to alter the landscape, physical and human. The power once thought of as the exclusive province of individuals or government—the power to control others—is now held and executed to a large extent by business corporations. Where government has such power, we have established measures to protect the individual. Not so with the corporation. Though government cannot deprive a person of free speech, a corporation can deny employment, thereby withholding the paycheck essential for the survival of such expression. Specific multinational corporations wield power beyond the boundaries of any national jurisdiction. Anyone concerned about the future must ask whether mechanisms to control (to make accountable) this power should be adopted, and if so what they should be. If we remain committed to the principle that the health and welfare of individuals who make up our society is the fundamental reference point in evaluating our society, then the exercise of all forms of power that can affect those individuals must ultimately be accountable to them.

The Consequence of Power

The history of our legal tradition makes it clear that individuals can assume risk. What is less clear in its legal or even social ramifications is the modern fact that societies and institutions within them can *impose* risk on individuals. Increasingly—and as a necessary function of the drive toward high technology and more centralized production—technologies such as those involving synthetic chemicals, electromagnetic radiation, and radioactive materials, through both public and private mechanisms, assess risk and then impose it on individuals who have no choice whether to assume it. For instance, if the release of a given chemical will cause one excess death per 100,000 population as a hypothetical example, it may be imposed on a society in which no one knows who that one will be. Society can explicitly consider such inherent effects of technology and could seek to avoid assessing and imposing risks that cannot be, in any meaningful sense, assumed by individuals. Love it or leave it is obviously one alternative, but not in any meaningful sense of choice. Whenever such risks are imposed by society, it must be through the most democratic of processes—perhaps even referenda. There remains a question how much a region can do to influence these types of patterns or decisions which affect them. But any consideration of the future must take them into account. To the extent, however, that a region moves toward less obtrusive technology, it can avoid some of these "imposed" risks.

Management of Chemicals and Resources

It has become routine to characterize the socioeconomic system of the United States as "linear" in respect to its movement of material: exploit, transport, use, transport, discard. This is in marked contrast to (for example) ecological patterns of cycling in other living communities. The norm, against which performance in the management of matter is measured, should be no release (meaning no loss of custody) of chemicals in production and product use. Special burdens of justification, "fundamentally compelling" reasons, should be established before activities or systems are permitted which do release chemicals into the environment—especially chemicals that are not normally found in the biosphere.

Any consideration of the future leads to the conclusion that continuing to assume, as our culture does assume, that chemicals may be released to the uncontrolled movement in the biosphere is not a prudent course of action. Since the 1920s, the annual production of synthetic chemicals has risen from a few thousands of pounds to the current rate, now reaching hundreds of billions of pounds. It is folly and extremely costly to perpetuate a culture that attempts to control these chemicals and their effects after release. Over time we can develop no-release methods for most forms of production and use of chemicals. That is the objective we must continually strive for as we continue technological development.

Linear pathways of chemical and resource use are inherently wasteful. With nonrenewable resources such patterns represent a tremendous imposition on future generations. With renewable resources such patterns dramatically reduce our sustained yield capacity. Our management of materials should represent a stewardship that envisions the future and respects the resource problems represented by the life-support needs of succeeding generations. Against such a consideration our present behavior is extravagantly wasteful.

Some agree that the perception of the current trend is toward a "megasystem" but take the view that individuals, even regions, are incapable of altering basic patterns in the flow of chemicals or resources. It is claimed that national and international marketing precludes any action that would, for instance, place requirements on a regional institution to move toward no-release production, because that would operate to the competitive disadvantage of such institutions. Only federal solutions seem appropriate. Such a perception has a firm basis, but it should not cause paralysis. A longer view of the future can result by identifying actions that can be taken at a regional level.

For instance, the Northeast is now resource poor. It imports most of its resources and products. Yet after use they are irretrievably discarded, often because the current markets are not there for recycled products. But the markets could be created if during a transitional phase those imported materials, after use, could be stored in depots (not deposited). Metals, plastics, paper—all could be segregated and stored for future use—to create future "mines" as it were. Over time this could lead not only to decentralization but to a regional resource.

Effects of Current Activity on the Future

The evaluation of how any action—any development of technology, of a system of production, etc.—or logical extension of such an action is likely to influence the near future should not be limited to resource availability. Vulnerability as a function of dependence admits to similar review. For instance, with even rudimentary foresight huge centralized systems for producing autos could have been predicted to hold our socioeconomic system hostage for their continuation. Creating such rigidities drastically reduces the system's adaptability. We must protect and maintain the system regardless of its objective or purpose. In an evolutionary sense it is akin to creating synthetic flowers to maintain hummingbirds if because of evolutionary change the flowers that provided nourishment should become extinct. Decentralized, diverse, cultural patterns are the most adaptable, enabling the adjustments necessary to provide both security and freedom in a changing world. The further creation of large megasystems *can* be avoided, and New England, as it faces the future, is in a position to assure that future development does not carry such a dependency relationship. Yankee tradition is fully supportive of such alternatives.

In addition to affecting dependency, actions taken by man vary in the extent and length of time in which such action will affect the biosphere. Contrast fission by-products with thousand-year half-lives to the clearing of land for agricultural production. After cessation of the activity, one action can affect the environment and health for centuries, but the other leaves only traces of the agricultural activity after forty years. In New England the hillsides returning to forest were not many years ago landscapes of intense agricultural activity. Actions can be evaluated against the future and the course chosen which will have the least impact.

These differences will ultimately be reflected in conventional economic terms. For instance, the burden of decommissioning a nuclear power plant after its useful life (about thirty years), or after accidental damage such as that to Three Mile Island, is as tremendous as it is unnecessary. It would seem obvious that any technology that creates inescapable burdens for the future should be avoided.

In addition to the duration of impact, some activities—(1) electric power generation by nuclear fission, (2) the production of certain long-life chemicals, (3) certain modifications of the earth's surface (building a dam, a water distribution system like Boston's Quabbin Reservoir, major urbanization), and, (4), albeit crystal-ball gazing, certain biological products of genetic engineering—require constant and almost infinitely long care or management into the future. As a result of some of these activities, increasingly large expanses of land are effectively precluded forever from any other use. In addition, energy and resources must be committed to them effectively in perpetuity, representing a real and unavoidable drain on the energies of future generations. Before we tie our hands and those of our successors in this manner, we must ask if it is fundamentally necessary. The health and welfare of individuals in society can be enhanced only by avoiding such lock-stepping of the future.

Impoverishment of Life

One of the most alarming signs that mankind does indeed stand at a turning point is the current evidence on extinction of biological species. Conservative estimates project that in the next twenty years as many as 15 to 20 percent of all species on earth will be lost as a result of overharvesting, pollution, and destruction of habitats. An erosion of the richness of the biosphere on this scale and in such a short time carries with it unimaginable consequences. Like so many other patterns it suggests that only global or at least national action is effective; regions are helpless. But again this is not true; all levels of human organization, without waiting for others, can and must take action to reverse the tide of biological destruction.

Any major alteration of the environment in New England as well as elsewhere should be undertaken only after assuring that there will not be placed at risk of existence any biological species or representative ecosystem, terrestrial or aquatic. The protection of the biological, physical, and chemical integrity of the biosphere is a general criterion against which human actions can be judged. It is necessary for a long-term stable life-supporting biosphere, and while action in a region such as New England is not alone sufficient it is not meaningless, even in the global context. It certainly is not meaningless in the more immediate sense of preserving the biological richness and amenities we associate with the region and which supports in large measure the quality of life we associate with New England.

Development Choices

It is possible to review the character of development in the United States and all regions within it and draw from it generalizations concerning assumptions supporting that development. When we look to the past for lessons to guide the future, a previous assumption that stands out is investment in ephemeral systems—structures and products. It can be postulated that this characteristic was and is a function of cheap, readily available materials and energy. The luxury will not be available in the future—not for New England, not for the United States, and not for the rest of the world. We have skimmed, even squandered, the resources we once thought inexhaustible: oil, ores, soil are now becoming precious.

Thus in the future the inexorable tendency of all material and energy to move to higher levels of disorder must be recognized in our investment in, and choice of, life-supporting techniques and systems. Whenever a system is developed, inescapably associated with it will be the capital costs of development and operation and maintenance (life cycle costs) as well as replacement costs. One principal reason American cities are in such financial trouble is the need to replace much of the earlier installed life-support requirements—especially water, sewer, and housing stocks—on which the second law of thermodynamics has taken its toll.

The scarcity of resources must drive our systems to recycle, to reuse, and to move away from linear systems. It must drive our system (and all human communities) to redesign and rebuild things to withstand the second law for the greatest time rather than, as at present, counting on it for rapid turnover or what we once glowingly referred to as "planned obsolescence."

Summary

So we return to the original question: Are modern industrial societies and regions within them at a turning point in history? The answer of this observer is decidely yes. Against the measures I have defined, the alternative directions for society are distinct. And they are major. The existing path can be characterized by increasing centralization and uniform standardization of basic life-support delivery: food, energy, water, materials. Larger and larger populations will be dependent on such systems. The systems will be characterized by complicated technology controlled and controllable by only a few experts neither elected or accountable. The systems when not subject to intentional or accidental malfunction, to which they will be extremely vulnerable, will deliver massive amounts of material goods. With the rapidly advancing capability for behavior control inherent in such technological power, the system will strive to satisfy the ever-increasing demands for material goods it creates. The systems will be governed by isolated individuals. A long, hedonistic life will be its principal attribute.

The alternative path would be characterized by decentralized systems, diverse and smaller technology, more accessible to and manageable by average, trained, educated citizens. The society would be characterized by community sharing and interaction. Reduced dependency on centralized systems would allow greater diversity of cultural patterns and life styles; emphasis would be on such human values as compassion, brotherhood, and community rather than on materialistic and sensual pleasure. Decentralization of basic life-support systems would provide more resilience between and among regions of the nation, making them less subject to wild oscillations in any component of life support.

There is still time to choose which path we wish to take. It is neither utopian nor idealistic, but rather very pragmatic to consider these choices. They cannot be relegated to the philosopher any longer. They must be addressed by citizens, because whether we like it or not the society we create makes them.

These choices can be addressed most effectively at a regional level, where it is possible for citizens to conceptualize alternatives and their manifestations. Although not all necessary elements of change are under the control of a region, enough are to begin to control our destiny. With control comes the possibility of citizen involvement and participation—a marked contrast to the increasing detachment citizens feel from the events that determine their lives. We would then see citizens fulfilling the promise of both our knowledge and our values—controlling our destiny in conformance with the human spirit and character.

AN HISTORICAL PERSPECTIVE

Benjamin W. Labaree

HOW A PEOPLE acquired land and used its resources is an important part of their history, but one that until recently has drawn little attention from professional historians. Over the past twenty years or so, however, studies of specific New England towns have shown how important land policy is to understanding a community and its value structure. Works on Andover, Plymouth, Dedham, and Sudbury, to cite but a few, have illuminated the role played by land in the formation of these towns. By inference, we can conclude that the distribution of these resources and their subsequent use by succeeding generations of owners have greatly influenced the development of the entire region. In an agricultural society such as New England's was, predominantly, until the beginning of the present century, access to the land conveyed not only the possibility of economic security but also social acceptance and a political role. For the community as a whole, land bestowed an identity, distinct from its neighbor's, and a territory to manage and defend. In short, control over a particular part of the North American land mass was a major factor in making New Englanders the kinds of people they had become by the beginning of the twentieth century.

Definition

For most people New England is easily defined as the six-state region comprised of Maine, New Hampshire, Vermont, Massachusetts, Rhode Island, and Connecticut, but for some the matter is not so simple. A New Hampshire man I know with three married daughters was asked whether any of them had remained in New England.

"Only one," was his disappointed response. "She's living in Ipswich." The others, it turned out, had moved to Williamstown, Massachusetts, and Ridgefield, Connecticut. Once over the Mohawk Trail in western Massachusetts or past New Haven or Bridgeport in Connecticut, one was apparently no longer in this man's New England, regardless of the fact that the state boundaries lay some miles beyond.

Perhaps my New Hampshire friend has something there. His concept of territoriality derives from the "castle-and-border" behavior observed among most creatures. The further a bird or animal gets from his nest or lair the less secure he becomes as he approaches the territory of another creature. Border areas are rarely well defined and are often in dispute, but creatures seem to know when they are no longer on safe ground. So do men from New Hampshire. According to this view, New England emanates from its center or hub in all directions and for great distances. A New Englander senses he is no longer in the region not primarily when he has covered many miles or has crossed a state border but when he begins to feel that he is under the influence of another center. One could travel northeast from Boston for nearly 400 miles without encountering a different culture, but go less than half as far in the opposite direction and feel increasingly drawn toward an alien center—New York. Well into New Brunswick to the northeast and upstate New York to the northwest, on the other hand, one can observe that the influence of New England remains virtually unthreatened by gravitational pulls toward other centers.

From a political standpoint, of course, it makes sense to define New England by governmental borders. No matter how much like New England upper New York may be, it is subject to the laws of a different state government. By the same token, Connecticut's Fairfield County must be reckoned a part of New England even if its ways are strange to residents in other corners of the region. Yet propinquity alone does not constitute a region, as, for instance, the combination of Pennsylvania, West Virginia, Maryland, Ohio, Indiana, and Kentucky amply demonstrates. Nor can we claim too much for similarities of topography and climate if the variations between New Hampshire and Rhode Island or between Virginia and Louisiana mean anything. At the foundation of any region must lie a common history. Without it, similar physical conditions cannot unite an area; with it, people who live in diversified surroundings will coalesce into a region, to the exclusion of their neighbors. A shared past is at the heart of regionalism.

The actual area encompassed by the name New England has an interesting history. In 1614 Captain John Smith explored the coast north and east of present-day Cape Cod and published his observations with a map two years later under the title *Description of New England*. The name apparently caught on, for in 1620 a company calling itself the Council of New England was formed to receive from the crown all the lands between 40 and 48 degrees north latitude—that is, from the middle of New Jersey to Newfoundland. Gradually, the area to which the term applied narrowed somewhat. One of the Pilgrims reporting on conditions in Plymouth in 1624 entitled his tract *Good News from New England*, and five years later the "Massachusetts Bay Company in New England" received its royal charter to the land lying between the Merrimack River and Charles River valleys. In 1643, when the colonies of Plymouth, Massachusetts Bay, Connecticut, and New Haven joined together in a defensive league, they called it the United Colonies of New England. Despite a slight relapse in 1686, when the newly formed Dominion of New England was expanded to include New York and New Jersey, by the end of the seventeenth century the term encompassed the four colonies (later to become five states) east of New York, namely New Hampshire, Massachusetts Bay (which by then had absorbed Plymouth and included Maine), Rhode Island, and Connecticut (which had absorbed New Haven Colony). Vermont, which to many people is the archetypal New England state, did not exist as a political entity until the end of the eighteenth century.

The name New England, unlike the merely geographical terms later assigned to other regions—"the South," for instance, or "the Middle West"—suggested a homeland, Old England. This effect was greatly heightened when Prince Charles, soon to become Charles I, randomly attached to John Smith's manuscript map of 1614 the names of some of his favorite English places, such as London, Sudbury, Boston, and even Plymouth. Only the latter actually continued to refer to the same location after English settlement, but with such familiar names, colonists might expect a land hospitable to their desire to make a fresh start in a new-world setting. In a sense, then, the name New England became a self-fulfilling prophecy as to it flocked a remarkably homogeneous group of immigrants. Many of them had been neighbors in the counties of Norfolk, Suffolk, and Essex in East Anglia. Others came from villages in Cornwall or Devon, and they often arrived in cohesive groups complete with parish ministers and other community leaders. Furthermore, they came to New England, as they said, on "an errand into the wilderness," to establish their communities according to the laws of God as they interpreted them. Most of the groups who followed came because they knew that their religious precepts, political principles, and economic activities would meet a favorable reception.

The Land

The land to which the colonists brought their hope for a fresh start was not quite so hospitable as its name implied. Only 12,000 years before, the last of a series of glaciers had begun its retreat from the region, leaving behind the till accumulated by previous advances. Meltwater flowing from the glacier's face etched deep gulleys into the surface and washed debris down and across the coastal plains. Along the shores of Maine the rising ocean drowned the valleys and created a bold, rocky coastline, but elsewhere land and sea met in sandy dunes and gently sloping beaches.

Thirty or forty miles in from the coast ran a belt of hills interspersed with many lakes and ponds and transected by numerous rivers coursing their way to the sea. The soil was more fertile here than along the coast, and the denser vegetation added each year to the gradually accumulating rich humus. But here also the glacier had left behind a vast quantity of stone and boulders, often at depths of several feet, some of which the frost heaved to the surface each year.

A hundred miles or more from the sea rose New England's own highlands, the White Mountains of New Hampshire and the Green Mountains of Vermont. Between them the mighty Connecticut River ran out from its narrow mountain sources south across the uplands of Massachusetts and through the coastal plain of Connecticut to the sea at Long Island Sound. Along its flood plains, as well as those of lesser rivers like the Kennebec, the Merrimack, and the Housatonic, deposits of fertile silt accumulated.

New England's climate also differed markedly from that of Old

England. The immigrants from the West Country would find no salubrious effects of a warm North Atlantic curent sweeping by their shores, nor would East Anglians discover the cool summers and moderate winters that had kept their pastures green throughout the year. Instead, New England was a land of climatic extremes—summer days considerably hotter than those experienced in the old country and winters desperately colder, accompanied by heavy snowfall and chilling winds. Because of its lower elevation, the southwest winds, and the proximity of the ocean, the coastal plain enjoyed more moderate conditions than did the interior valleys and uplands, where a greater proportion of the annual precipitation fell as snow. Throughout the region, spring came somewhat more slowly than in the old country, but the summer warmth lingered through a long autumn, making it perhaps the pleasantest season of the year.

Differences in soil, climate, and elevation throughout New England assured a wide variety of forest cover as well. Along the sandy coastal plain was a belt of pitch pine and scrub oak, with the trees growing to fuller proportions further inland away from the salt spray and where the soil was more fertile. The line of hills beyond the coast was covered at its southern end with stands of oak, maple, chestnut, and other hardwoods. Farther north, softwoods predominated, such as tamarack, hemlock, and particularly white pine. In the mountains of western Massachusetts and northern New England, beech, sugar maple, and birch were the more common hardwoods, while magnificent stands of white pine and hemlock were joined by red spruce and balsam fir.

The coastal waters of New England harbored a wide variety of fish: schools of herring and mackerel on their annual migrations along with tuna and swordfish. The warmer waters of southern New England were carpeted with oysters and scallops, while further north were found lobsters, mussels, and clams in great abundance. Up the brackish rivers each spring shad, alewives, and Atlantic salmon struggled against the current to deposit their eggs, and in the smaller streams and ponds of the interior lived several varieties of trout. The coastal marshes provided cover for migrating waterfowl twice a year, and eagles and ospreys made their seasonal homes there as well. The inland forests teemed with turkey, pheasant, and other birds, while vast numbers of passenger pigeons crowded the flyways overhead on their semiannual migrations. Commonest of the mammals inhabiting the coastal regions were undoubtedly rabbits, squirrels, chipmunks, and other small species. The white-tailed deer preferred somewhat more remote regions, and in the deepest recesses of the inland forest dwelt the moose, black bear, wolf, and bobcat.

Possessing the Land

English claims to the territory of North America were based primarily on the so-called right of discovery, devolving from the voyages of John and Sebastian Cabot in the last years of the fifteenth century. Largely because of continuing internal disunity, the English crown was unable to follow up these claims with any significant effort to colonize, as the Spanish had done in the Caribbean. Only with the death of Elizabeth in 1603 and subsequent unification of the realm under the Stuarts were English entrepreneurs willing to risk their capital in support of overseas adventures. By that time, however, English claims to North America were challenged by France. In a series of wars stretching over two centuries the two nations would fight for control of the continent, until in 1759 on the Plains of Abraham outside Quebec, English troops drove the French from their last major bastion in Canada. A century earlier, in 1664, the British had seized Dutch-held New Netherlands, the only other significant European colony north of Spanish Florida not originally settled by England.

When the English forces assumed sovereignty over New Netherlands and renamed their conquered territory New York, no effort was made to dispossess Dutch landholders of their property as long as they were willing to accept their new sovereign. The English policy was in keeping with general practice in almost all European wars. In Canada as well, with one exception, the British followed the principle of nondispossession. French-speaking landowners continued to enjoy their property rights under the British flag, and as we know, the new rulers went to great lengths to permit the development of a binational culture throughout the province. The only significant divergence from this policy involved French Acadia, captured by the British and renamed Nova Scotia in 1713. At the renewal of war in 1755 between France and England, the Acadians refused to take an oath of loyalty to their British sovereigns, and about six thousand were exiled to English colonies further south. Although many ultimately returned to their homes, undoubtedly a considerable number were in fact permanently dispossessed of their lands without compensation.

Although both the Dutch and the French had minor outposts in the territory that became New England, the principal claimants to those lands were, of course, the Indians already in occupation when the whites arrived at the beginning of the seventeenth century. Mostly members of the Algonkin family, the Indians had themselves invaded the northeast section of the continent many centuries before, succeeding in their turn to several still earlier occupants. Algonkins were divided into numerous tribes. The major ones in what became New England were the Pequots, Narrangansetts, and Wampanoags along the southern coast, the Pocumtucks, Nipmuks, and Massachusetts in the central region, and the Penacooks and Abnakis to the north and east. Each tribe exercised sovereignty over particular territories, usually well defined but occasionally subject to dispute along the borders with neighboring tribes. The males of each tribe were free to hunt and fish throughout these areas, title to which was generally held by the sachem or other recognized tribal head. Individual families held rights to tracts of land for planting corn and other vegetables. These claims, which most experts agree were something less than outright ownership, were usually handed down through the female line, since the women of each family did most of the work on the land itself.

Land, its ownership, occupation, and use, would soon become the major issue of confrontation between the Indians native to the northeastern section of the continent and the Englishmen who sought to establish new homes in the region. To understand the clash, we must understand more fully the attitudes and expectations of the white settlers themselves.

Most of the Englishmen who immigrated into New England in the seventeenth century had lived off the land in the old country and fully expected to become farmers or husbandmen in the new. English authorities knew well that the best way to attract settlers to overseas colonies was to offer them the opportunity to become landholders. In contrast, both the French and Dutch distributed land to seigneurs and patroons, who then attempted to attract settlers to take up leaseholds on terms similar to those in France and the

Netherlands. Why they expected peasants to leave France in order to remain peasants in Canada is difficult to imagine. England did not simply pay lip service to the principle of broad distribution of New World lands. It in fact adopted an extremely effective system for getting lands into the possession of the individual quickly and efficiently.

Massachusetts Bay will serve as an illustration. A group of Puritans backed by influential London businessmen formed in 1628 the New England Company, for the purpose of developing the fish, timber, fur, and other resources of the New World. To secure a base of operations they sought and received the following year a royal charter confirming their claim to the lands lying between lines three miles north of the Merrimack River and three miles south of the Charles River and running all the way to the "South Sea." They also received a new name, the Massachusetts Bay Company, and a free hand to govern their own affairs from headquarters in New England if the directors so desired (which they did). The company had little trouble finding potential settlers from among the many disaffected Puritans living in East Anglia and others from the West Country around Devon and Cornwall. With the arrival of John Winthrop's fleet with about 1000 settlers on board at Boston in the spring of 1630, the new colony was underway, and its governing board, called the General Court, began its quarterly meetings that autumn.

It is not necessary for us to trace the various routes by which this body emerged within a decade as a representative legislature for the colony of Massachusetts Bay. Suffice it to say that in addition to making such rules and regulations that were deemed necessary to establish the kind of colony its members wanted, the General Court's primary task was to preside over the distribution of the land granted the Company in its original charter.

The process varied somewhat in detail from case to case, for no official guide existed to instruct would-be settlers along the proper path, but within a decade after 1630 a general pattern had begun to emerge as a model for the future. First a group of settlers, usually numbering thirty or forty adult males, who were discontented with some aspect of their previous residence (or who had just arrived) petitioned the General Court for a grant of land for the purpose of founding a new community. In making such a grant, the Court generally gave leaders of the group considerable latitude in selecting the site, so long as it was not too distant from existing communities.

Defense against Indians, social cohesiveness, and religious conformity all argued in favor of a cautious plan of expansion. An explora-
tory committee for the new group looked for an unoccupied region
well endowed with natural meadowland, ample water, good woodland, and accessibility to the more settled parts of the colony. Such a
tract might include about forty to sixty square miles, although the
founders of Dedham received a grant five times as large, and others
varied widely.

Indian claims to the area had next to be extinguished, generally
through a treaty negotiated by the General Court. Much has been
written of the heavy-handedness of English settlers dealing with Indian claims. Unquestionably the white man was determined to possess these lands with or without the consent of the natives, but the
evidence is strong that, in New England at least, newcomers legal-
ized the transaction by purchasing the land, usually with such trade
goods as the metal tools the Indians badly wanted. At the time, the
natives seemed to consider that such an exchange of scarce metal-
ware for a part of their vast holdings a fair trade, especially as they
were customarily permitted to continue hunting and fishing in the
unoccupied parts of their former territory. Puritans of the seventeenth century would have strenuously denied any conscious inten-
tion of cheating the natives. That the Indians' growing dependence
on European goods directly contributed to the ultimate breakdown
of their society was a result that neither whites nor Indians anticipated. Nor could it have been prevented short of wholesale withdrawal of whites back to the Old World, a remedy hardly in keeping
with historical realities.

With a clear title to their grant, leaders of the proposed town next
drew up a covenant setting forth the principles upon which their
new community was to be founded. Dedham's covenant was perhaps typical for the period. First came a commitment to Christian
love as the governing principle of the intended inhabitants' daily
lives. Secondly the covenanters agreed to "receive only such unto
us as may be probably of one heart with us" in their determination
to lead godly lives. There would be no room in Dedham for dissen-
ters or malcontents. In the realization that differences would inevitably arise even among loving men and women, the next section of
the covenant provided for the mediation of disputes by impartial
third parties. On a still more practical level, the fourth part of the

covenant pledged the property owners in the town to pay their share of the public costs and to obey all laws and ordinances adopted to further the peace and orderly progress of the community. Men received into the town at its founding were to sign the document not only for themselves but for their successors forever. The principles upon which Dedham was founded were therefore intended to continue in perpetuity.

With the covenant prepared, the founders of the new town turned to the difficult task of selecting men to join them in the undertaking. Applicants residing in the old town or nearby might be known well enough, but what of the young man from Salem or the older one freshly arrived from England? Did he agree with the proposed method of distributing land? Was he a man of some substance in his previous community? Why had he left? Was he a church member? Answers to these and other searching questions could best be discovered by personal interview. As each man was accepted into the group, he "owned" the covenant and earned the right to examine subsequent candidates. It was not entirely a buyer's market, for every town needed certain individuals and was prepared to offer extra land to an inspiring minister, an experienced miller, and perhaps a skilled blacksmith. Gradually the numbers increased until at last the limit was reached, a number determined perhaps by the house lots available or by an estimate of how many families the land might initially support.

Meanwhile, the difficult task began of "ordering" the town, the process by which inhabitants acquired their land. Once again precedents were scarce, alternatives were plentiful, and critical decisions had to be made by imperfect men. A land committee had already made a more precise survey of the town's grant. Its members chose a suitable location for the village center, if possible on a site that could be easily defended, perhaps alongside a river, like Newbury's, or on top of a gentle rise, like Deerfield's. An adequate water supply was another requirement. The basic choice of land systems—between "open field" and "enclosed field" or some combination of the two—had probably been made by the original petitioners in favor of the system they had been accustomed to in the old country. Each plan had its own advantages. Open fields meant that scarce equipment could be shared, labor pooled, and the cohesiveness of the community preserved, because some of the land was set aside for all to cultivate cooperatively. But it often demanded a greater spirit of cooperation than many were capable of sustaining. Except for the home lot, a family's holdings were scattered about in several areas around the perimeter of the village. An enclosed system, on the other hand, by granting individual plots of one hundred or more acres, quickly led to the dispersal of population as men moved out from their village houses to take up residence on their tillable acreage.

Finally came the actual division of the land according to the system agreed upon. The committee that had examined applicants for admission assigned each successful candidate a specific place within the group. In Sudbury, for instance, the minister Edmund Brown was ranked number one, a wealthy investor came second, the miller third. Edmund Rice held eighth position, perhaps on the strength of his position in his former village of Berkhamsted. These rankings usually determined the size and location of one's lands within the town, leading citizens receiving the more favorable grants. Thus Edmund Rice received a fine four-acre home lot fronting the central Commons on Mill Road, thirty-three acres of river meadow, and fifty-four acres of upland across the river. He also received strips of open fields, and since only a small proportion of the town's grants was initially distributed, Rice could look forward to shares of future divisions. By right of being an original settler, Rice became one of the town's proprietors, who exercised exclusive control over all common lands. Later arrivals to the town might qualify to vote in town meeting, but they could become proprietors only by invitation or by the purchase of a proprietor's share. Now a vacant tract of wilderness was about to become a new town within the colony of Massachusetts Bay.

Settling In

With the initial distribution of the land completed, the first inhabitants could at last move out to their new grants. Here they raised crude houses on the lots around central commons, began the long process of clearing common fields and their own upland plots for cultivation, and started to fence in pasture lands to restrain their livestock. In the succeeding months the residents would also establish a church and a town government.

In ordering most Massachusetts towns, the founders used considerable care in selecting the site for the first habitation. In some cases house lots were laid out around a central green or common, but sometimes terrain or other considerations required that the town be planned along a single central street, one end of which might lead into an open market square. Complementing the dwellings constructed in the heart of the village were several other buildings of importance—the meetinghouse, the parsonage, the school, a tavern, several shops, and perhaps one or two garrison houses for defense against Indian attacks. The green itself was usually left as open space on which to muster the local militia, graze livestock, or simply enhance the village prospect. In many towns construction had to conform to certain regulations. Some enforced a minimum setback rule; others regulated the size of dwellings or the materials used. No one seemed to argue with the necessity for such rules. Most towns prescribed the pattern of streets as well as their width and other characteristics. Only a few villages developed helter-skelter without any plan at all, but the topography of a town like Boston, say, surely gives credence to the popular myth that cows rather than people laid out most of the original streets.

The essence of seventeenth-century Massachusetts life lay not so much in the village center as in the land around it. Whatever else we should know about these men and women in their scores of little villages, we must come to sense their closeness to the soil: each day determined not by the whims of man but by the requirements of nature; each year given to the planting, cultivation, and harvesting of the fields according to a schedule not of man's making but of the seasons; a lifetime devoted to the gradual acquisition and clearing of land whose worth reached far beyond a lifetime into the future. Each day's labor was an integral part of the year's endeavors, and each year became a part of a lifetime goal. As a man worked for his own survival, so, too, he worked for his children and for their children. At the end of a lifetime of toil he might have little in the way of worldly goods to pass along, but he did leave his land to mark the essential achievement of his being—the home lot itself, with house and barn, garden and orchard; pastures carefully fenced by stone or rail; the upland cleared of stumps and under cultivation; the forest beyond, waiting its turn to be subdued.

The center of family life was the farm. At first scattered about in several parcels, the typical seventeenth-century farmer forsook his village home as soon as practicable and settled anew on some larger lot of land closer to his major holdings. A kitchen garden under the watchful care of the wife yielded beans, cabbage, and other fresh vegetables in season and a variety of produce for winter keeping in the root cellar. Nearby the farmer might have planted a number of fruit trees. Now apples, pears, cherries, and plums could be enjoyed in the summer and early fall, with enough left over for preserves as well as sweet and hard cider. Outbuildings with various yards and pens for livestock and poultry completed the usual home-lot arrangement.

The fortunate farmer possessed among his grants several acres of natural meadow of abandoned Indian fields, where he could graze his livestock and put in an initial crop of corn or grain without much preparation. But most of his land very likely was heavily forested. That, of course, ensured a plentiful supply of wood for his fireplace, for fencing, and for the construction of his dwelling place and outbuildings; but as families increased or as old fields lost their meager fertility, it became necessary to clear new lands. The best way was to girdle the large trees, then wait for the next season and fell them. Timber not needed or unsuitable for other purposes was burned along with the branches and underbrush, to enrich the soil. Next came one of the most difficult tasks—removing the stumps. Grubbing around the roots helped to loosen the soil, but sometimes several teams of oxen were required to haul out the remains. Another onerous task was digging out the rocks and large boulders, which seem to grow like weeds in New England. Even after the rocks were disposed of—by building stone walls or a cairn—the first ploughing was no easy matter. Oxen had to work a heavy plow through the tough topsoil and entangled roots, and over deep stump holes, before the farmer could plant his first field crop. A hard-working landowner with a good yoke might be able to clear one or two acres each year without neglecting his other duties. A man could not help becoming part of the land that he himself brought from wilderness to cultivation.

Once cleared, the fields were ready for their first crops. Indian corn, wheat, and rye were the most common, although peas and beans, oats, barley, and other grains were also raised in considerable quantity. Calculations based on Plymouth records show that in the

·1640s an acre of land could produce eighteen bushels of corn worth £2 3s. When sown to wheat, however, an acre of typical Massachusetts soil yielded only eight bushels, and other grains fared no better. The inventory of a Plymouth farmer who died in 1650 discloses total holdings of about 30 acres, of which 5½ were planted to corn, 2½ to wheat, 2½ to rye, and 1 to peas. The balance of his land supplied his timber and served as pasture for his livestock. This ratio of one acre cultivated in every three owned was typical for a midseventeenth-century farm, but during the next two generations the ratio might increase to two acres under the plow in every three.

Various breeds of English and European cattle provided milk and beef for the family. Oxen were a necessity, as we have already seen, and so was the family horse. Sheep and goats provided wool, mutton, and milk, and pigs were a common source of meat because they could fend for themselves and they reproduced at a prodigious rate. Chickens, ducks, and geese provided meat and eggs for the table with little trouble. For much of the year the farmer could let his livestock run free in pasture, but pigs had a bad habit of breaking loose and raising havoc in the garden areas. During the winter most of the farm animals were kept close by in the yard and were fed whatever oats, hay, and other grains the farmer had stored for the purpose. Autumn was the usual season for slaughtering, the meats being hung and then smoked or salted down for winter consumption.

To work his farm the owner required three basic tools—a plow, a harrow, and some sort of cart. Most seventeenth-century plows found in Massachusetts were simple wooden implements with an iron coulter to cut the soil ahead of the plowshare. The harrow consisted of several heavy timbers in the form of a rectangle or triangle mounting a number of iron spikes to break up the soil. Most carts were simple two-wheeled vehicles which could carry various cargoes, both material and human. Without a sturdy cart no farmer could manure his fields or harvest his crop. In addition to these major items were a wide variety of rakes, shovels, hoes, scythes, and other hand tools which the farmer could make himself.

In Plymouth Colony the fields were often dry by the middle of March so that the husbandman could get his plowing done and first plantings in by the middle of May. In interior regions, however, the farmers had to contend with a prolonged mud season, which often delayed plowing until late April or beyond. During the summer months the yeoman concentrated on getting in a good hay crop, and in a long summer he might well make two hayings. By the end of August it was time to begin harvesting the wheat and other grains. Corn, pumpkins, and winter squash were left till last. Through the darkening autumn weeks the family husked the corn, threshed the wheat, and put up preserves for the winter. The yield was disappointing by English standards, only eight or ten bushels of wheat per acre, and eighteen bushels of corn. The soil was thin, and the early settlers had neither the time nor the incentive to experiment with new techniques to increase productivity. There was plenty of land, after all. No need to devote scarce time and labor to intensify the yield from a few acres. The colonial way to greater production was to cultivate more land.

Despite their inefficient methods, the farmers of Massachusetts soon produced more foodstuffs than their families could consume. And as succeeding generations grew to adulthood and put more acreage under the plow, the aggregate surplus grew larger each year. At first the steady stream of newcomers into the province depended upon these foodstuffs for survival, but emigration fell off sharply after 1640 and new markets had to be found. By midcentury Boston was becoming an entrepôt for a number of communities as far away as Ipswich, Concord, and Dedham. Farmers found a growing market for a variety of country produce, particularly beef and pork, wheat, firewood, shingles, and staves. Even a farmer as far inland as William Pynchon at Springfield sent 1500 bushels of grain to Boston in 1652. The merchants then exported much of this produce overseas to the West Indies, the Azores, and other Atlantic islands, and to Spain. Taking their profits in sugar, wines, or bills of exchange, the shipmasters then called at London or Bristol to purchase return cargoes of woolens and other manufactures. By the end of the century, then, the average farmer of Massachusetts Bay was acquiring the means to purchase some of the goods that could raise his standard of living beyond the level of bare subsistence.

The idea of land as security for a paper currency became a popular idea in Massachusetts early in the eighteenth century as an answer to the chronic shortage of specie in a rapidly expanding economy. In 1714 the General Court established a public land bank in response to an effort by Boston interests to charter a private bank. The public institution issued bills of credit which were lent out and circulated as legal tender throughout the province. The system worked for a time but could not keep pace with new demands. Not only was the economy expanding but at the same time it was becoming increasingly complex and therefore more dependent upon a circulating medium of exchange. Another problem was the growing scarcity of land. New farmers were increasingly forced to purchase their homesteads from merchants and other businessmen who were investing some of their mounting profits in large tracts in western Massachusetts, New Hampshire, and Maine.

Then in 1740 England ordered the contraction of public paper money in its colonies, and a group of subscribers began to issue bills secured by borrowers' lands, annual repayment to be made in bills or particular manufactured articles. Almost any landowner could obtain a loan from the land bank by mortgaging his real estate and making payments in manufactured commodities. The proposal particularly appealed to farmers who needed additional capital with which to purchase more land, or perhaps to purchase a store, inn, or craftsman's shop. In short, the land bank combined the traditional value of real property as the basis of wealth with the modern need to borrow money for the improvement of one's economic position. The land bank particularly appealed to men on the rise. In a larger sense the land bank scheme symbolized a break taking place from an older pay-as-you-go economy in favor of a modern system built on credit and a faith in future growth. Unfortunately for its supporters, the land bank was ultimately disallowed by the Privy Council.

Patterns of land use remained little changed throughout the eighteenth century. The frontiers moved inland, of course, and up the river valleys into New Hampshire, southern Maine, and across the Connecticut into Vermont, a region hotly contested by New York and New Hampshire. But except for farms very close to the major seaports along the coast, self-sufficiency remained the basic pattern of agriculture. As a broad generality one might say that for most of the seventeenth century the New England farmers had been fully occupied with clearing land of trees, stumps, and stones, with building houses and outbuildings, with husbanding livestock and planting crops for family consumption. Of course these functions also dominated the lives of most farmers in the newly settled regions of the interior throughout much of the eighteenth century as well. As the century progressed, however, market farming became somewhat more common throughout southern New England. By the end of the Revolutionary period in 1790 possibly a majority of farmers in southern and central New England sent at least some produce to market, and by the Civil War, three generations later, one would be hard pressed to find more than a few farmers anywhere in New England who were unaffected by the economic world around them.

The Nineteenth Century

The typical farm of the early nineteenth century consisted of about 100 acres or somewhat more. Ordinarily about one third of the acreage was in woodland, or in swamp or other wastelands. Another third was pasture, some of it natural perhaps, the rest cleared. The balance of the farm was divided between mowing fields, orchards, and tillage, the latter category rarely taking up more than ten or twelve acres of a one-family farm. Most contemporary observers, both residents and outsiders, seemed to agree that New England farmers were considerably less efficient than their counterparts in the middle states or in Europe. They were less likely to pursue a regular schedule of crop rotation; they were careless in handling manure; and they seemed slow to take up new crops or otherwise to diversify from their principal reliance on Indian corn. Wheat did very poorly, at least in part because of overdependence on inferior strains, and they had to rely on barley and rye as their primary source of grain. Only farmers along the coast seemed interested in experimenting with different kinds of fertilizer to restore their fields. Here was available both an inexpensive source of fish (herring, alewives, whitefish) and also seaweeds of various sorts. Without the incentive of a market for the sale of surplus crops, however, and without a handy source of cheap fertilizer nearby, the farmers further inland were far less likely to adopt systematic restoration of their lands.

One major resource available to almost all landowning farmers was the woodlot, for as we have noted, fully one third of most holdings was in forest lands. Here again, however, basic attitudes affected the way in which men used (or abused) a resource. From the earliest settlements of the seventeenth century, Americans had considered forests to be one of the greatest obstacles to progress in the new world, and they bent every effort to clearing the land. A few trees, of course, were used for firewood and for the construction of houses, barns, fences, and housewares, but for the most part the tree, like the Indian, was considered an enemy to be driven from the land. No one anticipated a time when timber would be of sufficient value to justify measures of conservation, let alone management of any sort.

Thus nineteenth-century farmers had to overcome deep-seated prejudices of almost two hundred years' duration in order to recognize that the forest resources of southern and central New England were in fact becoming scarce. Even so, few farmers had the patience to practice selective cutting; rather, they clear cut one plot after another, with only vague expectations that each would restore itself in time to its original condition. This, of course, rarely happened, with the result that second-growth forests were often of inferior quality. By the middle of the nineteenth century, therefore, the interior and hill-country forests of northern Maine had taken on increased value and provided a fairly good source of income for their owners for several decades thereafter.

The ways in which nineteenth-century New Englanders used their land resources were as varied as the land itself and the demands put upon it by outside developments. After a slow recovery from the disruptions of the Revolution, New England's economy resumed the expansion it had experienced throughout much of the eighteenth century, with new opportunities enhancing more established paths to prosperity. Perhaps the most significant development was the rapid expansion of foreign commerce at the outbreak of the Napoleonic wars in 1793. This affected the use of land in several ways. One major commodity in the trade was West Indies sugar, and in order to obtain it for shipment to Europe, New England merchants had to send to the Caribbean quantities of produce from both forest and farm. Lumber and other wood products, particularly shingles, clapboards, and staves, were in great demand, as were all sorts of foodstuffs. Fish generally led the list, but beef and pork, corn, peas, onions, lard, butter, and cheese were also popular items in the Islands. As a result, New England farmers could count on a steady demand for their surplus produce in the seaport cities of Boston, Newburyport, Salem, and Providence, which were heavily engaged in the so-called "neutral trade" boom from 1792 to the outbreak of the War of 1812.

Not only were these surpluses wanted as outgoing cargoes, but the seaports themselves represented a major market for farm produce. During the quarter century of prosperity some of them expanded in population by 50 percent or more, far outgrowing the foodstuffs that could be supplied by the few farms within their own town limits. Inland farms therefore experienced a considerable expansion in their domestic markets within New England itself as well as in the port cities farther south, particularly New York, in the Chesapeake Bay region, and along the Carolina lowlands. Although the boom in commerce was sharply curtailed during the four years of war with Great Britain, by 1815 the larger ports of Boston, Providence, and New York succeeded in reestablishing profitable overseas routes and enjoyed a resumption of commercial prosperity. By no means were the other seaports doomed, however, because much of the capital that accumulated during the neutral trade was invested in manufacturing establishments, particularly cotton and woolen cloth but later also the shoe, leather, and hardware industries. This meant that the expansion of communities into cities continued, even after their prosperity as seaports declined, and of course they continued to be profitable markets for the farmers of the interior. Finally, it should be noted that new industrial centers sprang up in the first half of the nineteenth century where only farming villages or no communities at all had previously existed. Lawrence, Lowell, and other mill towns of the Merrimack Valley; Hadley, Holyoke, and Springfield in the central Connecticut River Valley; and still further inland towns of the Upper Valley—including Bellows Falls and Brattleboro, for example—also became markets for the produce of New England farms.

A smaller market that should not be overlooked was composed of the business and professional men and the artisans who lived in almost every rural village. Although many of them may have continued to maintain a small kitchen garden in the back of their home lot along with some livestock, they also depended on neighborhood farmers for at least some of their foodstuffs. Of course, all town dwellers also needed firewood and such other products as cider, potash (for soap), and hay (for their horse and other domestic animals). In the smallest communities much of this exchange must have been done on a barter basis, but in the larger towns farmers could sell their produce at the local store, where customers paid cash for the quantities and qualities they needed.

But transportation systems at the beginning of the nineteenth century remained so poorly developed that only farmers within ten or fifteen miles of these growing centers could take full advantage of their markets. The principal routes for moving bulk commodities were limited to waterways, public roads, and a few turnpikes just then coming into existence wherever traffic was fairly heavy. Natural bodies of water like Long Island Sound, Narrangansett Bay, Massachusetts Bay, and the Great Bay region of New Hampshire made it possible for farmers to move their goods along the shore. Only a few New England rivers were navigable for more than a few miles into the interior, however. The Connecticut offered the most promise, with tidewater reaching all the way to Enfield, Connecticut, a few miles above Hartford and sixty-five miles from the mouth of the river at Old Saybrook. In Massachusetts the Merrimack River could be used as far inland as Haverhill, about twenty miles upstream. Above the fall line only small craft could travel on the rivers, and they had to rely on locks and canals to get them around the many rapids.

Regular roads were hardly adequate for the carriage of heavy goods. In fact, a man on horseback often had difficulty going from one town to the next, especially in the muddy season or during inclement weather. Consequently the movement of bulk commodities was usually limited to trips of fifteen miles or so, the distance a farmer might be able to cover in a day by ox-cart or wagon over the better roads. With the appearance of turnpikes in the eastern sections of Massachusetts and parts of Connecticut, matters improved somewhat. Not only were the road surfaces usually a little better than on public roads, but the carter could find accommodations along the way so that he could reasonably plan to reach markets several days' distance from his farm. As of about 1810, however, probably only 10 percent of New England's farmers had much hope of marketing significant surpluses in urban centers or through seaports to the southern states and the West Indies. These were the fortunate few who lived along the southern coasts of Connecticut and Rhode Island, near the shores of Massachusetts Bay or whose farms were located in the Connecticut River Valley or near the market towns already mentioned. The remaining 90 percent of New England's farmers were forced to remain self-sufficient until well into the middle of the nineteenth century.

One way in which farmers who were located at a considerable distance from markets could still sell some of their produce was to raise livestock. A few tidewater farmers of the seventeenth century had specialized in cattle, and the idea spread up the Connecticut Valley, especially in the following century. Not only was the product more valuable per pound than vegetables, but the animals provided their own means of transportation to market. By the 1830s, according to one authority, some 8000 head of cattle and 5000 sheep arrived each day during the season at the Brighton Market outside Boston from the farms of the interior. Prosperity of at least modest proportions brought with it not only a general sense of contentment but a gradual increase in population of the interior towns as well.

High Water

By the middle of the nineteenth century, most historians agree, the agricultural phase of land use in New England reached a high-water mark. This is not to say that in several subsequent periods farming would not again prove attractive in New England, but conditions were at their best throughout the region as a whole for the generation that thrived in the years 1840–80. Such a judgment is difficult to prove, of course, but certain facts do stand out. By 1880 both the number of farms and the amount of acreage devoted to agriculture had peaked in New England. Thereafter, both figures would steadily decline. And if the experience of the Connecticut Valley area of Massachusetts was of any significance to the region as a whole, the amount of acreage under tillage dropped even more rapidly. The value of farms reached its highest level of the century in 1880 as well, not to be topped for another thirty years, by which time other factors in land use raised values all around.

One development that brought prosperity to the farms of New England was the steady growth of cities throughout the region. In 1840 less than 20 percent of the region's population lived in urban areas (towns of 2500 or more). Forty years later, however, slightly more than half of all New Englanders lived in such towns. In the three southern New England states the concentration of urban dwellers was even greater, of course. Altogether by the year 1880 over two million New Englanders were dependent on a slightly smaller number of inhabitants for all of their foods.

Such a development would have been meaningless—in fact it probably could not even have taken place—were it not for a technological innovation that encouraged both the concentration of population and the ability of a minority of inhabitants to support the majority's need for foodstuffs. The innovation was the railroad. From 1840 on, the miles of track laid in New England increased so rapidly that by 1880 there was hardly a nook or cranny of the region not linked by rail with the population centers of central and southern New England. No longer did farmers have to live within a few miles of cities to send their goods to market. The iron horse overcame all of the topographical obstacles that had prevented most of the interior farmers from sending surpluses to the coast. With proper incentives those farmers could now expand their production to meet the challenge of a rising urban population.

Some economists have attempted to minimize the impact of railroads by asserting that without them the gross national product would have lagged behind its actual pace during the latter half of the nineteenth century by only three or four years. But surely such innovations as the railroad cannot be measured in dollars alone. In New England at least, the coming of the railroad profoundly altered not only the way farmers used their lands but ultimately their entire life style. Nor was the innovation an unmixed blessing. For the first time the region became accessible to the farms of the Middle West. Produce from Ohio, Illinois, and Wisconsin could and did undersell goods grown in New England itself because of the greater fertility of the soil and the opportunity mid-Western farmers had to make full use of mechanical devices and thus take advantage of economies of scale.

In response to the demands of the market, New England farmers altered the ways in which they used their lands throughout the middle decades of the nineteenth century. The first new development was the rise of the sheep industry beginning with the introduction of the Merino sheep from Spain just before the War of 1812. Sheep proved particularly adaptable to the hill country of northern and

western New England, with the clip steadily increasing in value until the mid-1840s. Raw wool fed the mills of the Merrimack Valley
and other industrial regions of New England, and a fair amount
reached overseas markets. Beginning about midcentury, however, a
number of factors brought about a steady decline in the sheep industry. Protective tariffs against the importation of foreign wool
gave way to steady pressure from advocates of free trade; competition from western farmers increased as railroad lines improved; and
a gradual change in clothing fashions from wool to cotton affected
the market. By 1880 the number of sheep in New England had declined by almost 60 percent from the heydays of the 1840s, and the
industry would soon thereafter become virtually insignificant as a
source of income in the region.

Fortunately a new opportunity awaited the New England farmer
at about the same time, for as the sheep industry declined, dairying
began a rapid increase. Railroads provided milk runs, so that farms
more distant from the urban centers could now join with the establishments closer in to supply the growing cities with fresh milk, butter, and cheese. Simultaneously, there seemed to be a rise in the
per-capita consumption of dairy products, particularly of fresh milk,
so that market conditions greatly encouraged the region's farmers to
switch to dairy herds. Besides, pasturage and fodder had always
been in plentiful supply in New England, and when in the 1880s
the idea of silage from corn began to catch on, farmers could now
make full use of the grain that grew best in the region. By the end of
the century the familiar cylindrical silo was appended to virtually
every barn throughout the six-state area, particularly in Vermont
and Massachusetts, where the herds could be supported through
the long winters without dependence on outdoor pasturage.

Other farmers took advantage of an expanding market for poultry
products. Fresh eggs could now reach the cities by train and coastal
steamer from the most remote farms in Maine and New Hampshire.
Fresh-killed chickens, ducks, and geese were also popular in the cities. Where necessary, the railroads put on refrigerated cars to assure that various farm cargoes would arrive in the best possible condition. Farmers in particular areas within New England began to
specialize in other produce as well. In the Connecticut Valley the
cultivation of tobacco, especially for cigar wrappers, underwent rev-

olutionary expansion in the middle decades of the century. From the modest crops of the 1840s, tobacco became a major money-maker for farmers in the broad plains of the Valley by 1880. Two vegetables became the special products of two other regions within New England—the potato and the onion. The potato grew particularly well in soils of Maine's Aroostook County, and the coming of the railroad into that area at the end of the century meant that Maine potatoes could reach markets all over the east and middle west. As for onions, they had long been a staple product of the lower Connecticut Valley around Wethersfield, but in the latter part of the nineteenth century production increased rapidly in the Central Valley around Hadley.

The development of canning as a commercial process was probably a predictable eventuality. Farm wives had for generations put up their own vegetables and other preserves for winter consumption, but by the latter part of the nineteenth century the process had become commercialized and was revolutionizing the meat and fish industries as well as farming. Canners bought hundreds of thousands of dollars worth of corn, beans, and other vegetables for marketing under brand names that would soon become household words throughout the eastern seaboard. The fresh vegetable market also grew rapidly in the shrinking farmlands that still surrounded the major urban centers of New England. Improved public transportation made it possible for farmers or wholesalers to truck each day to a central produce market, where retail storekeepers, restaurateurs, and even knowing city housewives could buy fresh vegetables in season directly each day. Grapes, strawberries, and cranberries, especially along southeastern Massachusetts and Cape Cod, were other specialties, and of course everywhere in New England apples were sold—fresh in season and in the form of ever-popular cider in the fall and winter.

By the last two decades of the nineteenth century, however, two of the very forces that had brought a degree of prosperity to the farms of New England bore the fruit of decline as well. The railroads, which gave almost all farms of the region access to the markets of the city, also brought in the produce of the Middle West, where soil conditions and economies of scale made it possible for farmers to undersell easterners in their own backyard. Further-

more, this same network offered cheap transportation for the rest-
less or ambitious youngsters of rural New England who were willing
to try their luck in the lands further west. In the second place, the
cities of southern New England, which constituted the markets for
Yankee farms, also offered job opportunities at wages that seemed
most attractive to young country folk eager to get into the main-
stream of modern America. Neither of these developments was
new—New Englanders had been moving west since the first days of
the colonial settlement in the seventeenth century. What was new
after the Civil War was the vast improvement in transportation that
the railroad brought. Other rural New Englanders had been moving
into the urban areas of the region since the seventeenth century,
especially during periods when the future for agriculture seemed
dim and the opportunities in the cities seemed, at least by compari-
son, to be attractive. By 1900 the number of New England farms
had declined by almost 10 percent from the high-water mark of
1880; acreage fell a little less sharply. Clearly an era was coming to
an end; trends that would continue into the twentieth century had
already been established in the last decades of the nineteenth.

The Twentieth Century

As one looks back from the 1980s to the beginning of the present
century one is pressed to find more than one or two new developments in the way New Englanders used the lands around them. Perhaps the most significant development, not strictly an innovation,
was the remarkable rise in the use of rural areas for recreation. Industrialization had increased both the number of people with leisure and the amount of time available for vacations, and these facts
combined with the widening contrast between city and country to
attract increasing numbers of people to the woods, seashore, and
country villages of New England for a few weeks of relaxation each
summer. This trend provided jobs for rural folk in the inns and
hotels throughout the countryside and, for those still farming, a
nearby market for their produce. Furthermore, the search for places
suitable as second homes helped sustain the value of properties that
had outlived their usefulness as working farms.

Farmers who stayed in the business found for the first time that at least some elements in the urban industrialized society around them were concerned about the land and its continued production of necessary foodstuffs. Many farmers scorned the government expert and university scientist as having nothing practical to offer the working farmer, and this attitude persists among many rural folk to this day, perhaps not entirely without cause. But for those who would listen, the state agricultural colleges and the government extension services and experimental stations began in the early twentieth century to address themselves to some of the serious problems confronting farmers in New England and elsewhere. In dairying, still the single most important agricultural industry in the region, the threat of tuberculosis from impure milk continued to hang over many herdsmen. Other blights could carry off an entire flock of chickens, wipe out a potato crop, or destroy a promising apple season virtually overnight. The scientists got to work devising methods to detect such dangers before they occurred and then either developed disease-resistant strains or the means of protecting flock or crop from attack. Not all of the methods worked and progress was slow, but at the turn of the century science did begin to make a meaningful effort, with encouraging results.

Yet the number of New Englanders living on farms, after reaching a temporary new mark of 892,000 in 1900, began a long decline, slow at first but gaining momentum through the latter decades. The number decreased by 29 percent to 1920, by another 36 percent in the next thirty years to 1950, and by a further 68 percent in the twenty years to 1970. The number of farms and the amount of acreage in agriculture also declined precipitously, although at somewhat slower rates. Not surprisingly, however, the value of farm land increased throughout the twentieth century, first at a steady pace and then, since the end of World War II at a sharp rising rate, until by 1970 the average New England farm with its buildings was worth about $63,000. A look at the longer view tells the real story: as recently as 1900 slightly over half of New England's total acreage was devoted to agriculture, but by 1977 the farm share had dropped to less than 12 percent. What happened to the nearly 16 millions of acres that were in farmland at the beginning of the century? Some of it has obviously given way to the expansion of cities and towns into what have become suburban areas, but by far the greater portion of

abandoned farmland has reverted to forest. As of 1978 slightly over
50 percent (32,461,000 acres) of New England was classified as forestland and about 8 percent (5,200,000 acres) as farmland.

The Forests

We have already noted in passing that New Englanders made good
use of the forests almost from the moment of first settlement in the
seventeenth century. No matter how much timber was needed for
home construction, for domestic utensils of all sorts, for shipbuilding, fence-building, and firewood, there was more than enough left
over for export to less well forested parts of the Atlantic world. The
southern colonies had ample reserves of their own, but the West
Indies were less well endowed. In addition to lumber for buildings,
they required enormous quantities for barrel hoops and staves for
the shipment of their principal products—sugar, molasses, and rum.
Timber, then, played an important role in New England commerce,
along with fish and foodstuffs, for it enabled the merchants to buy
West Indian produce to exchange in England for highly desirable
manufactured articles like cloth goods, hardware, and chinaware.

Of equal importance was the use of New England timber in shipbuilding. Though most colonists of the region wanted nothing to do
with the sea, fishing and commerce nevertheless soon became significant activities, not least because of the abundance of timber
close to the shore or along river valleys that reached far into the interior. Oak for keel and frames and pine for planks and spars were
the principal woods that went into Yankee-built vessels. Throughout the colonial period the region could turn out ships at about two
thirds of the cost of vessels built in Great Britain. As a result, New
England merchants could compete with their counterparts in England for the carrying trade of the empire, and in fact they had no
difficulty selling their own vessels in the mother country at a considerable profit.

One of the most interesting markets for the forest products of
New England was the British navy. The gradual exhaustion of its
own timber resources had forced the mother country to find needed
supplies elsewhere. The Baltic served for a time, but access was dependent on cooperation of the Danes, who controlled the narrow

waters through the Belt, and they were not always dependable allies. Throughout the war-torn years from 1650 until the American Revolution more than a century later, England looked to its New England colonies for some of the timber necessary to build and maintain the "wooden walls" that were its first line of defense. Particularly desirable were the tall white pines needed for the masts and other spars for the giant ships of the line. The forests of Maine and New Hampshire became the major sources for these valuable trees. The most desirable were those with a diameter of at least three feet over a length of at least one hundred feet. The mast trade quickly became involved in imperial politics as Parliament insisted by 1729 that thereafter all American timber, masts, and naval stores (products like turpentine, pitch, and resin made from pine) could only be sent to the mother country. Furthermore, the king's surveyors were empowered to commandeer for the navy all trees of the proper size. Anyone harvesting a tree, even on his own property, marked by the king's broad arrow was subject to severe penalties.

The coming of steam in the nineteenth century greatly increased the demand for timber as fuel first for the boilers of steamboats operating along the coast and rivers of the region and later for the railroads. The inefficient engines of midcentury consumed enormous quantities of wood. As railroads expanded in this period, they required timber for rail ties, for trestle construction, and finally for the telegraph poles that paralleled many of the more important routes. Most of this wood came from small lots harvested by their farmer-owners as a part-time occupation. They worked mostly in winter after the fall harvest was completed and when the snows facilitated the task of getting the timber to market. Another demand for what we might call wood-lot timber was as domestic firewood, and for the lime kilns, iron smelters, and other industrial processes that were becoming increasingly common during the century. Coal did not emerge as a major source of fuel in most parts of New England until after the Civil War.

Paralleling these demands for timber was the expanding lumber industry. As we have already seen, wood from New England's forests was always in considerable demand as sawn lumber, shingles, clapboards, and other products needed in the construction of buildings. Demand rose as the area of settlement expanded across the continent, although of course new sources of timber supply increased as well. By the Civil War the upper Midwest had replaced New England as the leading producer of lumber in the country, although the forest products of Maine and New Hampshire remained in great demand. For one thing, wooden shipbuilding continued apace, especially in Maine, where yards along the Kennebec launched the increasingly large square-riggers called Downeasters, along with hundreds of coastal schooners used in the lumber, granite, and later coal trades along the coast. This activity lasted well into the twentieth century. In the 1880s a whole new market for timber in commercial quantities sprang into being with the change from cloth rags to pulpwood as the principal raw material for the making of paper. With growth of urban populations and the expansion of the packaging industry, the use of newsprint and paperboard expanded rapidly.

The major difference to note in the timber business is that the first-mentioned small-scale operations were principally carried out by individual farmers from their own wood lots, while the large-scale industries involved extensive forest areas owned by merchants, manufacturers, and professional men acting as investors. Of course these men did not get out the timber themselves, as did wood-lot owners. They hired woodsmen, built roads, set up sawmills, and employed managers to supervise the whole operation. Originally the farmers had obtained their land through the town as a grant to those who were willing to settle there. The large-scale owners, on the other hand, more often acquired their extensive holdings directly from king or colony as a result of political patronage or military reward. Later, wealthy merchants and others bought up large tracts as investments, hopeful perhaps that the tide of settlement would soon reach their land and increase its value. Often enough that is precisely what happened. But in the meantime it was worth while in many cases to harvest the timber on the more accessible acreage. Still later, groups of investors formed companies, or existing companies expanded their operations; as a result, in the twentieth century much of the timberland of northern New England is no longer in the hands of individuals. This outcome evolved slowly through the centuries but perhaps inevitably, since it was never likely that these areas would become as densely populated as more southerly parts of the region.

Other Land Uses

Almost all of the land used by New Englanders from the first settlements to the present has been for farms or timber and forest reserves. The remaining acreage is accounted for by a wide variety of other purposes, the most obvious of which has been for private residences in urban and suburban areas. In point of economic value, this use has long since become dominant as the density of population has grown each decade. Aside from housing, however, one must reckon in a number of enterprises other than agriculture and lumbering to explain the importance of land to New Englanders of the past. Some holdings have been valued for the stone and minerals that lay exposed or just beneath the surface. Granite deposits along the coast from Maine to Connecticut and marble in Vermont have been of great significance as a building material. Other tracts have borne limestone for the manufacture of plaster and cement, sand, and gravel. Even iron ore deposits of commercial quantity and quality were found in the bogs along the coast and in the northwest hills of Connecticut.

There is yet another factor to be considered in the determination of land values—location in respect to other natural advantages. For example, lots along the water, either the ocean itself, or harbors, rivers, and streams, have always been more valuable than other plots not so situated. Land fronting on a natural harbor invited the construction of a wharf, the launching of vessels, and the establishment of contact overseas or to the fishing grounds. A riverfront property was ideally suited for a factory because fuel, raw materials, and finished goods could all be transported by water, and waste products could simply be dumped into the stream. When leisure homes became a factor toward the end of the century, ocean- and lake-front sites were greatly enhanced in value, as were locations that commanded a scenic view of mountain ranges.

The Meaning of Land

From king to company, from company to town, and finally from town to individual, the land of New England inexorably passed into the possession of ordinary settlers. For most of them the ownership of land played an absolutely essential role in their lives and in the lives of their descendants for many generations thereafter. Indeed, land has fulfilled several of the same functions throughout our history. First, and most fundamental, land provided the New England settler with a place to live—a site for his house, room for a shed or barn for his livestock, space for his garden and perhaps a few fruit trees. In the villages of New England this piece of land was invariably know as the home lot. Often it was located in the middle of the settlement along with other plots surrounding a central green or common. But wherever it was found, this lot provided that place most essential to all creatures, a home.

The home lot was not only important as a means of providing basic subsistence for the family; it was equally important for the sense of psychological orientation it provided. "Be it ever so humble there's no place like home" reflects the deep-seated need of humankind to fulfill a sense of place. It is in the best interests of society that there be some means of assuring each of its citizens a place to call home. This principle is strengthened in Anglo-Saxon law by the well-buttressed doctrine that a man's home is his castle. Without such a system that made possible the acquisition and retention of a home, the strong and wealthy would soon dispossess the weak and poor, perhaps taking the common resources as well. Conversely, the homeless will often seize homesites, as on the plains of Kansas during the midnineteenth century, or in abandoned buildings of New York City today. Finally, the home lot fulfilled the need most of us have to identify ourselves (and others) in geographical terms. The answer to the universal question "Where are you from?" seems to reveal much about the respondent—perhaps less than we think, but nevertheless something, or else the question would not be asked so frequently. Whether the response is "I'm from Boston," or "I'm from the Back Bay," or "I'm from Commonwealth Avenue," each answer conveys some sort of message in the shorthand of American culture. Land as home, then, carries with it vastly important values of material, psychological, and social significance.

While the home lot usually contained enough acreage to include a small "kitchen" garden, it was never intended to remain the sole means of support for its owner and his dependents. For that purpose either a single tract of perhaps thirty or forty acres or several pieces of land including arable, pasturage, and woods, along with rights to the "common and undivided land" of the town was granted to each original settler. In many towns the home lot and farm lands were at first separate from each other, both physically and in concept. Only later did farmers in those "open-field" communities move their homes from the town center and take up residence on their working farms. Thereafter they followed the practice of working and living in the same place, but that should not obscure the fact that their land fulfilled an economic function distinguishable from its status as a home. Land as a means of earning a living, then, is a second meaning, one on which we have devoted much space and attention in this essay. As we have seen, land put to agricultural use supported non-farming communities as well, just as other land-based enterprises contributed to economic activities often far removed from the land in question.

A third meaning for land has been the means of establishing and maintaining a close bond between the individual landholder and the community in which he lived. We have noted that the original settlers in a New England town received a grant of land. The offer of such a gift could be and was used to attract additional settlers to the community as a means of adding to its strength. Most often, men with special skills, a minister, a miller, or a militia captain, for instance, would be given especially generous grants to draw them to towns without such people. Once there, the original settlers and their descendants were encouraged to remain in the town by the promise of shares in future divisions of the common lands. And so land was used not only to attract people to the community but to keep them there as well.

From the beginning, local communities relied on property holders as the primary source for tax revenues necessary to support such various public programs as the construction and maintenance of public highways, bridges, and schools, and care for the poor. There was probably no more effective way to link people and community than by the process of taxation. In fact, of course, the revenue was raised and disbursed by the taxpayers themselves, for in establishing their towns the colonists followed the principle of John Locke that only those with a stake in society should be entitled to participate in its political affairs. Until well into the nineteenth century the New England states all had property qualifications for voters and town meeting participants. Although one might meet the requirements with personal property, the common way to qualify was by the possession of real estate worth a certain minimum amount, enough to assure that the resulting electorate would act responsibly, since it also constituted the majority of the community's taxpayers.

In New England towns, furthermore, delegates to the colonial and later state legislatures had to own property and be residents of the town they represented. In contrast, Great Britain had no such residential requirement; to this day members of Parliament do not have to reside in the districts in which they stand for election. As a result, the concept of representative government in this country took on territorial implications from the start and has remained an integral part of the American political system. We expect our congressional delegates to represent the interests of our districts and states not only in competition with other parts of the country (witness the competition for defense contracts) but sometimes against the better interests of the nation as a whole (regional opposition to the 1980 grain embargo, for example). Although the formal property qualifications for both voter and officeholder have long disappeared from the scene, the candidate who can bill himself or herself as a "native of Nantucket," or a "local taxpayer" has an overwhelming advantage over opponents unable to make such claims. In short, the possession of land has held a central place in the structure and operation of our political system, bestowing upon the landholder a right to his political voice implicitly stronger than that of an ordinary resident and giving to our representative form of government a special meaning not found in the mother country or in most other European nations.

Yet another meaning of New England land has been investment. Much of the forest land of northern New England, as we have already seen, was granted to or was purchased by wealthy merchants, government favorites, or other entrepreneurs, not for immediate use but for either later development or sale. Until well into the nineteenth century there were relatively few ways in which a successful merchant could invest his profits. Banks were scarce and of uncertain security, and the same was true of manufacturing corporations. Successful men, not wanting to plough all of their profits back into their principal business, looked to purchase in lands as a means of diversifying their investments.

At first the goal was more a matter of security than profits. The intelligent observer could easily conclude, however, that the steady increase in population would ultimately bring a rise in the value of land as well, and that would more than offset the carrying charges of taxation and minimum supervision. This did happen during the agricultural era of the colonial period and first three quarters of the nineteenth century, during which the farming population increased several fold; it has remained valid even as New England's people have moved off the land into urban areas. One reason is that lands put on the market by one farm family were usually bought up by neighbors who added the acreage to their own establishments, increasing the value of both parcels. Furthermore, the many other uses for rural acreage—forestry, primary housing, and second homes, for example—have helped to maintain a steady demand for all but the most remote or impenetrable property.

The value per acre of New England farm land and buildings has continued to increase in remarkable fashion throughout the twentieth century. From 1900 to 1950 it increased nearly fourfold while general prices rose only about three times. In constant dollars this represented a real increase of about 15 percent, at a time when the total of farm acreage fell by almost 40 percent. Since 1950, the figures show, any investor able and willing to keep his money in actual farmland has been richly rewarded. For the real value per acre has increased about two and one-half times between midcentury and 1978. One would expect, of course, that as agricultural acreage is converted into residential uses or reverts to forest, the value of the remaining farmland would increase simply in response to the effects of diminishing supply. The fact is, land has been and continues to be an excellent investment for those patient enough to forego present earnings for future capital gains.

Perhaps the best way to grasp the significance of holding land in New England is to think about what happened to the people who were deprived of it—the American Indians. In the long run it really mattered very little whether they lost their land by military conquest or by legitimate purchase, the consequences of that loss are significant. Without land the Indians of New England no longer had a home, except on so-called reservations left for them by the whites. Prohibited from retaining or purchasing land within white settlements, the Indian was effectively segregated from that society without any hope of becoming assimilated into the dominant culture. In the second place, without access to land other than the isolated and usually unproductive acres of the reservations, the Indians could barely support themselves either by the traditional means of hunting and gathering or by agriculture. Cut off from markets by distance, social ostracism, and relative ignorance of a cash economy, they had little hope of rising above the level of self-sufficiency. And unless they were permitted to invest their gains in land, what good would profits have been? A romantic view might suggest that self-sufficiency was a blessing in disguise, except that the Indians' inability to "progress" was constantly viewed by whites as a sign of their racial inferiority and became its own justification for continued deprivation.

Thirdly, by depriving the Indian of land, the dominant society denied him a political voice and thereby of any meaningful place within the system. His views and interests remained totally unrepresented in town, state, and national levels of government, for the simple reason that the Indian was not a resident landowner in any political district. Francis Jennings has noted in his perceptive work *The Invasion of America* that "property and liberty were synonymous in the seventeenth and eighteenth centuries. When the Indian was dispossessed of his land he lost all hope of finding any niche in the society called civilized, except that of servant or slave."

Had the Indian been permitted to retain landholdings within the white community as had the Dutch in New York, for instance, cultural differences might still have delayed assimilation for many generations. But surely the Indian would have in time found a place within that society far more promising than was his actual fate. For the possession of land was above all else the only way to find a home and get ahead in the first two centuries of New England's history.

TOWARD A WORKING
RURAL LANDSCAPE

Mark B. Lapping

IT HAS BEEN SAID by more than one student of New England agriculture that had the recent independent truckers' strike lasted one more week, New Englanders would have learned that the food on supermarket shelves was all there was to be had! No region lacks food storage and processing capability as much as New England does. Indeed, the six states of the region import 80 percent of their foodstuffs from other regions and nations. Prices tend to be higher for basic foodstuffs, and with the cost of transportation rising, in large part because of increasing fuel prices, New Englanders will pay increasing amounts for food.

It was not always that way. A century ago agriculture was one of the preeminent industries in New England, and most of the commodities New Englanders consumed came from the farms and forests of the region itself. Now there are fewer farms and fewer farmers. The survivors have become exceedingly productive, .but they produce fewer products.

Cycles of New England Agriculture

Even before the arrival of the first white settlers, agriculture and forestry were important activities of the Indians who dwelled in New England.[1] And from the earliest time of settlement by Europeans, each successive generation of Yankees has maintained a dynamic relationship with the land. The forests provided fuel, building materials, cooperage, maple syrup, and nuts. The farms produced all manner of meat, dairy products, fruits and vegetables, and homespun. The rural land base of the region emphasized the township system of land settlement and local village government, which nurtured and sustained the family owned and operated farm. For many years to come this was to be the predominant pattern of New England society and its physical landscape.

Early New England farms were categorized by a high level of self-sufficiency. As one writer has noted of Vermont's early farms, "cattle were kept to supply butter, cheese, milk and beef, as well as leather for shoes, harnesses, and other farm purposes. Sheep were kept to supply mutton and wool. Swine, turkey, geese and other poultry were kept for family use. Maple products were used in place of imported sugar. Wheat, corn, oats and other crops were grown to supply the family needs and to feed livestock." [2]

The high point of New England agriculture, defined as the greatest number of farms and amount of land in agricultural production, was reached in the late nineteenth century. According to the 1880 Census of Agriculture, there were over 200,000 farms in the region operating on some 21 million acres. [3] With the exception of Maine, whose land mass was dominated by forests, agriculture was, by far, the major use of land in all states. The farms were manifestly productive, for the region was self-sufficient in all major crops and livestock categories and food exports to other regions and nations were substantial.

Although this self-sufficiency existed throughout the nineteenth century, changes in the structure of the region's agriculture were beginning to emerge. Perhaps the most profound was the gradual movement toward specialization of production as a market economy evolved and matured. At the same time, competitive production centers in the Middle West and West, began to claim many of New England's markets and more than a few of its young. Alternative em-

TABLE 1. *Percentage of Land in Farms*

State	1880	1940	1970
Maine	33	21	9
New Hampshire	64	31	11
Vermont	82	62	32
Massachusetts	67	39	14
Rhode Island	78	33	10
Connecticut	79	49	17

SOURCE: U.S. Census of Agriculture, 1880, 1950, and 1970

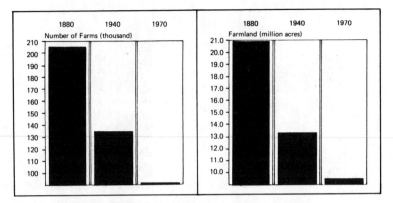

Figure 1. New England's Disappearing Farms.

SOURCE: U.S. Census of Agriculture, 1880, 1940, 1970, modified by Wayne Worcester in "Farmland for New England's Future," *Yankee* (October 1978).

ployment opportunities, both within and without New England, also added to a general decline. Gradually, the number of farms decreased—the "hill farms" going first[4]—and less land was devoted to agriculture, though farms remaining in production tended to increase in size and in their level of mechanization. The diminution in numbers and acreage has yet to be reversed.

By 1940—after World War I, the Great Depression, many market adjustments, and the growing agricultural dominance of other regions—New England's agricultural picture looked significantly different. Only Vermont remained predominantly agricultural. With few exceptions, the region's farms were producing less of the commodities noted above. The exceptions were potatoes, hay, dairy products, poultry, and apples. Milk production, on a cow-by-cow basis, was rising substantially. Even more profound changes in agricultural land have occurred since 1940. By 1970 both the number of farms and land in farms had declined further, and no New England state was predominantly agricultural. The enormity of these decreases is clearly demonstrated in Figures 1 and 2.

A concomitant development has been the sharp reduction in farm employment and those working in the agribusiness sector. In the years between 1958 and 1978, total farm employment fell over 54

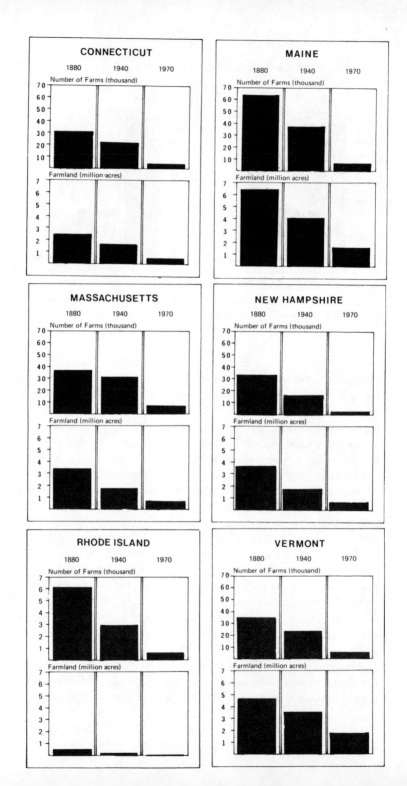

TABLE 2. *New England Farm Real Estate Values[a] and Average Dollar Value Per Acre of Land and Buildings[b]*

Year	Maine	N.H.	Vermont	Mass.	R.I.	Conn.	Average
1959	83	105	81	310	380	444	234
1964	100	132	109	386	485	561	292
1970	161	239	224	565	734	921	474
1974	341	564	462	961	1500	1525	892
1977	400	661	541	1126	1758	1779	1044
1979	485	802	567	1366	2133	2158	1270
% change (1959–79)	+484%	+664%	+711%	+331%	+435%	+386%	+442
% change (1970–79)	+200%	+235%	+193%	+131%	+191%	+134%	+169

SOURCES:
[a] U.S. Census of Agriculture, Farm Real Estate Market Development, U.S.D.A., E.S.C.S., July 1972/August 1979.
[b] Does not include machinery, equipment, livestock, etc., just land and permanent buildings.

percent from 171,000 to 78,000. Cash receipts for New England farm commodities increased, thus demonstrating the relative efficiency of the farmers that remained in production. Between 1964 and 1978, these cash receipts increased 81 percent, from $724 million to $1.3 billion.[5] All of this is reflected, in part, in farm real estate values, which have increased significantly.

Finally farmers in New England, with the exception of Vermont, have become minority owners of the region's farmlands. This situation contrasts with the nation as a whole, where farmers and ranchers have a greater degree of control over the future disposition of farmlands. The tenure factor, noted in the following data, remains a hidden dimension of land use that can no longer be ignored.[6] Strategies of farmland retention that do not address this issue may fail to create a stable and viable agricultural base.

This current period of farmland loss is, generally speaking, different from that of previous decades. Where in the past the "hill farm" was being abandoned, much of the land lost to farming in more recent decades has been converted to other land uses, usually

Figure 2. Vanishing Farmland in Six New England States.

SOURCE: U.S. Census of Agriculture, 1880, 1940, 1970 modified by Wayne Worcester, "Farmland for New England's Future," *Yankee* (October 1978). Reprinted by permission.

of a more urban variety. This has been the result of numerous government policies, expecially tax codes, the continued growth of the
region's metropolitan areas, a casual policy toward future food needs,
and the kind of short-term allocations which the market-place makes
so effectively and efficiently.

Where, then, has all the farmland gone? Though much of it has
been urbanized, especially in the past three decades in southern
New England, the New England farmland of yesterday has become
the New England forest of today. For then as now, the forest and the
farm have been dynamically related, often to the point of ecological
juxtaposition. When farms were created, the forest was cut. When
farms were abandoned and declined, forests grew. This is the key to
understanding New England's contemporary rural landscape. As
Table 4 on regional land use for 1969 indicates, forest is the predominant land use in the region in all states.

Forest lands now cover over 80 percent of the land area of New
England. Maine has the largest percentage, at 90, and Rhode Island
the least, at 60.[7] Every New England state is predominantly forested,
a marked contrast with the 1880 statistics, when all states but Maine
were dominated by agricultural uses. In approximately one century,
then, New England's land use has essentially turned from agriculture to forest. Once again, this represents a return to the historical
structure of rural land use at the time of settlement by Europeans.

TABLE 3. *Percentage Distribution of Farmland Acreage Owned in New
England, by Occupation*

State	Farming[a]	White Collar	Blue Collar[b]	Retired	Other	No Response	Total
Connecticut	26.2	19.3	10.3	26.6	2.8	14.8	100.0
Maine	30.6	26.6	20.0	14.2	3.8	4.8	100.0
Massachusetts	21.6	21.6	24.4	27.1	2.0	3.3	100.0
New Hampshire	28.5	39.9	7.9	17.6	1.9	4.2	100.0
Rhode Island	3.8	37.6	23.2	22.9	0.5	12.0	100.0
Vermont	55.4	20.7	6.7	10.6	4.0	3.6	100.0
United States[c]	53.6	13.4	7.6	15.8	4.1	5.5	100.0

[a] Includes farm managers and farm laborers.
[b] Includes private household and service workers.
[c] Excludes Alaska.
SOURCE: 1978 ESCS Landownership Survey (USDA).

TABLE 4. *Regional Land Use for 1969*

State	Agricultural Lands[a]	Forest	Developed	Other	Total
Maine	909	17,605	807	468	19,789
New Hampshire	255	5,046	294	182	5,777
Vermont	1,157	4,384	250	140	5,931
Massachusetts	337	3,412	1,219	14	5,009
Rhode Island	37	429	201	4	571
Connecticut	306	2,119	654	33	3,112
New England	3,001	32,995	2,425	841	40,289

[a] Includes pastures.
SOURCE: H. T. Frey, "Major Uses of Land in the United States, 1969," in *Agriculture, Rural Development, and the Use of Land*, Subcommittee on Rural Development, U.S. Senate, 93rd Congress, Second Session (Washington, D.C. 1974), p. 156.

Current Policies to Preserve Farmland

To date the policies of the New England states have centered on the need to retain farmlands.[8] The most widely used mechanism has been the differential tax assessment. Although there are subtle differences between programs, all differential tax systems employed in the region rest upon the assumption that a reduced property tax burden will aid farmers. Such a lower levy is brought about by the assessment of working farmland at its use and value for farming, rather than its market value if put to some other use. For a number of reasons, differential assessment has not proved to be an effective means of farmland retention. Perhaps the most obvious reason is that owners of land near the region's growth centers, who are most susceptible to development and conversion pressure, are noticeably unwilling to participate in such programs. This is especially the case in Maine, Massachusetts, Rhode Island, and Vermont, where penalties are laid upon landowners who convert lands to nonqualifying uses during a specified time period. Yet the most likely reason for the inability of differential assessment to control farmland conversion is that tax concessions under these programs are very largely overshadowed by the opportunities associated with development. Another criticism is that such tax programs could reduce the tax base of a jurisdiction and thereby reduce local government revenues. The ability of a county or town to supply certain services might be sharply curtailed if a significant amount of land were

brought into differential assessment programs. Efforts to make adjustments for this loss require the increase of property tax burdens
on nonfarm landowners. It has been argued by some that such an
adjustment program creates serious problems of justice and equity.
To date only Vermont has sought to address this issue by means of
reimbursement to local towns of lost tax revenues from the state's
general revenues.[9]

The failure of the differential tax program has spawned other responses throughout New England. Connecticut, Massachusetts, and
New Hampshire have begun to implement programs to purchase
farmland development rights. Under this method a farmer sells to
government his right to develop his land. The farmer keeps the fee
interest except for this one right, retaining all of his other rights,
including the right of possession. The encumbrance runs with the
land and thus binds all subsequent purchasers as well.

The public acquisition of development rights presents several
clear advantages over other methods. Buying development rights is
likely to be cheaper than fee simple purchase, and the landowner
retains ownership and control of his farmland. Landowners receive
a cash payment for giving up their right to develop, and this capital
could be utilized further to enhance the farm operation. Following a
favorable ruling from the Internal Revenue Service, governments
could pay farmers for the development rights over a number of
years, rather than all at once, spreading the federal capital gains tax
and keeping it in manageable proportions when it has to be paid.
Farmers who sell their development rights still have to keep their
lands on the tax rolls, but when the development rights are transferred to government, the farm can be taxed only on its agricultural
use value. Moreover, the expense of maintaining the property is not
transferred to a governmental agency, and the farmer can continue
to keep his property in a productive, though limited, use. A more
subtle though very important attribute of the program is that it addresses in a direct way some of the equity issues related to farmland
retention.

All too often a farmer's land is at once his hospitalization plan, insurance policy, child's college tuition, and personal retirement fund.
Consequently, farmers are clearly concerned about the issue of
compensation when they perceive land use controls to be limiting
their options. When compensation is provided, as in the purchase

of development rights, members of the agricultural community are more likely to participate. The point is that techniques to keep farmland in agricultural use often require that the development potential for agricultural lands will no longer be available to farmers. For a program to succeed, it clearly has to have the endorsement of the farming community. One way to obtain such support and cooperation is to deal openly and directly with the issues of justice and equity.

The great problem of buying development rights is cost; the purchase of such rights can be expensive. In rural areas, where development pressures are less intense, the cost of buying development rights is lower. But in areas under conversion pressure, the cost of acquisition would be high, and the reduction in the local tax base is significant as lands have to be assessed at use value. One way to reduce such costs might be to target such purchases selectively so that only farms under pressure for direct development would have their development rights purchased. Still, funding is required for such a program, and it appears that bonding, either by local or state governments, is the most appropriate source of capital for the program. As a consequence, there may be a tendency to purchase developments on particular farms because it makes good political sense rather than sound economic judgment. Whether the public purchase of development rights will prove to be an effective method to preserve farmlands remains to be seen.[10]

Vermont is the sole state in New England, indeed the nation, directly intervening in the farmland market through a capital gains tax. Under Vermont's program, variations in the tax rate depend on both the degree of gain from a land transaction and the length of time the land is held prior to sale. The rates rise as the percentage of gain from a sale increases, but decrease over time. Long-time owners are taxed far less than short-term, fast-turnover owners. The highest tax rate is 60 percent if the gain is 100 percent or less. As each year passes after the initial purchase, the rate drops in each gain class until the sixth year, when the tax is eliminated altogether. The purpose of this law is to tax the capital gains on land so heavily that speculation and the rapid turnover of land lose much of their profitability. A number of evaluations of this program suggest that the results are mixed at best. Where land markets soften, it would seem that the capital gains tax has been of aid in slowing the loss of agricultural lands. But where the market is intense, sales remain brisk.[11]

A "Business As Usual" Scenario

A recent USDA study of American agriculture plays out a "business as usual" scenario for the region's agriculture. It suggested that if "current trends in the Northeast continue for the next 20 years, there will be further decreases in the number of farms and more decline in acreage of lands in farms. The land taken out of production will be abandoned, consolidated into on-going units, or used for non-agricultural purposes."[12] The title of another USDA publication puts it succinctly: *Fewer, Larger U.S. Farms by Year 2000.*[13]

Clearly, predictions of this sort are easily upset and are highly dependent on a large variety of complex factors, such as the nature of regional food demand, demographic changes, alternative sources of supply, availability and cost of capital inputs, including land, and many others. Nonetheless, the continued diminution of New England's agricultural base is inevitable unless these factors change their present complexion in most fundamental ways or unless policy is altered.

Of course, not all changes in present policy would be favorable. In fluid milk production, a sector of the region's agricultural economy of the most fundamental consequence, federal policy has been directed to protecting New England farmers. Under the present milk-marketing order system, competition from other areas in New England's traditional market—the "Boston milkshed"—is largely prevented. Likewise, the prohibition against selling reconstituted milk at prices lower than fluid milk also works to the region's benefit, since major producing areas, like the Upper Midwest, could supply and ship powdered milk to eastern markets at (theoretically) lower prices than those at which regional farmers can supply fluid milk.[14] Finally, import restrictions also insulate and protect New England dairy farmers, though clearly other sectors of society pay for such policy initiatives. Current discussions in Washington, D.C., are focusing on substantial changes in the price-support structure of milk production, and this could influence the region's dairy industry in a profoundly negative way. The point is that policy manipulation is of critical importance to the future of the region's agriculture; it is not to be overlooked or taken lightly. Moreover, any policy cuts several ways, and somewhere along the line, someone's ox will be gored!

Economic Strategies

Current programs to preserve farmland evade the real question: how to enhance farming as a profitable pursuit? It makes little sense to maintain a farmland base unless there are farmers willing and able to produce food. Methods to retain farmlands have been successful only to the degree that they are part of a larger effort to enhance the economic viability of agriculture.[15] Nearly all of the states maintain the official mythology that land retention and economic support for farming can be handled independently of each other.

A popular saying that reflects much conventional wisdom goes something like this: there is nothing wrong with Vermont agriculture which a few more dollars in the farmer's pocket wouldn't solve. If New Englanders are to retain their farms and reach a higher level of food self-sufficiency, producers will need to have a greater earning capacity. It may be argued that only a national commitment to end the cheap food policy will ultimately create the proper economic climate for agriculture, but states within New England can take important steps toward greater agricultural economic viability. Paramount among these is the creation of a climate and posture favorable to farming. Historically, state agricultural departments and agencies have been regulatory in nature. The time has come when that need must be complemented with an aggressive advocacy posture. It can be done in a number of ways, and New England states have made some moves in that direction through programs to promote agricultural production. Thus the From New Hampshire Fields to New Hampshire Tables program and the Vermont Seal of Quality project, among others, are important initiatives. Programs that would stimulate greater purchases of locally produced commodities would be enormously helpful. Such programs as Meals on Wheels and School Lunches should have as a priority the purchase of local produce and commodities. This would represent a transfer of public funds to the local private agricultural sector and would constitute a substantial commitment to local farmers. Likewise, programs can be fashioned to promote local produce and commodities in the region's huge tourism and recreation sector. Barriers to such cooperation betweeen local producers and consumers can be lowered through an extensive effort in consumer education. Emphasis should be on buying locally, and this can come about only when preferences are directed away from cosmetics toward freshness and quality. Regional marketing organizations like those which operate in the region's fluid milk industry can be developed for other commodities. Such organizations not only aid farmers through their pooled resources and capability, but also meet the needs of industrial and institutional consumers by helping to guarantee a steady supply and quality control. Indeed, few things are more fundamental to longterm profitability of a marketing strategy than is quality control, and this can be jointly provided by state departments of agriculture and the producers themselves. Quality control, strictly enforced and adhered to, builds consumer confidence and sustains local marketing options.

Farmers' markets as one means of direct marketing can be most successful, though an urban location appears to be more successful than a rural one, given the tendency in farming areas to have too much in-season produce because both consumers and farmers are often growing the same commodities. One New York study has determined that the main limitations on such new markets has been the difficulty in obtaining city administration support.[16]

Government at all levels can stimulate the formation of such markets through a number of programs. One of the most outstanding examples is provided by West Virginia, which operates a number of highly successful markets. Networking systems, utilizing hotlines like California's, may also be successful in the New England context. The aims of public policy in this area should be to nurture and support—in modest ways—such direct marketing systems. As two Maine researchers have noted, a catalytic approach for government is most desirable in that it:

entails a more gradual development of new markets, with stress on farmers taking as much responsibility and committing as much of their own funds as possible right from the start. It builds slowly from venture to venture as farmers become ready to commit themselves to expansion. In effect, the goal is to render themselves obsolete in each successive venture. They remain accessible to assist when necessary, but their main task is to catalyze action—to explore the marketing terrain and map out new ventures.[17]

A comprehensive program for encouraging such projects might include provision for physical sites, venture capital in the form of limited start-up money, development of management shields, and withdrawal of restrictions on direct marketing.[18]

Energy Vulnerability

One of the most important reasons for seeking greater agricultural self-sufficiency in New England is the uncertainty of energy supplies and costs. High energy costs mean high production costs. Because the region imports the vast majority of its food from other areas, additional expenditures will be made by consumers to reflect these rising transportation, storage, and processing costs. Lyle Schertz of USDA sums up the situation this way: "Transportation costs take on special meaning because the region will continue to import food from other parts of the country. Prospective further increases in prices of gasoline and diesel fuel and wage increases associated with inflation, will increase the costs of transporting food from other parts of the country to the Northeast."[19] Also, American agriculture is highly dependent upon massive amounts of fossil fuels, and impending scarcities will force up the cost of commodities that rely upon such inputs. Over 16 percent of all fossil fuels consumed in the United States are related, one way or another, to the food systems.[20] Perhaps more significantly, energy inputs into the country's agriculture are often three times greater than energy use in all sectors of the economy in many developing nations! Recent studies on energy used in agriculture in New England illustrate major inefficiencies.[21]

Higher energy costs, either at the production end or the processing/transportation end, translate into higher food costs for all consumers.[22] When both ends of this continuum require greater inputs of expensive energy, the situation is more severe and the vulnerability greater. Such is the situation in New England. Moreover, given the lagging economy of the region, the large number of poor and elderly on fixed incomes, and the inability of the region to meet all of its food needs internally, the prospects strongly suggest the need for action.

The transportation component of New England energy use can be reduced through the greater utilization of rail transport, which has a demonstrable advantage per energy-ton mile over truck transport. This would represent a significant reversal of current trends, which have seen trucks replacing rail systems. The reluctance to use rail transport for agriculture may be the result of inefficiencies inherent in the region's railroad system or the flexibility of truck use. Some of these problems can be overcome with a greater public commitment to rail transport systems. For example, as fuel prices increase, the movement of some commodities (such as fluid milk) in rail cars as against bulk milk truck haulers will be economically justifiable. If something of a revival in New England agriculture takes place, reliance upon far-away food sources and suppliers will decrease, and costs may be reduced as a reflection of this transformation.

Perhaps exciting changes in the energy and farming equation can take place on the farm itself. Two are especially important: increase in the use of forages in dairy production and production of manure-based biogases.

The structure of the region's agriculture is very much defined by the prominence of dairying. Feed grains for cows, imported into New England from other areas, are a major cost factor in the dairy economy. Historically, the low cost of such feeds, even with high transportation costs, permitted New England farmers to develop a dependency upon their importation. As the cost of producing such grains increase—they require significant energy and petroleum-based inputs—and the cost of transportation also rises, the region's dairy farmers will find themselves paying considerably more for their feeds. Forage crops like alfalfa, hay, silage, pasture, and grass can be grown within the region and can provide the major share of the regional dairy-feed requirement. A greater shift in the direction of forage-crop utilization is to be preferred for a number of reasons. First, New England is ideally suited to forage production. Indeed, considerable amounts of such forage are already being introduced within the region. If more can be grown and utilized in the regional dairy-feed mix, less New England farm income will leak outside the region to pay for the importation of such grains. Second, the expansion of forage crops in New England will bring back into production many pieces of land currently underutilized to the point that they are moving into marginal forestland. Third, in terms of energy produced per unit consumed by cows, forage crops have a higher yield. Moreover, energy inputs to produce forage crops are lower than those required for grain feeds.[23] The major constraint against greater utilization of forages relates to the quality of milk produced. Suffice it to say that improvements in forage will lead to a concomitant improvement in milk quality. What has historically worked against that has been the lack of intensive management of forage, which is the direct result of low monetary returns per acre for such production. If the price of grain continues to escalate and grain shortages emerge, as some predict, the price situation for forage replacement of feed grains will improve substantially. Its benefits for New England are many.

Finally, New England agriculture can reduce its dependence on expensive, imported, nonrenewable energy sources through the production and utilization of more farm-derived energy sources. The animal agriculture of the area is well suited to produce bio-energy from manures, for instance. Though this is not a new idea, cheap substitute fuels, such as fossil fuels, prevented substantial utilization of manure-based fuels in the past. Now the equation has turned around because of the movement of United States fuel prices toward world scale. It has been estimated that nearly all dairy farms have the ability to generate more energy from manure than they consume.[24] Additional benefits of utilizing manure for energy include the better management of wastes through recycling, the concomitant reduction in water pollution, and the utilization of nutrients abundant in such wastes. Aside from the economic disincentives which in the past frustrated the use of biogas, a number of institutional issues have operated as well. Leadership in the greater use of manure for energy can come from state governments, again through start-up funds and technical assistance from state energy offices and the agricultural engineering units of the state land grant universities.

These potential developments in the energy use aspects of agriculture lead almost automatically to the advocacy of a more diversified production system. To date, diversification—the ability to supply a greater variety and number of commodities locally and regionally—has been carried out by part-time, small-scale units. Indeed, an increase in the number of farmers in New England, documented by the 1980 census, is explained by the inclusion of these agriculturists in the census definition and reporting scheme. The value of commodities has increased as well. In Vermont, for example, the value of locally grown fruits and vegetables was just under two million dollars in 1975. By 1979 the value was over $5.3 million. Many of these producers were organic farmers.[25] The diversification of the region's agriculture, which will include a large number of organic units, has initially been a choice of life style or an economic necessity because of limited resources. Gradually, even large-scale farms are diversifying and some are choosing the organic option as well. One survey of 174 midwestern organic farmers who manage 100 or more acres of cropland indicated that over 85 percent were once "conventional" farmers.[26] A USDA study on organic farming found that in 44 percent of the case studies analyzed the subjects had thirty years or more of experience in farming.[27] Even among traditional hardliners on organic farming, a change in attitude is observable. A University of Missouri agricultural economist has noted that "organic agriculture points the way all agriculture must go [for] it is increasingly evident that a more labor-intensive, resource-conserving, re-integrated crop-and-livestock agriculture offers more potential for maximum output than using ever heavier machines to disgorge ever larger quantities of chemicals over the surface of the land."[28]

Here again, marketing expertise and educational outreach can be supportive. Much of it can be provided by the extension services of the state universities.[29] Research for organic farming and unit diversification should receive support from the agricultural experiment stations of New England. In assembling a regional research agenda, some of the following areas must be evaluated: the necessity of crop-rotation systems on organic farms; pasture systems and crop-rotation; soil testing for organic farming; biological control of insects; nutrition; and economies of scale for organic farming and commodity diversification.

As one travels through New England farming areas, one is struck by the fact that many individuals farm several parcels of land, some of which may be several miles from the main farmstead. Often these scattered lands are leased. One study of farmers in the Lake Champlain basin of Vermont estimated that 40 percent of the farmed land was leased.[30] This dependency upon leased lands reflects another vulnerability in the region's agricultural structure. Distances between leased or owned parcels exacerbate the problem in that farmers must increase energy expenditures to reach these farmlands, and the security of machinery and structure cannot be guaranteed given the lack of surveillance occasioned by distance. This scatter effect, together with the dependence upon the land of others, suggests the need for a farm land rationalization program. Approaches of this type have been tried in such diverse places as Taiwan, Sweden, and at least three provinces in Canada. Essentially, farmland rationalization programs operate through a governmental body that has oversight powers over land transactions in a given area. If there is a willing seller and a willing buyer, this public agency can intervene in a land transaction to prevent the movement of an important parcel of farmland to a person or group who would convert the land to a different use. Under this type of approach, the willing seller sells the farm at a negotiated price to the governmental body which then attempts to attach the farmland to an existing farmstead of a local farmer. In essence, government has the right of first refusal in land sales. By enlarging and rationalizing the farm unit, local farmers can operate more efficiently and with a greater degree of security. The farmers purchase the land, usually at favorable rates, often subsidized by the government. Both efficiency and economies of scale may be achieved; large areas may be preserved; and mixing land uses, which can be so detrimental to farming, may be prevented. Also, enough farming units may be retained to provide the critical mass necessary to support local agribusiness, which is of fundamental importance to the agricultural community.

A land rationalization program for New England provides a mechanism for the consolidation of important farmlands under the control of working family farmers. Such a system would make the purchase of development rights in rural areas largely unnecessary, thus freeing public funds for targeting in urban / rural fringe areas. Finally, a rationalization program might help alleviate the difficult problem of entry for young farmers. Under present conditions it is exceedingly difficult for would-be farmers to enter the industry unless there is a farm in the family; even then, young farmers often lack sufficient capital to purchase their parents' farms.

Land rationalization approaches can also be handled through a land trust approach. Saskatchewan operates a farmland trust with more than half a million acres in the program. Under this system, applicants who meet eligibility criteria are able to lease lands from the province. This reduces taxes paid by operators and also eliminates the immediate need for large amounts of capital that would be sunk in a land purchase.[31] Yet farmers involved in this program become rent-paying tenants instead of owner-operators, and a tenant is less likely to make the substantial investments in the land or machinery often required for truly successful, long-term productivity. Community trusts, which might allow farmers to obtain fee-simple titles restricted only by conservation and land use restrictions, might be a more attractive option for New England communities and regions.

Entry into farming, a critical problem, will be addressed only partially through such a land-reform program. Ultimately, capital at favorable rates must become available for farmer entry. Additionally, venture capital must be created if New England farmers are to take advantage of changing technologies and innovative practices. A move toward greater forage-crop production will require an interim period of adjustment for farmers. Over the past several decades, public-sector credit has begun to fill the void created by shrinking private-sector resources. Of the top one hundred banks lending to farmers in the nation, only one is in New England.[32] Means must be created to extend private credit back into the region's rural areas. A partnership between private and public capital sources, operating through a nonprofit organization, would help to create a capital supply necessary for the agricultural community. Needless to say, inflation and investment options for capital other than agriculture make the commitment of monies for farming a difficult goal to achieve.

This issue of capital for agriculture is truly a national one and probably requires a reordering of national policy on agricultural financing. A recent USDA study argues for the following credit goals:

(1) Assuring that agriculture has competitive access to private capital markets at competitive rates.

(2) Augmenting private markets to provide loans, insured loans, and guaranteed loans to those unable to compete for them or where broad social goals would be achieved.

(3) Reducing the growing dependence of farmers on emergency credit by switching them to an actuarially sound disaster-insurance system.

(4) Refocusing programs, such as the Farmers Home Administration, to those in agriculture demonstrating real need.[33]

It can be argued that a more vital agriculture in New England will attract all the capital it needs. Conversely, inputs of capital appear necessary to revitalize segments of the region's agricultural economy. This is the kind of chicken-and-egg problem which resource-constrained regions like New England have always faced.

Environmental problems also create a degree of uncertainty for the region's agriculture. Although soil erosion and compaction are not as great as in some other regions, they must remain a matter of concern. For instance, 1977 erosion rates in the South have been calculated at approximately ten tons of soil per acre per year on as much as 32 percent of the lands producing row crops. In the Northeast the figure is ten tons of soil per acre per year on only 9 percent of the lands producing similar crops.[34] These forms of land degradation occasioned by poor farmland management and practices can be reduced. For New England this is vital, given the shallow soil base of so much of the region and its already limited productivity.

Air pollution and acid rain—a problem too little understood by Americans—appear to have negative impacts on farm production. The National Academy of Sciences reports that tobacco and potato production in the once rich Connecticut Valley have shown marked decreases since the 1960s as a direct consequence of air pollution.[35] The limited research on acid rain and its effect on agriculture suggest that the surfaces of plants, especially leafy crops like lettuce and spinach, are particularly vulnerable. Moreover, the rate of nutrient cycling in soils and the mechanics of photosynthesis may also be impaired. Though certain crops may be benefited by increased acidity, on balance the effects of acid rain "would be more detrimental than beneficial."[36]

Problems of erosion and soil degradation are local; acid rain and air pollution are national and even international. But policies and programs that ignore the integrity, health, and fertility of the region's soil are profoundly shortsighted and self-defeating.[37]

The Working Rural Landscape

A final rationale for new initiatives and investments in New England farming is rooted in the need for a rural development strategy for the region. A key element in such a policy ought to be reestablishing within New England, a working rural landscape—one which provides livelihood, familyhood, and community. It is not enough for the landscape to look healthy; it must be intrinsically healthy, and that means it must be productive both for individuals and communities. This is fundamental if there is to be a "stay" option for rural New Englanders. Indeed, the number of New Englanders who reside in rural areas has increased substantially over the past several decades. As Table 5 and Figure 3 demonstrate, all New England states have grown in population. When growth is mapped, however, it becomes apparent that the distribution of population growth is far from equal throughout the region. With the exception of just one, all rural counties in the region have witnessed growth, many at rates in excess of the national average. At the same time, nearly all of the region's urban counties show a decline in population.

This growth in rural New England is part of a general rise in rural population throughout the United States. Demographers have labeled the phenomenon the "counterstream" or "turnaround."[38] The sources of rural residential growth appear to be varied: expansion of rural, nonfarm employment opportunities; life style and residential preferences; age-structure changes in an aging society; and others. The result has been to focus greater pressures on rural economic and social systems. Historically, the farms and forests of New England provided the basis and strength of the region's rural system. That they may do so again is problematic, though any well-conceived rural development policy for the region must be directed toward this end.

A rejuvenated agriculture as a mode of rural development has clear advantages. First, unlike other elements of a rural "staples" economy,[39] agriculture tends to be locally owned and controlled. That local people have such power over and responsibility for the basis of the local rural economy is necessary to building secure and mature communities. Second, as more of the constituent elements of agriculture are locally derived, less capital will flow out of the region to pay for food and production requirements that previously had to be imported from other areas and nations. The availability of this capital is necessary for the further development of "interior" economies within the community and region. This becomes especially acute for local capital formation and accumulation, which is basic to the nurturing of local entrepreneurialism. Third, agricul-

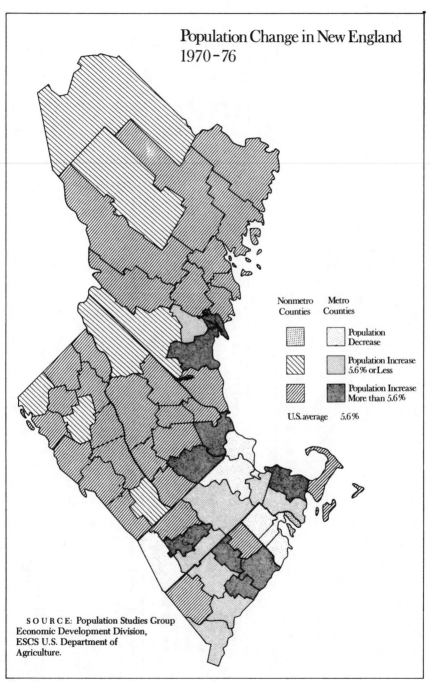

Population Change in New England
1970-76

Nonmetro   Metro
Counties   Counties

Population
Decrease

Population Increase
5.6% or Less

Population Increase
More than 5.6%

U.S. average   5.6%

SOURCE: Population Studies Group
Economic Development Division,
ESCS U.S. Department of
Agriculture.

Figure 4.

TABLE 5. *New England Population by States, 1950–1980 (based on 1978 estimates)*

State	1950	1960	1970	1980 Est.	Increased Number	Percentage
Connecticut	2,007,000	2,536,000	3,032,000	3,097,000	1,090,000	54
Massachusetts	4,691,000	5,149,000	5,689,000	5,726,000	1,035,000	22
Maine	914,000	969,000	994,000	1,124,000	210,000	23
New Hampshire	533,000	607,000	738,000	919,000	386,000	72
Rhode Island	792,000	859,000	950,000	946,000	154,000	19
Vermont	378,000	389,000	455,000	511,000	133,000	35
Six State Total	9,315,000	10,509,000	11,828,000	12,323,000	3,008,000	32
Fifty State Total	150,697,000	179,323,000	203,235,000	223,869,000	73,172,000	48+

SOURCE: A. M. Woodruff, "Comments on a Land Policy for New England," a paper presented to the New England Regional American Assembly, Hartford, Conn., April 20–22, 1981.

tural development has a significant economic multiplier effect, and much of the capital so derived will stay within the immediate region. This has the potential to create employment opportunities with local agribusiness and other support systems. Though rural industrialization should also be encouraged, it must be noted that such development very often brings in new residents rather than employing those already there. Agricultural development, on the other hand, is at a scale more appropriate to rural and small-town living and infrastructures. An expanded New England agriculture will be capable of producing more and varied high-quality and fresh foodstuffs for the ever-expanding population of the region. In sum, a rural development strategy built upon an invigorated farm and forestry sector will create an array of options for rural New Englanders as well as provide others in the region with quality foods, substantial open space and scenic amenities, and greater balance through diversity.[40]

That the problems of New England agriculture are numerous few will deny. A rejection of the business-as-usual scenario is required, though warmed-over Jeffersonianism is not enough. An economically sustainable agricultural economy capable of meeting many—though not all—of the region's needs should be the objective. Policies must be articulated that encourage diversification and new agricultural investments at all levels in production, processing, marketing, and distribution. Capital investment strategies that do not place growth-inducing elements like sewer systems and highways in farming areas are required, lest the land squeeze on farmers be further exacerbated. Appropriate credit systems must be fashioned so that sons and daughters may work their parents' farms, and others may enter the marketplace as well. Land-use and tenure programs that promote the family farm—still the most efficient form of agricultural production—are vital. These and other elements looking toward a working rural landscape are critical if this present generation is not to be that of the last-stand Yankees.

NOTES

1. See Howard S. Russell, *A Long, Deep Furrow: Three Centuries of Farming in New England* (Hanover, N.H.: University Press of New England, 1976), pp. 3–24.

2. Frederic O. Sargent, *Trends in Land Use, 1673–1964* (Burlington, Vt.: Agricultural Experiment Station, University of Vermont, 1964), p. 3.

3. Counting farms and farmland is never easy. I have relied upon federal census data, though census definitions have changed from time to time, and this makes the reliability of the data somewhat suspect. The problem of counting remains with us today; note the difficulty for the National Agricultural Lands Study in developing statistics on farms and farmlands.

4. H. F. Wilson, *The Hill Country of Northern New England: Its Social and Economic History, 1790–1930* (New York: Columbia Unversity Press, 1936).

5. This statistical material comes from Mark Lapping, *The Land Base for Agriculture in New England* (Washington, D.C.: National Agricultural Land Study, USDA-CEQ, 1980); see also Lapping, "Of Farms, Forests and Open Lands: New England's Rural Landscape," paper presented at the Conference on Taxation and Farmlands, Lincoln Institute of Land Policy, Cambridge, Mass., November 23, 1980.

6. Gene Wunderlich, *Who Owns America's Land: Problems in Preserving the Rural Landscape* (Washington, D.C.: USDA, 1974); Wunderlich, *Facts About U.S. Landownership* (Washington, D.C.: USDA, Bulletin 442, 1978).

7. Carl H. Reidel, *The Yankee Forest: A Prospectus* (New Haven, Conn.: School of Forestry and Environmental Studies, Yale University, 1978); Ernest M. Gould and C. H. Reidel, "The Yankee Forest," *Journal of Forestry*, 77 No. 9 (1979).

8. M. Lapping, "Agricultural Land Retention: Responses, American and Foreign," in A. M. Woodruff, ed., *The Farm and The City* (Englewood Cliffs, N.J.: Prentice-Hall, 1980).

9. M. Lapping, "Agricultural Land Retention"; M. Lapping, R. Bevins and P. Herbers, "Differential Assessment and Other Techniques to Preserve Missouri's Farmlands," *Missouri Law Review*, 42, No. 3 (1977), pp. 369–408. J. Keene, et al., *Untaxing Open Space: Evaluation of the Effectiveness of Differential Assessment of Farms and Open Space* (Washington, D.C.: Council on Environmental Quality, 1976); N. Roberts and H. J. Brown, *Property Tax Preferences for Agricultural Lands* (Montclair, N.J.: Allanheld, Osmun, 1980).

10. Lapping, "Agricultural Land Retention."

11. Lisle Baker and Stephen Anderson, *Taxing Speculative Land Gains: The Vermont Experience* (Washington, D.C.: Environmental Law Institute, 1980).

12. L. P. Schertz, "The Northeast," in Schertz, et al., *Another Revolution in U.S. Farming?* (Washington, D.C.: USDA, 1975), p. 275.

13. T. McDonald and G. Coffman, *Fewer, Larger U.S. Farms by the Year 2000—and Some Consequences* (Washington, D.C.: USDA, Agricultural Information Report, No. 439, 1980).

14. R. Fallert and B. Buston, *Alternative Pricing Policies for Class I Milk under Federal Marketing Orders—Their Economic Impact* (Washington, D.C.: USDA, Agricultural Economics Report, No. 401, 1978).

15. M. Lapping, "Agricultural Land Retention Strategies: Some Underpinnings," *Journal of Soil and Water Conservation*, 34, No. 3 (1979), pp. 124–126.

16. E. M. Stuhmiller, *Farmer-to-Consumer Direct Marketing Operations Selling Fruits and Vegetables, New York, 1979* (Ithaca, N.Y.: Agricultural Experiment Station, Cornell University, Agricultural Economics Report, No. 80-7, 1980), p. 17.

17. D. Vail and M. Rozyne, *Small Farm Marketing: The Experience of 31 Farmers in Maine* (Brunswick, Me.: Bowdoin College Small Farm Project, 1978).

18. See G. G. Williams, ed., *Marketing Alternatives for Small Farmers* (Muscle Shoals, Ala.: Tennessee Valley Authority, 1978).

19. Schertz, "The Northeast," p. 275.

20. D. Pimentel and M. Pimentel, *Food, Energy and Society* (New York: John Wiley and Sons, 1979), p. 137; J. Steinhart and C. Steinhart, "Energy in the U.S. Food System," *Science* 184 (1974), 306–316.

21. Center for Studies in Food Self-Sufficiency, *Energy Utilization in Vermont Agriculture* (Burlington, Vt.: Center for Studies in Food Self-Sufficiency, 1978).

22. D. L. Van Dyne, R. D. Reinsel, T. J. Lutton and J. A. Barton, "Energy Use and Energy Policy," in *Structural Issues of American Agriculture* (Washington, D.C.: USDA, Agricultural Economics Report, No. 438, 1979), p. 202.

23. P. A. Oltenacu and M. S. Allen, "Resource—Cultural Energy Requirements of the Dairy Production System", in *Energy Use in Agriculture* (West Palm Beach, Fla.: CRC Press, 1979); D. Pimentel, *Livestock Production Systems: Energy and Land Conservation* (manuscript in preparation).

24. P. J. Catania, ed., *Uses of Agricultural Wastes: Food, Fuel and Fertilizers* (Regina, Sask.: University of Saskatchewan, 1974); J. A. Alich, *An Evaluation of the Use of Agricultural Residues As an Energy Feedstock* (Menlo Park, Calif.: Stanford Research Institute, 1976).

25. Neil Pelsue and Edward Bouton, *Small Fruits and Vegetables Production Survey* (Burlington, Vt.: Agricultural Experiment Station, University of Vermont, Research Report No. 10, 1981). Information also contained in the Commissioner's Report, Vermont Department of Agriculture, 1977.

26. W. Lockeretz and S. Wernick, "Organic Farming: A Step Towards Closed Nutrient Cycles," *Compost Science* 12, No. 3 (1980), pp. 40–46.

27. *Report and Recommendations on Organic Farming* (Washington, D.C.: USDA, 1980), p. 11.

28. H. Breimyer, *Economics of Organic Agriculture* (Columbia, Mo.: University of Missouri, Department of Agricultural Economics, Paper No. 1980-35), pp. 3–5.

29. Two excellent examples of such outreach include F. French, *Management of Maine Small and Part-time Farmers* (Orono, Me.: Cooperative Extension Service, University of Maine, 1977) and J. W. Sumner, *Diversify Vermont Agriculture* (Burlington, Vt.: Cooperative Extension Service, University of Vermont, 1979).

30. M. Lapping and R. Feldman, *The Economic Viability of Agriculture in the Champlain Basin* (Burlington, Vt.: Lake Champlain Basin Study, New England River Basins Commission, 1979).

31. Kim Young, "The Saskatchewan Land Bank," *Saskatchewan Law Review*, 40 (1974–75), 1–24.

32. "Shawmut Invests in New England Farming," *New England Business*, 3, No. 1 (January, 1981), pp. 42–43.

33. *A Time to Choose: Summary Report on the Structure of Agriculture* (Washington, D.C.: USDA, 1981), p. 123.

34. National Association of Conservation Districts, Soil Degradation: Effects of Agricultural Productivity, for the National Agricultural Lands Study (Washington, D.C.: NALS, Interim Report No. 4, 1981). See T. Jorling, "Protecting Land Resources," *Journal of Soil and Water Conservation*, 33, No. 5 (1978).

35. National Academy of Sciences, *Agricultural Production Efficiency* (Washington, D.C.: NAS, 1975), p. 101.

36. R. H. Shaw, "Climate Change and Future of American Agriculture," in S. Batie and R. Healy, *The Future of American Agriculture as a Strategic Resource* (Washington, D.C.: The Conservation Foundation, 1980), p. 271.

37. Winston Way, "Soil for Northeastern Agriculture," *Proceedings, Northeast Agricultural Leadership Assembly* (Amherst, Mass.: Center for Environmental Policy Studies, University of Massachusetts, 1979), pp. 299–308.

38. See G. Fuguitt, P. Voss, and J. Doherty, *Growth and Change in Rural America* (Washington, D.C.: The Urban Institute, 1979); D. Brown and J. Wardell, *New Directions in Urban-Rural Migration: The Population Turnaround in Rural America* (New York: Academic Press, 1980).

39. The concept of a staples economy is a major element in the tradition of Canadian political economy and has particular relevance for understanding rural systems. See H. Innes, *The Fur Trade in Canada: An Introduction to Canadian Economic History* (Toronto: University of Toronto Press, 1930); H. Innes, *The Cod Fisheries: The History of an International Economy* (Toronto: University of Toronto Press, 1940); M. Watkins, "A Staples Theory of Economic Growth," *Canadian Journal of Economics and Political Science*, 29, No. 2 (1963).

40. M. Lapping, "A Conceptual Premise for Rural Planning: Building a Theory for Action," unpublished manuscript, 1981.

AIR POLLUTION STRESS
AND ENERGY POLICY

F. H. Bormann

THE LANDSCAPE, that particular mix of mountains, forests, fields, streams, villages, farms, and lakes, is at the heart of the concept we call New England. At the same time a shaper and a product of human history, the landscape provides an ambiance that permeates our thinking, makes our corner of North America unique and weighs heavily when we are tempted to migrate to other regions. New Englanders have not been unaware of their landscape and its importance. Emerson, Thoreau, and Marsh down to present-day conservation commissions have seen the value of landscape and fought against its unnecessary disruption in the face of development. Probably nowhere else in the United States is the conservation ethic so strongly entrenched as in our region, and its past successes are in no small part responsible for the desirability of living in New England today.

Despite our outstanding conservation efforts, it is my opinion that almost all of the New England landscape is under serious air-pollution stress. Stress may well increase to the further disadvantage of the landscape as many politicians, industrialists, and other energy users seek "cheaper energy" bought at the cost of more air pollution. Policy-makers may fail to perceive the landscape as a living dynamic entity using solar power to perform an elaborate array of nat-

I wish to thank James Galloway, John Skelly, Gene Likens and Wallace Reed for information, comments, and suggestions, and many others for making data available. Especially, I am indebted to Christine Bormann for assistance and many hours of fruitful discussion. Finally, I acknowledge the valuable financial support provided by the Andrew W. Mellon Foundation. This essay was written while the author was a visiting professor at the Center for Advanced Studies of the University of Virginia.

ural functions basic to the well-being of society. This can lead to
energy policies that increase air pollution and diminish natural
functions.

Such limited and short-sighted policy is self-defeating. Natural
functions of the landscape, powered by solar energy, are provided
free of charge. Destruction or diminution of these functions requires, if we are to preserve the quality of life, substitution of fossil
or atomic energy to maintain or replace these natural services.
Hence, "cheap energy" is not really cheap in the long run. For New
Englanders an energy policy that fails to give fair weight to nature
has the further disadvantage that it will degrade the landscape, de-
tract from the New England ambiance, and possibly speed flight to
the sunbelt.

A national energy policy is needed, one that not only helps to restore the health of our economy but also understands and seeks to
optimize the solar-powered contributions our landscape makes to
the economy and our well-being. A policy that seeks these objectives will conserve fossil fuels and reduce the assault of air pollution
on the landscape. This paper will consider such a policy after discussion of the function and value of landscapes; natural cycles and air
pollution; transportation of pollutants over long distances; air pollution in New England; the effects of air pollution on the landscape;
and prospects for reducing air pollution.

The Function and Value of Landscapes

Certain values of landscapes are well known and used by environmentalists in current debates on alternative land use. Natural ecosystems such as forests and fields are valued for their aesthetic
contributions; as recreational resources, such as hunting, fishing,
and bird-watching areas and nature appreciation sites; as gene reservoirs preserving plant and animal species; as sites for the production of renewable resources such as paper and wood products and
wood for energy. What is less well known is the critical role natural
systems play in maintaining the quality of our lives through regulation of the hydrologic, biogeochemical, and erosion cycles and the
moderation of local climate.

Approximately 75 percent of New England is covered by forests
and fields. These terrestrial ecosystems use solar energy, directly

and indirectly, in a variety of ways. About one percent of the solar energy falling on a forest ecosystem is captured by plants and chemically fixed in the process of photosynthesis. About 55 percent of this energy is used to sustain the life processes of plants, the remaining 45 percent is called net primary productivity (NPP) and is built into the organic plant structure (for example, leaves, roots, wood). Forest and field ecosystems therefore contain a considerable amount of solar energy that is stored in the organic matter of living plants and animals and in dead organic matter in the soil. This living and dead organic matter mediates important functions of the ecosystem and serves as a source of energy for all other organisms within the ecosystem. One of the major mediating functions of living organic matter is carried on by leaves of plants. This is transpiration, the absorption of solar energy and its utilization to evaporate or transpire water from leaves. The process of transpiration is at the core of the terrestrial ecosystem's ability to moderate humidity, to regulate amounts of stream water and erosion, and to influence local and perhaps even regional climate.

The amount of solar energy utilized by natural terrestrial ecosystems in New England is enormous. About 3×10^{15} Btu's (3 quads) of solar energy is fixed by forests and fields each year (Wood and Botkin, unpublished). Energy used in transpiration would account for an additional 84 quads of solar energy. To give some perspective on these numbers, all sources of fossil and nuclear energy used by man in New England during 1978 are estimated to total 3 quads (Report of the New England Energy Congress, 1979). Thus natural ecosystems use about thirty times more energy than is currently being used by man.

The forests and fields of New England use this vast amount of solar energy coursing through them not only to produce the values discussed earlier, but also to do work. To understand the vital natural tasks performed by a working forest ecosystem, it is necessary to conceive of an ecosystem as a volume of space occupied by a community of organisms. For example, a one hectare (2.47 acres) forest ecosystem would be bounded by the horizontal extent of the hectare, by the top of the forest canopy above, and by the deepest depth of the roots below. Materials (for example, rain, dust, chemicals) and energy (for example, solar energy, wind) may cross the boundaries of the ecosystem. It is through inputs and outputs of ma-

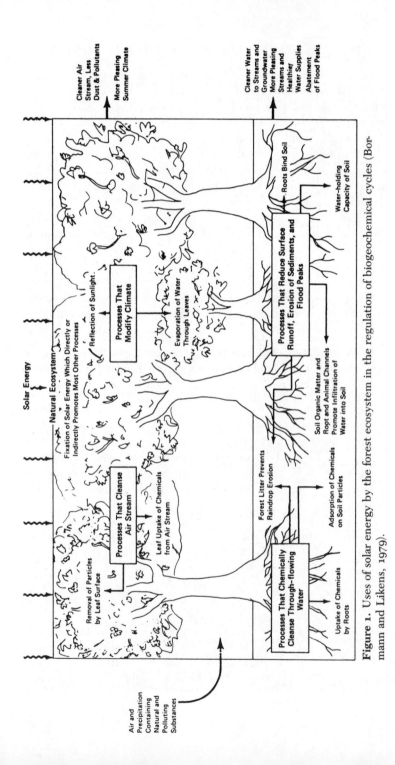

Figure 1. Uses of solar energy by the forest ecosystem in the regulation of biogeochemical cycles (Bormann and Likens, 1979).

terials and energy that the individual ecosystem is connected with the larger biogeochemical cycles of the earth. The behavior of the ecosystem is in large measure determined by the inputs and, in turn, the ecosystem affects the behavior of other interconnected ecosystems by its output. For example, the quality and quantity of water entering a lake ecosystem within a forest ecosystem is largely determined by the nature of the outputs from the forest system which constitute inputs to the lake system.

Through the use of solar energy, the ecosystem carries out a number of processes (work) that determine (1) the form in which solar energy entering the ecosystem is stored and/or returned to the atmosphere, (2) the chemical make-up of the streams of air and water moving through the ecosystem boundaries, (3) the proportion of water that will leave as liquid or vapor, (4) the proportion of liquid water which leaves as surface runoff or seeps into the ground to recharge groundwater, and (5) the amount of material eroded from the ecosystem (Figure 1). The sum of these activities may be thought of as biotic regulation of biogeochemical cycles. Through biotic regulation, the forest and field ecosystems of New England determine in large measure the quantity and quality of air leaving the ecosystem and the nature of local or even regional climate.

It is extremely difficult to measure the work performed by ecosystems. For New England, however, considerable data has been acquired from the Hubbard Brook Ecosystem Study in West Thornton, New Hampshire. For two decades, scientists there have measured the response of second-growth forest ecosystems to various kinds of experimental manipulation.

At Hubbard Brook about 4 trillion Btu's of solar energy are received each year on one square kilometer (1 km² = 100 ha = 0.39 sq. mile) of forest. Through the process of photosynthesis, one half of one percent of the energy is chemically fixed into plant substance (NPP) and 18 percent is used to transpire water. Of the approximately one billion liters of precipitation received by 1 square kilometer of forest, about 38 percent is evaporated into the air, while the remaining 62 percent is drained from the area as streamwater or groundwater (Bormann and Likens, 1979).

This forest ecosystem has a remarkable effect on the chemistry of water moving through it. Streamwater leaving the ecosystem is chemically very different from precipitation entering it. For example, calcium, magnesium, potassium, and sodium are significantly more concentrated in streamwater than in precipitation, while ammonium and hydrogen ions are significantly less concentrated (Bormann and Likens, 1979). In terms of nutrient budgets, each square kilometer of forest annually receives 218, 58, and 89 kilograms of calcium, magnesium, and potassium in precipitation, and loses 1370, 313, and 189 kilograms of these elements in streamwater. The difference is made up within the ecosystem by the chemical breakdown of rock particles (Likens et al., 1977). On the other hand, 650 kilograms of nitrogen enter the system dissolved in precipitation, while 400 kilograms are lost in streamwater. Each square kilometer of forest is accumulating about 250 kilograms of nitrogen, which is incorporated into living and dead organic matter.

The physical and chemical nature of the air stream passing through the ecosystem is also changed. These changes are not as dramatic as those occurring in water moving through the system but nevertheless are of great significance on a regional scale. For example, a fifty-five-year-old forest ecosystem adds about 500 million liters of water vapor to the atmosphere each year for each square kilometer of forest, while removing a net of about 0.7 million kilograms of carbon dioxide, and 610 kilograms of gaseous or aerosol sulfur. In the same period about 1400 kilograms of gaseous nitrogen are converted into biologically fixed compounds.

These biotic regulatory activities of natural ecosystems have special significance in relation to man-made air pollutants. Forests and fields act as giant filters or detoxifying systems, removing pollutants from both the air and water. As an illustration, about 90 percent of the hydrogen ions and 99 percent of the lead in acid rain are removed and stored within the system as rainwater passes through the soil at Hubbard Brook (Likens et al., 1977; Smith and Siccama, 1981). Pollutant gases like ozone, sulfur dioxide, or carbon monoxide can be removed from the gas stream by reactions with living organisms within the ecosystem. It should be stressed, however, that while the removal of pollution by ecosystems is beneficial for man because it results in cleaner air and water, it may not be good for the ecosystems. Too much pollution will cause a natural ecosystem to degenerate and thereby diminish its filtration capacity and other functions.

Finally, biotic regulation is linked to the capacity of the ecosystem to maintain itself through time. Every ecosystem is subject to an array of external energy inputs: radiant energy, wind, falling and running water, and gravity. All of these represent potentially destabilizing forces that could diminish or destroy ecosystem organization. For an ecosystem to grow and/or to maintain itself, it must be able to meet these destabilizing forces in such a way that their full destructive potential is not achieved within the ecosystem (Bormann and Likens, 1979). Stabilization is the net effect resulting from the ecosystem's use of solar energy to regulate energy flow, and to exercise some control over hydrologic, nutrient, and erosion cycles. Thus biotic regulation is largely responsible for the New England landscape appearing as well-vegetated topography rather than thinly vegetated, highly eroded topography or even bare rock.

A critical relationship fundamental to understanding the role of New England's landscapes is the connection between nature's use of solar energy and human use of fossil and nuclear energy. Humankind constantly applies pressure on natural systems in the form of outright conversion to other uses, management for the production of goods and services, and by indirect assaults, such as air pollution. As natural systems are destroyed or degraded, they lose some of their capacity to carry out natural functions; to maintain stable landscapes and biological diversity; to moderate temperature; to filter air and water; to recharge groundwater; to control erosion and yield sediment-free water to streams; to provide aesthetic and recreational enjoyment; and to produce forest and forage products.

If natural functions are damaged or destroyed, they must be replaced by human intervention if the quality of life is to be maintained. Such intervention requires substitutes for wood products, breeding and establishment of pollution-resistant crops and vegetation, building of erosion-control works, addition of lime to lakes and fertilizers to forests, enlargement of reservoirs, upgrading of air-pollution control technology, installation of flood control and water purification facilities, increased air conditioning, and development of new recreational facilities.

These man-made substitutes require a considerable capital and energy expenditure to maintain functions formerly provided on a continuing basis by natural ecosystems using free solar power.

Clearly, as our population grows and as our material (man-made) standard of living increases, rearrangement or loss of natural ecosystems is unavoidable. However, much of what we do to nature may be unnecessary and costly and may contribute to the trend of greater amounts of man-generated energy necessary to maintain the landscape. In an age of increasing awareness of the limitations of the world's natural resource base, this is a hazardous path indeed.

Natural Cycles and Air Pollution

Throughout the earth's history, the atmosphere has functioned as a primary biogeochemical pathway for gases, water, and particulate matter moving through the biosphere. Practically all substances that occur naturally move through the atmosphere in some amount, including a large variety of elemental and molecular ions, organic compounds originating from biological sources, and inorganic minerals from soils, volcanoes, or the sea. To some degree, ecosystems have adapted to the materials or inputs they receive from the atmosphere, such as the amount and distribution of rainfall. Naturally occurring atmospheric inputs are not always in harmony with ecosystems. Changes in inputs resulting from shifts in climate, volcanic activity, and similar modifications may cause major and long-lasting changes in the structure and function of local or regional ecosystems. Natural ecosystems, however, are thought to be adapted to a range of naturally occurring fluctuations in atmospheric inputs resulting from the vagaries of year-to-year changes in local climate.

Human society, taking into account fluctuations, depends upon some historically established range of ecosystem performance. For example, the landscape is expected to yield some average amount of water; major floods are expected to occur within some predicted time schedule; dams are expected to be filled with sediment in some number of years; and forest and agricultural production regulated by nature is expected to fall within some range. In other words, much social planning is based on the notion of landscape durability.

In the United States and Canada, industrialized man is heavily influencing biogeochemical pathways through air and water pollution. Throughout human history, pollution has caused substantial damage to local ecosystems, but now the problem is much larger. There is some evidence that, for the first time, man-made pollution may be causing fundamental changes in regional landscapes covering millions of square kilometers not only in New England but over a large area of northeastern North America. We must now ask ourselves if pollution is weakening the ability of natural systems to provide the stable base upon which man plans his activities.

Operations such as generation of electricity, transportation, industrial processes, space heating and cooling, smelting, mining, refuse burning, and agricultural activities add a surprising variety of substances to the atmosphere and often in very large amounts. The estimated amount of five major pollutants emitted into the air of the United States in 1977 was about 200 million tons (EPA, 1978) not including substantial substances emitted in Canada and Mexico or all types of pollution. (For our purposes, all substances injected into the atmosphere as a result of human activities are considered as pollutants because of their potential to alter the natural situation. It should be clear, however, that not all pollutants or all levels of one pollutant are harmful to man or natural ecosystems. Some may even be beneficial in the sense of increasing productivity of an ecosystem or ameliorating some naturally occurring limiting factor.)

Air pollution is considered from two points of view—as emissions into the air and as pollutants of the ambient air. Emissions are released into the air from some point source, as from a smoke stack or from an area source like a burning dump, the exhaust from all the cars in an area, or pesticides released into the air during crop spraying. Ambient air pollutants are those occurring in the air at some distance from the site of emission. They are of two types: primary pollutants and secondary pollutants.

Primary pollutants are those emitted directly into the atmosphere. The most important from the standpoint of amounts are total, suspended particulate matter, sulfur oxides, carbon monoxide, hydrocarbons, and nitrogen oxides (EPA, 1978). However, a large variety of inorganic and organic substances also qualify. Primary pollutants, especially sulfur dioxide, hydrocarbons, and nitrogen oxides, may act as precursors or starting chemical substances, which undergo chemical reactions within the atmosphere, often of a photochemical type promoted by the energy of sunlight, and produce new substances called secondary pollutants. Precursors, given sufficient time (seconds to days) in the air, will react with other substances in the air or with one another to produce an array of such secondary pollutants as photooxidants (for example, ozone and peroxyacetal nitrate), hydrogen ions, nitrate, and sulfate. Some of these substances, like nitrate and sulfate, may also be emitted from a source and thus qualify as primary pollutants as well as secondary pollutants.

An important aspect of the chemical nature of air pollution is that many pollutants are exactly the same as substances found in nature, while others are new to nature; creations of modern chemistry like DDT, PCB's, PAH, and organic pesticides. It can be assumed that organisms have evolved to process or tolerate most concentrations of naturally occurring substances, but man-created chemicals may present new hazards to some species composing local or regional ecosystems. The well known effects of DDT on the reproductive function of some fresh and saltwater fish and birds of prey are examples.

Suspended particulate matter, sulfur dioxide, nitrogen dioxide, carbon monoxide, ozone, and a few other pollutants are regulated by law through the National Ambient Air Quality Standards (NAAQS). To determine air quality conditions and whether an area is conforming with the standards, pollutants are measured at ground level by various monitoring devices. Areas with measurements exceeding the NAAQS are said to be in violation. Control of air quality is sought by regulations designed to limit emissions through mandated actions, such as the installation of scrubbing devices or burning less polluting fuel.

Emissions of sulfur and nitrogen oxides and hydrocarbons are of particular importance to New England, since they are both primary pollutants and precursors to secondary pollutants. Sulfur dioxide emissions per unit area of land in Connecticut, Rhode Island, Massachusetts, southern New Hampshire, and southeast Maine are relatively high, while Vermont, northern New Hampshire, and northern Maine have relatively low emissions.

There is, however, a large area of intense emissions to our west (Figure 2). Of the approximately 33 million metric tons of sulfur dioxide produced in the United States and Canada in 1980, approximately 65 percent was produced in the area upwind of New England bounded by the southern border of Tennessee and North Carolina, the western border of Illinois, Wisconsin, and Tennessee but also including Missouri, and to about the 48° parallel in Canada.

Nitrogen oxide emissions in southern New England are relatively

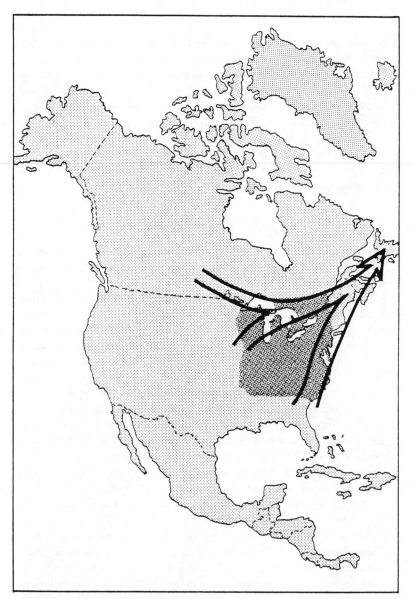

Figure 2. Mean monthly tracks of frontal storms, 1885 to 1980, in eastern North America (Hayden, personal communication). 65 percent of all sulfur dioxide and 49 percent of all nitrogen oxides produced in North America are emitted in the dark stippled area to the west of New England (Benkowitz, personal communication).

high, while those in northern New England are relatively low. The total of nitrogen oxide emitted in the United States and Canada is about 21 million metric tons of which about 49 percent is produced in the upwind area west of New England, defined above. Of special interest, however, is the very high rate of emissions of nitrogen oxides in the so-called Northeast Corridor that runs from southeastern Maine to northern Virginia.

Hydrocarbon emissions in the United States in 1978 were estimated at 27.8 million metric tons (EPA, 1980), with high emission densities in the Northeast Corridor (EPA, 1978).

Transportation of Pollutants over Long Distances

Materials emitted into the atmosphere may be transported great distances. Smoke from forest fires in Canada has been observed in Europe 8000 kilometers away (Reed, 1976); ash from the Mount St. Helens eruption passed over New England; dust in Barbados has been identified as originating in the Sahara Desert 7000 kilometers away; arctic haze is thought to originate from sulfur emissions in northern Europe 10,000 kilometers away (Kerr, 1979). We have long known that airborne radioactivity from testing nuclear weapons has been distributed world wide.

Obviously we know that New England receives and exports pollutants to and from adjacent areas. The crucial question, however, is whether the amounts are large enough to cause a significant pollution problem in our region. If this is so, New England must have a primary interest in political decisions governing emissions in the emitting area, just as Canadians must have an interest in decisions governing emissions in our area.

Most of the air reaching New England passes over the area of intense emissions defined in Figure 2, and accumulating evidence suggests that a large part or even the bulk of the secondary pollutants affecting New England are transported into our region from the west.

Some of the most convincing evidence for the long-range transport, as a common phenomenon, comes from Scandinavia (Likens, 1976). Analysis of precipitation data collected by a network of monitoring stations in northwestern Europe has shown that precipitation has become increasingly acidic. Hydrogen ion concentrations in rain and snow have risen, and acidity has become geographically more widespread. Acid rain is a complex secondary pollutant composed of hydrogen ions, sulfate, and nitrate anions. It is derived from sulfur and nitrogen oxide precursors that have been chemically changed as an air mass moves from the site of emission to other regions.

Significant increases in acidity have occurred in southern Sweden and Norway where hundreds of lakes have become acidified and have lost their fish populations. In the mountainous tip of southern Norway, an area of low population and little industry, considerable acid rain falls. Winds carrying the acid originate to the south and travel over 100 to 700 kilometers of sea. If the flow of the air parcels is traced backward, it becomes clear that the precursors originated in industrialized northern Europe up to 1500 kilometers away (Nordo, 1976).

As in Europe, precipitation falling in the northeastern United States and adjacent Canada since about 1930 has become acidified (Likens, 1976); the acid appears to come from pollutants carried long distances (Galloway and Whelpdale, 1980). As in Europe, acidification of precipitation is related to high emissions of sulfur and nitrogen dioxide.

Several lines of evidence indicate that long-range transport plays a major role in the secondary pollution of New England. Frontal storms release much of the rain and pollutants that New England receives. In general these storms move from west to east, but analysis of data from 1885 to 1980 indicates that low-pressure cyclonic storms tend to follow two major tracks, one through the northern Great Lakes region and the other along the Atlantic Coast. They converge in the vicinity of New England (Hayden, personal communication). The pattern of flow guarantees that most low-pressure cells that deliver rain to New England receive substantial amounts of air that has transversed the high emission areas to our west (Figure 2).

The Hubbard Brook Experimental Forest in central New Hampshire is among the more acidified locations in the United States. A hundred-kilometer circle drawn around Hubbard Brook encloses an area of low population density and relatively little industrial activity. Prevailing winds are from the north and west, making it likely that acid rain falling on Hubbard Brook is derived from emission centers far to the west and north of New England. Cogbill and Likens (1974) found that winds bringing acid precipitation to central New York were primarily from the northwest and southwest. These winds passed over midwestern industrial areas before reaching New York. Apparently sulfur and nitrogen oxides emitted into an air parcel over a period of several days were oxidized to sulfuric and nitric acid, part of which fell out on central New York. Another study in the New York City region indicated that air parcels flowing from south to northwest produced precipitation that was from three to ten times more acidic than air parcels originating in the northwest to northeast sector which included New England (Wolff et al., 1979).

Recently, considerable effort has been invested in studying the transport of sulfate aerosols (very fine air-borne particles). In a recent sulfate episode, during which aerosol concentrations were considered a health hazard and which ultimately covered one million square kilometers of eastern North America, peak concentrations were found to move from west to east. Back trajectories of polluted air in Boston and Hartford indicated that two days earlier the air parcels had been over the Sudbury smelting region of Canada and the Chicago area (DeMarrais, 1979). Another sulfate episode was tracked from the United States–Canadian Great Lakes area, across northern New England, to Nova Scotia (Shaw, 1979). This high concentration of sulfates was in warm air south of a frontal system and appeared to move along with the system. In a major study in the New York City region, Lioy et al. (1980) found strong evidence that a major portion of the sulfate measured in the region came from the transport and oxidation of sulfur oxide emissions in the Ohio River Basin and from the Northeast Corridor.

Studies of photooxidants, primarily ozone, indicate that a large proportion of those detected in New England arise from precursors emitted to the south and west. Ozone is formed from nitrogen oxide and hydrocarbon precursors. Ozone concentrations sufficient to damage test tobacco plants on Nantucket Island were correlated with across-ocean winds from the New York to Washington area (Kelleher and Feder, 1978). A detailed study of movements of packets of air indicated that photooxidant air pollutants resulting from primary emissions in metropolitan New York and westward are transported on a 200 kilometer trajectory as far as northeastern Massachusetts (Cleveland and Graedel, 1979). At Fitchburg, Massachusetts, 66 percent of all recorded ozone values above the National Standard occurred when winds were from the New York City area. Primary emissions from even more distant areas were probably involved, since air entering the New York City region was often above the Federal Standard but well below ozone levels recorded in Connecticut.

Studies of New England by Spicer et al. (1979) indicate that ozone at any given location originates from a number of different sources. These include background ozone from natural precursors and the stratospheric ozone reservoir, ozone generated from local anthropogenic precursors, regional ozone generated from precursors in high-pressure air masses and transported hundreds of miles over several days, and ozone formed from precursors in urban plumes downwind from cities. Plumes may extend up to 400 kilometers. It was estimated that maximum contributions to the ozone burden over New England were background, 0.02 ppm (parts per million); rural precursors, .02–.045 ppm; regional associated with high pressure systems, 0.070–.150 ppm; and urban plumes, .150–.250 ppm.

In aggregate, the available evidence indicates that New England receives a large burden of transported pollutants that originate in an area stretching from southern Canada to the southeastern United States.

Air Pollution in New England

Acid Rain. Acidified precipitation is currently falling on all of New England, with northern New England reporting some of the most acidified precipitation in North America (Likens, 1976; Likens and Butler, 1981). Acid rain became a regional phenomenon between 30 and 50 years ago with acidity increasing markedly between 1955 and 1976 (Figure 3). Today precipitation is thirty to forty times more acid than would be expected for an unpolluted atmosphere, but individual storms may be five hundred times more acid than expected (Likens and Butler, 1981).

The acidity of precipitation falling on New England is due to a mixture of sulfuric and nitric acids (Likens et al., 1977), mostly derived from anthropogenic sulfur and nitric oxides (Likens, 1976). These oxides may come from natural sources but anthropogenic sulfur emissions in the eastern United States exceed emissions from natural sources by one to two orders of magnitude (Galloway and Whelpdale, 1980; Shinn and Lynn, 1979).

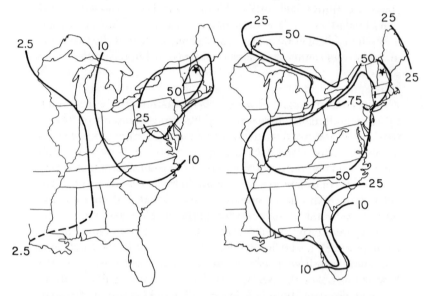

Figure 3. The distribution of acid rain in the eastern United States in 1955–56 and 1975–76 (after Likens and Butler, 1981). Micro equivalents of hydrogen ion per liter, μ eq/l are the values shown. Nonpolluted rain has a concentration of less than 2.5 μ eq/l (pH-5.6). Rain of pH 5.0, 4.5, and 4.0 contains 10, 32 and 100 μ eq/l respectively. Precipitation falling at Hubbard Brook in central New Hampshire, shown as a star, averages 71 μ eq/l (pH 4.15), but annual averages range from 60 μ eq/l (pH 4.22) to 95 μ eq/l (pH 4.02). One storm had a concentration of 1400 μ eq/l (pH 2.85).

Current measurements of acidity in rain and snow may seriously underestimate the severity of the acid rain problem (Kerr, 1981). Measurements of acid rain are primarily based on bulk samples, essentially open containers, but it is now thought that these samplers are not effective for measuring dry or gaseous deposition. Dry deposition can be in the form of very fine sulfur particles, filtered out of the air stream by leaves or other surfaces, or sulfur dioxide gas that dissolves in a lake or in moisture films on vegetation or around soil particles (Galloway and Likens, 1979). Dry deposit of sulfur is converted to acid within the ecosystem and can add appreciably to the acids entering the ecosystem in precipitation. At Hubbard Brook, about one third of the sulfur arrives in dry form, mostly as sulfur dioxide (Eaton et al., 1978). In general, dry deposition may account for up to one half of the sulfur reaching the surface of the earth, and under certain conditions it makes major contributions to the acidity problem.

Photochemical smog. Photochemical oxidants are the most damaging air pollutants currently affecting agriculture and forestry in the United States (Glass, 1979, *after* Jacobson, 1977). Smog is primarily an episodic pollutant rising to injurious levels during periods when precursor concentrations, meteorologic conditions, and photochemical conditions are right. Formed by the interaction of nitrogen oxides, hydrocarbon precursors, and sunlight, smog contains a host of undesirable secondary products, including ozone, peroxyacetal nitrate (PAN), acrolein, nitric acid, and sulfur compounds including sulfuric acid (Cleveland and Graedel, 1979). PAN and ozone can injure sensitive plants at low concentrations; ozone at concentrations below the NAAQS (Williamson, 1973). Sulfuric and nitric acid also contribute to acid rain, thus linking the photooxidant problem to the acid rain problem.

The NAAQ Standard for ozone was set at 0.08 ppm in 1971 but revised upward in 1979 to 0.12 ppm (King, 1979). In 1977 all but one of 34 monitoring stations in New England reported violations above the Federal Standard. New England as a whole was above the national average for ozone (EPA, 1978).

Areas of the United States that experience ozone concentrations above the Federal Standard show a heavy collection of violations in the Northeast Corridor reaching into all parts of New England except the northernmost part (Figure 4, Ludwig and Shelar, 1980). Next to the Los Angeles Basin, the Connecticut–New York City–Philadelphia area has the nation's worst photooxidant pollution (King, 1979). Coastal New England is most heavily impacted, with concentrations in Connecticut among the highest in the northeast (Cleveland and Graedel, 1979). In southern New England ozone has been a problem for some time (Heggested and Middleton, 1959). A crop loss of 5 million dollars due to ozone damage was reported in Connecticut as long ago as 1953. An analysis of ozone conditions in

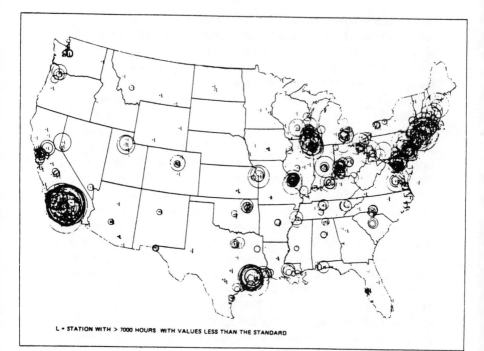

L - STATION WITH > 7000 HOURS WITH VALUES LESS THAN THE STANDARD

Figure 4. Areas where it is 95 percent probable that the NAAQS for ozone (0.12 ppm) has been exceeded during 1977 and 1978 (Ludwig and Shelar, 1980).

the Northeast Corridor from Virginia to Maine during 1975–77 indicated that most of the New England portion of the Corridor exceeded the National Standard with from 80 to 240 hours in excess of 0.08 ppm ozone concentration.

In general, levels of ozone in northern New England are more moderate than in central and coastal areas, but violations of the NAAQS do occur. In 1977 Burlington and White River Junction, in Vermont, and Franconia Notch and Berlin, in New Hampshire, reported 149, 78, 26, and one hour, respectively, of concentrations greater than the old NAAQ Standard of 0.08 ppm. At least half of the ozone detected is thought to have arisen from precursor emissions around Lake Ontario and Lake Erie (Ludwig and Maughan,

1978). Urban plumes containing high levels of ozone have been detected in the air between 2500 to 3000 meters over central Vermont (Spicer et al., 1979).

Toxic trace metals. In various regions of the world, the atmospheric fallout of trace metals, potentially toxic in small amounts to humans and other organisms, have greatly increased as a result of industrial activities (Galloway et al., 1981). Lead, zinc, manganese, silver, arsenic, vanadium, antimony, selenium, chromium, and nickel have been found to be ten to two hundred times more concentrated in some rural continental regions than in such remote areas as the South Pole.

New England is one of the regions markedly affected because of its downwind position from the intense anthropogenic emissions in the Northeast Corridor, the Midwest and midwestern southern Canada (Lazrus et al., 1970; Schlesinger et al., 1974; Groet, 1976). For rural regions of New England, depositions are generally greater in the southwest and decrease toward the northeast (Groet, 1976; Norton et al., 1980). Lead, copper, chromium, and nickel were more heavily deposited in southern New England; while cadmium and zinc depositions were higher in northern New England (Groet, 1976).

Study of an Adirondack mountain lake indicates that deposition of cadmium, copper, lead, zinc, chromium, and vanadium began to increase twenty to thirty years ago. Lake-of-the-Clouds atop Mount Washington, and Mirror Lake, West Thornton, New Hampshire, show similar patterns of accelerated deposition, although the time scale may be different (Galloway and Likens, 1979). Norton et al. (1980) report that deposition rates for lead and zinc in remote lakes in northern New England have increased more than thirty times the rates prior to elevated anthropogenic emissions. Their data also suggest that the deposition of lead and the acidity of precipitation may be positively correlated, indicating that the lead and acid rain problems cannot be easily divorced.

Information on lead deposition is the most abundant and therefore, the easiest to use in making comparisons. Urban areas of the United States have deposition rates that range from one hundred to several thousand milligrams (mg) of lead per square meter per year, while deposition in globally remote areas like Antarctica, Greenland, and mid-oceans range from a few tenths to several milligrams of lead per square meter per year (mg Pb/m²-yr, NAS, 1980). Depositions in rural regions of New England are well above globally remote areas, with some even approaching lower values for urban areas. Deposition of 44 and 85 mg Pb/m²-yr have been reported for Caribou, Maine, and Nantucket, Massachusetts, respectively (Lazrus et al., 1970). Values for rural areas in southern New England ranged from 29 to 43 mg Pb/m²-yr (Groet, 1976), while those reported for northern New Hampshire were from 15 to 37 mg Pb/ha-yr (Schlesinger et al., 1974; Groet, 1976; Siccama and Smith, 1978; Smith and Siccama, 1981). Lead concentrations in some rainstorms in north central New Hampshire have exceeded the United States Public Health Drinking Water Standards (Smith and Siccama, 1981).

About 98 percent of the lead falling on forest ecosystems of northern New Hampshire is retained in the uppermost level of the soil. Measurements at Hubbard Brook show that 860 mg/m² of lead have accumulated in the forest floor and that lead accumulation increased by 13 percent in four years (Smith and Siccama, 1981). In white pine forests of central Massachusetts, lead in the forest floor increased from 683 mg/m² in 1962 to 1161 mg/m² in 1978, an increase of 70 percent (Siccama, Smith, and Mader, 1980).

Some trace metals are apparently deposited in greater quantities in high elevation forests, perhaps because of greater rainfall, deposition of cloud moisture, or greater dry deposition (Schlesinger and Reiners, 1974; Vogelman et al., 1968). In a New England-wide study (Groet, 1976), the highest levels of cadmium deposition were found at high elevations in the Green Mountains of Vermont, as were the highest concentrations of lead, copper, nickel, and zinc, although the author thought the latter data were anomalies. In a study of trace metal deposition along an elevational gradient in central New Hampshire, the greatest accumulations were found in high elevation fir forests (Reiners et al., 1975). A similar positive relationship between lead in the forest floor and increasing elevation has been reported for the Great Smoky Mountains (Wiersma and Brown, 1980).

On Camel's Hump Mountain in Vermont, lead was measured in the forest floor along a 1000 meter elevational gradient (Siccama, personal communication). The highest amounts, 2580 mg/m², were found at the midslope (850 m). The midslope value was about two and one half times the average values for lead in seventeen forest stands in central Massachusetts and equivalent to high values measured in forests near urban areas in New Jersey and Connecticut (Andresen et al., 1980).

Other pollutants.   To illustrate further the deep complexity of the supply side of the air pollution stress problem, mention should be made of the large number of organic micropollutants that can originate in industrial areas, be transported long distances, and be deposited along with acid rain, toxic metals, and other pollutants. In samples of snow and rain from all over Norway, Lunde found dozens of organic compounds including PCB's and benzopyrenes (Overrein et al., 1980). In the United States nearly one billion pounds of pesticides are applied annually to agricultural crops to control insect pests, plant pathogens, and weeds. About 65 percent is applied by aerial spraying and of this, 60 to 80 percent reaches the agricultural target area; 20 to 40 percent of the pesticide enters the atmosphere; some is deposited in adjoining fields, but an unknown amount is deposited at great distances from the site of application (Pimentel, 1981). Unfortunately, there is very little information on the kinds and amounts of micropollutants reaching New England ecosystems.

To summarize, all of the New England landscape receives acid rain, with the northwestern part receiving some of the most acidic rain in North America. Coastal and central regions of New England have a serious photooxidant problem, ranking not far behind California. Modest levels of anthropogenic ozone have also penetrated northern areas around Lake Champlain and the northern part of the Connecticut Valley. Trace metals are entering land and water ecosystems throughout the region, with some mountain deposition of lead equaling amounts found around urban areas. Added to this is a large array of micropollutants, mostly unmeasured, but some of which are biologically active in minute amounts.

The Effects of Air Pollution on the Landscape

The critical issue is the effect that air pollution stress will have on the ecosystems of New England. It is possible to render an informed judgment on this subject. First, however, it is important to understand some of the complexities involved in studying the interaction of pollution and the ecosystem, and the difficulty, if not the impossibility, of gaining precise estimates of damaging effects. Those who cite failure to provide precise answers to these complex problems as a reason to weaken air pollution standards suffer from naivete or cupidity.

Effects are hard to measure because of the nature and impacts of the pollutants on highly complex ecosystems. Regional air pollution is a variable mix of acids, photooxidants, gases, trace metals, inorganic substances, and man-made organic chemicals with which nature has had no previous experience. This mixture makes it exceedingly hard to analyze effects of single pollutants. Furthermore, individual pollutants may be beneficial, neutral, or harmful to organisms, and they may be synergistic, with two or more pollutants together having an impact far greater than the sum of each alone. The effects on organisms or ecosystems can be direct or indirect, resulting from interactions triggered by pollution damage, and they can be cumulative and slow in expressing themselves. Finally, regional pollution can involve relatively low-level chronic pollution as well as occasional higher-level, episodic exposure.

The effects of regional air pollution on the structure and function of natural ecosystems such as forests, fields, streams, and lakes are difficult to measure. Because of their size, seasonal and yearly variation, developmental changes, and other subtle changes, large amounts of effort are required to assay even a small system. Furthermore, these systems contain thousands of species of organisms. New England contains about 2500 species of higher plants and several times that number of animals and microorganisms, and only a handful have been intensively studied in terms of pollution effects. Ecosystems also vary in space. They change in composition and structure with changes in geology, topography, and altitude. They also change through developmental processes like succession, and all have been affected in some degree by man's use. Finally, study of natural systems has always had a low priority when it comes to apportioning national research funds.

Despite these difficulties, ecologists have shown that forest ecosystems respond to increasingly severe pollution in a highly repeatable pattern (Gordon and Gorham, 1963; Woodwell, 1970; Knabe, 1976; Guderian, 1977; W. H. Smith, 1981). The pattern of decline of a forest ecosystem under increasingly severe air pollution stress—

made so either through long periods of exposure to some more or less constant level of pollution or by shorter exposures to increased levels of pollution—can be thought of as a series of stages leading to ecosystem collapse.

Stage O. Anthropogenic pollutant levels insignificant. Pristine ecosystems.

Stage I. Anthropogenic pollution occurs at generally low levels. Ecosystems serve as a sink for pollutants, but species and ecosystem functions are relatively unaffected.

Stage IIA. Levels of pollutants are inimical to some aspect of the life cycle of sensitive species or individuals. As a result, they are subtly and adversely affected. For example, plants may suffer reduced photosynthesis, a change in reproductive capacity, a change in predisposition to insect or fungus attack, or deleterious effects on nutrient cycling. Other organisms within the ecosystem, such as predators, parasites, decomposers, and symbionts may be affected, and ecosystem functions of decomposition and nutrient uptake altered. Smith (1981) has documented numerous examples of these effects determined by laboratory and field studies. Inorganic and organic pollutants may accumulate within the ecosystem. Some like DDT may undergo biomagnification in predators (Gill, 1972), but most are probably at concentrations too low to have toxic effects. The effects of Stage IIA are hard to pin down in field studies, but if continued over long periods of time they may lead to significant changes in the competitive ability of sensitive species and to the next stage.

Stage IIB. With increased pollution stress, populations of sensitive species decline, and their effectiveness as functional members of the ecosystem diminishes. Ultimately these species may be lost from the system, but a more likely fate is that some individuals will hang on as insignificant components. The death of sensitive plant species is probably due to a secondary effect, like fungal or insect attack, rather than to direct pollution damage (Miller and Elderman, 1976; Loucks and Willams, 1980). If a sensitive species is an important member of an ecosystem, its loss can have reverberating effects. For example, the success of seedlings of one species may depend on environmental conditions, like shade, provided by another species. If the latter species is sensitive to pollution, the former species may suffer (Treshow and Stewart, 1973). Animals tolerant of pollution may suffer if they depend heavily on sensitive plant species for their livelihood. Likewise, plants dependent on pollution-sensitive animals may suffer. Honeybees are particularly sensitive to air pollution, and deleterious effects on them might interfere with pollination of plants, seed production, and ultimately with the reestablishment of vegetation (Loucks and Williams, 1980).

An important aspect of Stage IIB is that ecosystem functions, such as biotic regulation of hydrology, erosion, or nutrient loss, *may* be little affected. The reason is that as populations of sensitive plants decline, their role in ecosystem function may be taken over by tolerant plant species that, in effect, prosper because of their release from competition with sensitive species for available resources within the ecosystem, or nonliving components may be capable of biotic regulation for several years despite declining ecosystem productivity (Bormann and Likens, 1979).

Finally, pollution stress can be an important agent of natural selection (Kettlewell, 1961). Genes favoring resistance to pollution stress will probably become more important in plant and animal populations. Whether these populations will trade off other important adaptive genes is unknown.

Stage IIIA.   With still more pollution stress, the size of plants becomes important to survival, and large plants, trees, and shrubs of all species die off. The basic structure of the forest ecosystem is changed (Woodwell, 1970). Gordon and Gorham (1963) describe this process as peeling off the layers of forest structure: first the trees, followed by tall shrubs, and finally, under the severest conditions, the short shrubs and herbs. During this phase, impoverishment of species continues and, most important, the structure of the forest ecosystem is progressively changed to one dominated by small scattered shrubs and herbs, including weedy species not previously present in the forest. Productivity is greatly reduced as the ability of the ecosystem to repair itself by substituting tolerant for intolerant species is surpassed. Toxic concentrations of accumulated pollutants may limit many species. The capacity of the ecosystem to regulate biogeochemical cycles, discussed earlier in this article, is severely diminished. Runoff is greatly increased, the loss of nutrients previously held and cycled within the ecosystem is accelerated, erosion is increased, and soil and nutrients are exported to interconnected aquatic systems. Local climatic conditions are changed. The capacity of the ecosystem to filter pollutants from rainwater is sharply lowered, and these substances may be transferred directly to stream and groundwater. Interconnected streams and lakes may be severely affected.

The probability of fire is markedly increased during the peeling stage. As layers of vegetation die, masses of highly flammable dead wood are left behind, increasing the probability that natural or man-induced fire will occur. If fire does occur, conversion to open shrub land will be speeded.

Stage IIIB. Ecosystem collapse. All ecosystems are subject to various kinds of naturally recurring disturbances, such as wild fires, strong wind storms, insect outbreaks, or forest cuttings. Usually they have a built-in ability to recover from these disturbances. After the perturbing event is over, in the course of several decades, the ecosystem will rebuild itself to predisturbance levels of structure and function (Bormann and Likens, 1979). On the other hand, some disturbances can so damage ecosystems through loss of species, ecosystem structure, nutrients, and soil that the capacity of the ecosystem to repair itself is greatly constricted. Even if the perturbing force is removed, these damaged ecosystems would take centuries or even millennia to achieve predisturbance levels of productivity, structure, and function. It is this type of degraded ecosystem that is found under the severest pollution conditions close to point pollution sources (Hutchinson and Whitby, 1976).

Based on various lines of evidence and inference, it is possible to judge the condition of the New England landscape in terms of the stress categories just defined. Given the extent and intensity of regional pollution discussed earlier, it seems safe to say that no part of New England is free from some form of air pollution stress. Some parts are now in Stage I, but a considerable area is probably well advanced into Stages IIA and IIB for reasons that will be presented shortly. The IIIA and IIIB responses are, at the present time, rare in New England. The best examples are found around large smelters like those at Sudbury and Wawa, Ontario, and Copper Hill, Tennessee, where hundreds to thousands of square kilometers of landscape have been denuded. Smaller examples are found in the Naugatuck Valley in Connecticut and around a zinc smelter at Palmerton, Pennsylvania. In general, the bulk of the New England landscape is quite far from a Stage III response under present levels of pollution. However, time, future emissions, and vulnerability of individual ecosystems are factors that could lead to Stage III responses in a number of areas. Three examples will be dealt with later.

Four categories of evidence are used to support the conclusion of widespread Stage II responses: sensitive species, potential effects of acid rain, growth responses of some tree populations, and productivity responses to air pollution.

Sensitive species.   There is abundant evidence that among wild plant species there is a wide range of tolerance to various air pollutants (Davis and Wilhour, 1976). We also know that air pollution stress by its selective action on sensitive species can bring about major changes in the composition and functions of natural ecosystems (Smith, 1980). A clear example of this process is seen in the mountains of southern California, which have been subject to photooxidant stress for more than thirty years. Two of the major tree species, Ponderosa and Jeffrey pine, are sensitive to photooxidants and in thirty years have had an enormous mortality, about 3 percent per annum, which means that hundreds of thousands of trees have died. Death is usually attributed to the western pine beetles which invade pollution-weakened trees. On one plot measured over a twenty-year period, the standing volume of timber fell by 28 percent (Miller and Elderman, 1976). Obviously air pollution stress of this magnitude on two dominant species will cause profound changes within these ecosystems. It is also of interest to note that photooxidant damage of economic proportions to these species is now occurring along the entire western slope foothills of the Sierra Nevada (Williams et al., 1977).

Extensive field and laboratory work has documented that many species are sensitive to sulfur dioxide and/or ozone (Davis and Wilhour, 1976), often at doses below the current NAAQS (Williams and Wong, 1980; Manning, 1979) and that loss of productivity can occur without any visible symptoms of injury (Sprugel et al., 1980). Some New England species sensitive to sulfur dioxide are large-tooth and trembling aspen, white and yellow birch, low-bush blueberry, red and white pine, staghorn sumac, and black willow. Tree-of-heaven, white ash, trembling aspen, concord grape, honey locust, white oak, tulip poplar, and sycamore are sensitive to ozone (Davis and Wilhour, 1976). Only a small fraction of the New England flora, however, (ca. 2500 species of higher plants) has been evaluated for pollution resistance. Of all woody plants that have been tested, about 28 percent are sensitive to ozone and another 29 percent, not necessarily the same species, are sensitive to sulfur dioxide (Davis and Wilhour, 1976). If we apply these percentages to the New England flora, somewhere between 700 and 1400 species might be expected to be sensitive to these air pollutants. Since southern New England is among the worst photooxidant areas in the east, and crop damage due to photooxidants was reported in all six states as long ago as 1971–72 (Naegele et al., 1972), and photooxidant damage has been observed on Nantucket Island, miles at sea, it seems very probable that many wild plant species have already been affected and are undergoing subtle population declines.

It does not seem unreasonable to conclude that in the face of current levels of air pollution, large-scale biological changes are occurring in our landscape. Whole-scale genetic changes are probably underway. Many sensitive species are probably in a state of decline, with decline most rapid in nodes or areas where local pollutants are laid over the regional patterns (Havas and Huttunen, 1976). Disease and insect outbreaks on plants may be related to the weakened conditions of hosts. The likely effects are a decrease in both plant and animal diversity and fundamental changes in ecosystem function. Unfortunately, long-term studies specifically designed to test effects of air pollutants on natural ecosystems have not been done.

Acid rain.   Although acid rain has been falling on New England for more than two decades (Likens and Bormann, 1974; Likens, 1976), only in the last few years has it begun to receive intensive scientific study as a regional phenomenon (Galloway et al., 1978). Laboratory, greenhouse, and field experiments with simulated acid rain have shown numerous effects on both crop and wild plants, including the leaching of nutrients from leaves, increased potential for infection by bacterial and fungal pathogens, synergistic effects of sulfur dioxide and ozone in damaging leaves, premature senescence of leaves (Galloway et al., 1978), and reduction in the establishment of tree seedlings (Abrahamson et al., 1976). Experimental work has shown effects on soils, such as increased leaching of nutrients, acidification, and increases in the availability of toxic metal. Acidification is also known to reduce soil processes like nitrogen fixation and decomposition (Galloway et al., 1978). Despite this impressive array of specific biological and soil effects of simulated acid rain, reliable evidence of acid rain resulting in *economic* damage to crops or forest trees is scanty (Galloway et al., 1978). Nevertheless, we know that certain processes accelerated by acid rain like foliar and soil leaching and increased availability of toxic aluminum in some soils are underway. In some ecosystems, long-term effects of this type could be serious. In aquatic ecosystems, the widespread and damaging effects of acid rain are well known. I will return to this topic later.

Forest tree population.   Eastern white pine is one of New England's major tree species from both an ecological and economic point of view. The species is moderately sensitive to both photooxidants and sulfur dioxide (Davis and Wilhour, 1976). Trees in permanent plots along the Blue Ridge Parkway in western Virginia have been noted to die following clinical symptoms of photooxidant damage; and an accrued decrease in annual wood production among all tolerance classes of 40 percent between 1955 and 1978 has been reported (Skelly, 1980).

   In a study of nine stands in central and southern Indiana and fifteen stands in central Wisconsin, 90 percent of all trees examined had symptoms of photooxidant damage which was judged to be moderate to severe throughout Indiana (Usher and Williams, 1980). Other workers have reported that mixtures of ozone and sulfur dioxide might have been reported in New England as early as 1908 (Skelly et al., 1979). Damage to thousands of acres of New England white pine by ozone and sulfur dioxide were noted by Naegele et al. in 1972. In view of photooxidant conditions throughout our region, it is probable that white pine in New England is under severe photo-oxidant stress.

Pitch pine is an important tree species in sandy areas of coastal New England, particularly Cape Cod, where it is probably the principal tree species. Johnson et al. (unpublished) in an examination of diameter growth of dominant open-grown trees in the Pinelands of New Jersey, found a dramatic reduction in the growth of many trees beginning in the late 1950s with no subsequent recovery regardless of age. The average decline in growth was 40 percent. Investigation of 200 pitch pines growing in Pennsylvania, New York, Massachusetts, and Connecticut indicated that about one third show the same precipitous decline in radial growth beginning sometime within the last twenty-five years. The authors suggest that acid rain may be an important contributing factor to growth decline, but photooxidant pollution may also be involved.

Red spruce, one of three major tree species in the extensive spruce-fir forests of northern New England and New York, is suffering a decline throughout its range. This phenomenon, to be discussed later in detail, is coincident with particularly severe air pollution in mountainous regions. Important tree species such as white ash, and white and yellow birch are suffering from decline or dieback in parts of New England (Houston, personal communication). Is widespread and increasingly severe air pollution implicated?

It has been observed that insect pests sometimes attack air-pollution-stressed forests more than pollution-free forests, and in forests under pollution stress even normally innocuous insect pests may cause plant mortality. Although air pollution alone can kill forests, in southern California it has been shown that insects, fungal-root pathogens and photooxidants form an integrated complex of destructive factors that speed up forest decline (Miller and Elderman, 1976; Loucks and Williams, 1980). Reports of this type raise a difficult question: to what degree has regional air pollution increased the incidence of insect and fungal disease among trees and other plant species? An intriguing case of mortality is seen in red pine plantations throughout Connecticut. This species, planted south of its natural range as part of a reforestation and watershed management program forty to sixty years ago, began to undergo massive die-off ten to fifteen years ago. Pathologists and entomologists more or less agree that death results from a dual attack by a scale insect and a root pathogen, but one cannot help wondering to what degree increasingly severe photooxidant pollution and acid rain predisposed these trees to attack.

Productivity.   There is accumulating circumstantial evidence that plant productivity (new tissues resulting from photosynthesis) may be substantially reduced by regional air pollution.

In California it has been estimated that wood production in pole-sized stands of Ponderosa pine growing in polluted air from about 1941 to 1971 had about 83 percent less volume than a similar stand growing in nonpolluted air (Miller and Elderman, 1976). This suggests a remarkable reduction in energy flow through the ecosystem. Loucks et al. (1980) have estimated crop and forest losses due to air pollution in the Ohio River Basin due to regional ozone pollution ranges from 5 to 26 percent for soybeans, 5 to 15 percent for corn, and 3 to 10 percent for wheat. Additional losses due to sulfur dioxide pollution around power plants range from 0 to 4 percent in the affected area. The reduction in annual wood production of all forests in the Ohio River Basin was estimated to range beween 0.7 and 3.4 percent in 1977. The authors suggest that if trends in lowered forest productivity hold, the diminished ability of forests to fix carbon by photosynthesis may contribute to carbon dioxide increases in the global atmosphere.

Field experiments using open-topped chambers through which either ambient air (containing pollutants) or filtered air (pollutants removed by various absorbants) have produced some remarkable results. In England, grain yields of barley in filtered chambers were nearly double those in nonfiltered chambers and about 60 percent greater than plots with no chambers. The polluting agents were sulfur dioxide, fluorides, and mercaptans but at concentrations previously thought to be at nondamaging levels (Brough et al., 1978). Another chamber study showed that sulfur dioxide concentrations in rural districts of England can depress the yield of a cultivated rye grass by 50 percent (Bell and Clough, 1973). They pointed out, however, that clones of wild rye grass collected in a polluted district and grown side by side with the cultivated rye grass were not affected by ambient sulfur dioxide levels.

In other chamber studies, Skelly has shown that growth of tulip poplar, green ash, and loblolly pine is depressed in nonfiltered air.

Skelly and Wilhour (1979), citing that oxidant levels in the southern Appalachians have increased 2 to 3 times in the last 10 to 15 years, conclude that oxidant air pollution is becoming increasingly inimical to forest productivity throughout the eastern United States.

Perhaps the most startling result using open-topped chambers was obtained by John Skelly and his associates (Duchelle et al., 1980). Filtered and nonfiltered chambers and field plots were established in an old pasture atop the Blue Ridge Mountains in northwestern Virginia. Some of the plant species involved were milkweed, field pea, strawberry, and raspberry—all important successional species. Plants in the nonfiltered chamber and in plots had well recognized symptoms of ozone damage, while those in the filtered air chamber were free of symptoms. At the conclusion of the 1979 growing season it was found that growth in the ambient air chambers and outside plots was about 32 percent and 57 percent less than in the filtered air. Ozone concentrations were below the NAAQS. This remarkable study illustrates severe damage by regional photooxidant pollution in a remote region.

Skelly's finding suggests that productivity (photosynthesis) of natural ecosystems covering large areas in the eastern United States may be depressed by the concentrations of ozone that exist today. Southern New England may be one such region, since photooxidant conditions there are far worse than those in the Blue Ridge Mountains (Ludwig and Shelar, 1980; and Figure 4).

The photosynthetic fixation of solar energy by plants is the cornerstone of all ecosystem activities. Consequently, chronic depression of photosynthesis raises questions of fundamental importance about indirect effects of air pollution on ecosystem function. Natural ecosystems are powered by solar energy fixed in photosynthesis and used in transpiration. Directly and indirectly, solar energy is used to do work. What would happen to this work if, for example, productivity were reduced by 10 percent because of chronic air pollution? Would this diminish transpiration and the ecosystem's effect on local climate? Would enhanced runoff and a greater loss of nutrients in drainage water result? Would the rate of erosion increase as productivity declines? Would species diversity be lowered in relation to energy flow? Would the ecosystem undergo degradation that would be largely imperceptible because of its slow rate?

Although there is much to be learned about the effects of local and regional air pollution on plants and ecosystems, there is no doubt that pollutants can markedly affect productivity even in remote areas. Effects can be severe, and both crop and wild plants can be affected. Effects can occur at levels below present Federal Standards and often without visible symptoms of damage. Finally, the geographical zone affected.by damaging photooxidant pollution is spreading. Given the intensity of our regional pollution, it is almost a foregone conclusion that significant changes in the New England landscape are underway.

Vulnerable ecosystems.   It is possible to consider the New England landscape as a collection of ecosystems ranging from those particularly vulnerable to those much less vulnerable to air pollution stress (Galloway et al., 1978; Norton, 1980; Hendrey et al., 1980; Hendrey and Lipfert, 1980; Flamm and Bangay, 1981). The vulnerability of each ecosystem is determined by the amount of pollution (input), soil (Galloway et al., 1978), slope and aspect, and so forth.

Clearly, the New England landscape may be viewed as an array of aquatic and terrestrial ecosystems of varying vulnerability to air pollution stress, with vulnerability itself varying with different types or mixtures of pollutants. We will now consider three types of ecosystems particularly vulnerable to air pollution stress: lakes, sensitive to acid rain; forests of intermediate fertility; and mountain forests of northern New England.

Acidified lakes.   The acidification of thousands of lakes throughout the northern hemisphere (Wright and Gjessing, 1976; Schindler, 1981) is the clearest example of drastic ecosystem alteration resulting from regional air pollution. Acidification results from acid precipitation, over a period of years, progressively increasing the acidity of hydrogen ion concentrations of lake waters. This has profound effects on the chemistry of the water, including an increase in biologically toxic trace metals. Some trace metals—like mercury, cadmium, and lead—enter with acid precipitation and are derived from the same anthropogenic sources that inject sulfur and nitrogen oxides into the atmosphere. Other trace metals like aluminum and zinc are leached by acid rain from soils surrounding a lake (Hendrey, 1981). As the lake water becomes more acid, far-reaching changes in the biota of the ecosystem occur (Hendrey and Lipfert, 1980; Hendrey et al., 1976). Progressively, numbers of some zooplankton, phytoplankton, molluscs, and amphipods will be reduced, and species of various kinds will be eliminated. Decomposition of organic matter will be slowed. The net effect of loss of species and reduction in rates of decomposition is a drastic reduction in the quality and quantity of food available for higher-level organisms like fish. With continued acidification, not only may fish suffer from food shortages but they may also be affected directly by acidity and a variety of trace metals whose toxicity increases with acidity. Together these factors lead to the disruption of their life cycles. Many species of fish begin to disappear at hydrogen ion concentrations of about 10 mg H^+/l (pH 5). Sport fishes are the most sensitive (Schindler, 1981). All fish are eliminated at concentrations of 32 mg H^+/l (pH 4.5), a level now detected in many lakes. Effects are not limited to inhabitants of permanent lakes, but are felt also by transient species, like osprey, ducks, loons, and blue herons dependent on lakes for their livelihood (Loucks, 1980).

The vulnerability of lake ecosystems to acidification is determined by many factors. Perhaps the most important is alkalinity, which determines the ability of a lake to neutralize acidity. Alkalinity, in turn, is determined by the geology and soils of the watershed surrounding a lake. Rocks like limestone provide high levels of alkalinity and an almost infinite capacity to neutralize levels of acidity expected from acid rain. At the other extreme, granites and related igneous rocks, their metamorphic equivalents, and noncalcareous sandstones yield minimal alkalinity and minimal acid-neutralizing capacity. Thus lakes whose watersheds contain these latter types of rock may be considered sensitive or vulnerable to damage by acid rain (Norton, 1980). Geological maps of areas potentially vulnerable to acid rain have been prepared and much of New England is underlain by rocks with little acid neutralizing capacity; hence many of its lakes and streams may be vulnerable to acid rain.

It should be borne in mind that acidification is not an all-or-none phenomenon with a lake one day neutral or slightly acidic and the next strongly acid. Acidification involves a slow lowering of alkalinity with little change in acidity. Once alkalinity of a lake is exhausted, relatively small additions of acid may bring about noticeable increases in acidity (Hultberg and Wenblad, 1980). Thus the

acidification process in a lake may be well underway before there is
a noticeable change in acidity.

The problem of acidification of surface waters reaches far beyond
the borders of New England and cannot be treated in the ultra-
simplistic cost/benefit terms of a David Stockman (see quotation pp.
123–29). Most of the northeast quadrant of North America, including much of the eastern United States, is subject to the acid rain/
trace metal problem (Figure 3). About one quarter of the total area
of Canada, underlain by hard rocks that yield minimum alkalinity, is
now receiving acid rain with 20 mg H^+/l (pH 4.7 or less). This is an
enormous area of 1,400,000 square kilometers, thirty percent of
which is covered by fresh water (Schindler, 1980). Large areas of
Scandinavia with abundant lakes are also geologically sensitive and
subject to acid rain. The exact impact is not known, but in Ontario
alone it is estimated that nearly 50,000 lakes are degraded, while
the government of Norway estimates that 20,000 lakes are already
severely affected, and 20,000 more are in imminent danger (Schindler, 1980).

Loucks (1980) has brought together information on the rate at
which lakes are currently being acidified in Ontario, Quebec, New
York, and New England. He has projected that by 1990 between
250 and 1500 lakes will become acidified each year, that is, lake
acidity will rise to levels known to have strong negative effects on
fish. He emphasizes that these projections are rough and perhaps
best considered as questions in need of answers.

As if the huge problem of acid lakes were not enough, anthropogenic acidification also affects streams, rivers, and groundwater-
elements, which for reasons of space cannot be treated here. Obviously, the economic implications are enormous, but of even greater
importance, acidification of lakes provides the first evidence of significant degradation of large areas of our globe resulting from anthropogenic air pollution.

Forests of intermediate fertility.   Extensive areas of commercially
important, mixed coniferous and deciduous forest in southern Quebec and Ontario are considered to be at risk from acid rain (Rennie,
1979). These forests, underlain by soils of intermediate acidity and
modest fertility, are thought to be especially sensitive to a progressive loss of nutrients, which could culminate in a significant loss

of productivity. Similar forests cover large parts of northern New England.

Careful experiments in England have shown that annual additions of ammonium sulfate fertilizer will cause increased soil acidity, depletion of calcium reserves, and significant declines in yields. Sulfate is converted into acid in the soil, and acid leaching causes the removal of calcium.

The amount of sulfate applied in England is not greatly different from that being deposited by long-range pollution in southeastern Canada. Although there is, as yet, no direct evidence of this effect on Canadian forests, the worry is that by the time a 15 to 20 percent loss in productivity has been documented, degradation will be too advanced to reverse.

High elevation forests.   If asked to choose the most likely New England candidate among forest ecosystems for a Stage III response, my choice would be the high elevation forests of northern New England.

These forests, which cover hundreds of thousands of acres, vary in composition and structure with elevation (Bormann and Likens, 1979). In the mountains of New Hampshire, for example, spruce-hardwood forests dominate at 600 meters (2000 feet); but with increasing elevation, most hardwoods drop out, and at 760 meters (2500 feet) the forest is dominated by red spruce, balsam fir, and white birch. At still higher elevations, red spruce decreases in importance, and above 1100 meters (3600 feet) balsam fir and white birch are the principal components of the forest ecosystem.

These mountain forests have many features that would seem to make them fragile and vulnerable to the stress of air pollution. Most are underlain by hard rocks with little acid-buffering capacity (Hendrey et al., 1980). Glacial till, which can contribute to buffering capacity, is thin or absent at many higher elevations (Thornthwaite, personal communication). The podzol soils are thin, acidic, and relatively infertile. They have virtually no sulphate buffering capacity. (Some soils can absorb sulphate and hydrogen ions and thus greatly diminish effects of acid rain—Johnson et al., 1979.) Most of these forests occur on steep slopes where erosion would be a threat if vegetation cover were lost. In many localities, the potential for landslides becomes increasingly important with increasing elevation

(Bormann et al., 1969). As discussed earlier, if a species sensitive to some form of stress is lost, its role in the ecosystem may be taken over by other species. This form of protection is minimal because the number of species composing these mountain ecosystems is relatively low and decreases with increasing elevation. Finally, even without pollution, the mountain environment is generally stressful, typified by short and erratic growing seasons, desiccating winds, and frequent wind and ice storms.

These high-elevation forests receive far greater pollution than nearby lowland areas, because of orographic precipitation, deposition of cloud moisture in the form of fog drip and hoar frost, and dry deposition. Not only does more precipitation (Vogelmann et al., 1968; Schlesinger and Reiners, 1974) and its contained pollutants enter the ecosystem, but cloud moisture often contains up to ten times the acidity of rain (Tomlinson et al., 1980; Falconer and Falconer, 1980). Coniferous trees, which predominate over most of the elevational gradient, are exceedingly efficient in removing cloud moisture, dry particles, and some pollutant gases (Mayer and Ulrich, 1980). Reiners (personal communication) and his associates estimate that the total of acidity, trace metals, and other pollutants strained out of the air stream by high-elevation fir forests is between the amount added in rain and snow and ten times that amount. Their preliminary modeling also suggests that fir forests have an extraordinary capacity to remove even low concentrations of sulfur dioxide from the air stream.

The deposition of pollutants by orographic rain, cloud moisture, or dry deposition is not uniform. Windward slopes receive an extra load, while slopes on the lee side or in sheltered positions receive less (Geiger, 1965; Nordo, 1976). Measurements of anthropogenic lead accumulated in the forest floor along a windward slope in New Hampshire indicate that about twice as much is found in high-elevation fir forest as in lower-elevation spruce-hardwood forest (Reiners et al., 1975). In an examination of windward slopes in the Green Mountains of Vermont, however, the highest levels of lead (three times that in spruce-hardwood) were found in mid-slope forests dominated by red spruce. In Norway it has been noted that the maximum acidity received in orographic rain is at mid-slope (Nordo, 1976).

Levels of sulfur dioxide and ozone in the air currently striking these mountains are generally modest. Ozone measured on White-face Mountain in New York, about 25 miles west of Vermont (Kadleck and Mohnen, unpublished; Pratt and Falconer, 1979) is generally below 0.05 ppm. During the growing season of 1974; however, 69 hours above 0.08 ppm were recorded, and during Juné of 1977 the average daily maxima equaled or exceeded 0.08 ppm. As noted earlier, ozone at these concentrations can damage some sensitive species of plants. Most of the ozone measured at Whiteface is thought to be of stratospheric origin—that is, not anthropogenic.

Given the intense levels of air pollution, we may ask what has been the effect on these mountain ecosystems? To judge, we must first consider some potential effects distilled from intensive research on acid rain during the last fifteen years. European and North American scientists see the effects of acid rain on high-altitude forest ecosystems as largely indirect. But as with forests of intermediate fertility, the addition of atmospheric acid to these poorly buffered forest systems may result in a reduction of fertility and eventually of forest productivity (Overrein et al., 1980).

Yet things may not be so simple. In relatively infertile forest ecosystems, nitrogen added as part of the pollutants may actually stimulate growth and productivity. Nutrients needed for growth, however, are needed in certain biochemically determined proportions, and nitrogen added in acid rain that at first stimulates growth may ultimately bring about nutrient deficiencies and poor growth (Overrein et al., 1980). Almost nothing is known of long-term synergistic effects that heavy metals, other pollutants, and acid rain may have on trees and other plants, and on animals and microorganisms that make up the ecosystem. Still another aspect of the acid-rain problem concerns the behavior of aluminum in soils. Study of a mountain forest in West Germany receiving atmospheric acidity from distant industrial sources has shown that an increase in soluble aluminum in the soil has occurred during the last thirteen years. Concentrations of aluminum in the soil are now at levels thought to be damaging to plant roots (Ulrich et al., 1980).

How do these things apply to the mountain ecosystems of New England and New York? We know these things: inputs of acid rain are among the highest in the world; trace metal depositions are above regional averages; and, because of diverse topography, inputs of pollutants will be variable—yet sampling of inputs has been very limited. All this suggests that even hotter spots of pollution-input exist but as yet have not been detected.

At both upper and mid-elevations in New Hampshire, substantial aluminum leaching in forest ecosystems has been measured in soils and groundwater and appears to be increasing coincidentally with acid rain (Cronan, 1980; Johnson, 1979). Levels of soluble aluminum in soils (Cronan, 1980; Mulder, 1980) are on the border of concentrations thought to be toxic to some plants (Ulrich et al., 1980).

What is the evidence of large-scale ecosystem effects? In high-elevation fir forests there are no clear-cut signs of degradation due to air pollution, except possibly symptoms of potassium deficiency in foliage (Reiners, personal communication). In lower-elevation spruce-hardwood forests, a sharp decline in the growth rate of the forest after 1960 has been measured (Whittaker et al., 1974).

The most dramatic change now taking place seems to be in mid-elevation spruce-fir forests. Measurements taken on four mountains in Vermont in 1964 and repeated in the same locations in 1979 indicate red spruce trees of all sizes are dying at a fairly rapid rate (Siccama et al., unpublished). A similar decline has been measured in the spruce-hardwood forest of New Hampshire, and observations suggest that a decline is also underway in the Adirondack Mountains. In the spruce-fir forests of New Hampshire, Reiners (personal communication) has observed that red spruce is not as healthy as it used to be. No place looks good, and dying spruce trees are common. Baldwin (1977) has reported that red spruce is not doing well on the higher slopes of Mount Monadnock, in New Hampshire.

Red spruce is a species of extraordinary importance in these northeastern mountain forests, particularly in mid-slope forests where spruce is one of the four important tree species. If these declining trends prove to be long lasting, and red spruce is severely diminished in importance, a Stage III response is not an impossibility. Such a response might be hastened by wildfire burning over the accumulations of dead wood left after the death of spruce.

A final word regarding the vulnerability of New England mountain forests to air pollution stress. What has been said so far represents an attempt to see the impact that current levels of pollution are having. If emissions of sulfur dioxide, nitrogen oxides, and hydrocarbons continue to grow, it seems likely not only that inputs of acid rain and trace metal will increase, but that two other pollutants that now seem to be relatively unimportant may become important. Two modeling efforts demonstrate this potential. Lincoln and Rubin (1980) forecast that the largest percentage increase in emissions of sulfur dioxide from industrial sources in the Northeast will occur in northern New England. Cleveland and Graedel (1979) have modeled the production of ozone from nitrogen oxide and hydrocarbon precursors. Their model shows that the more precursors emitted, the further from the precursor source will ozone be produced. Levels of ozone in central New England are already substantial, and increased production of precursors might well drive high levels of ozone into the mountains of northern New England. Thus already substantial acid rain and trace-metal pollution could be made still more acute by sulfur dioxide and ozone pollution.

Prospects for Reducing Air Pollution Stress

Current levels of air pollution have the potential to cause serious damage to the landscape of the northeastern United States, including New England, and adjacent Canada. What are the prospects of reducing stress on the landscape caused by air pollution?

Control of emissions is basic to any reduction, and clean-air legislation is the instrument of control. Emission records for the last forty years indicate that the Clean Air Act and its implementation by the EPA has slowed the rate of emissions. Emissions of sulfur dioxide increased from 21.5 million metric tons in 1940 to 29.8 million in 1970 with a slight decrease to 27.4 million in 1977. Nitrogen oxides showed a steep increase from 1940 to 1970, 7.9 to 19.6 million tons and an increase to 23.1 million in 1977. Hydrocarbons increased from 19.1 to 29.5 million tons from 1940 to 1970 and decreased to 28.3 million in 1976. Total solid particulates fell from 27.1 tons in 1940 to 22.2 tons in 1970 and then decreased to 12.4 tons in 1977 (Cavender et al., 1973; EPA, 1978).

In a general way, emissions are directly related to the use of fossil fuel, which is one aspect of economic growth. This relationship, however, can be modified by a number of other factors. For example, it can be affected by the quality of the fuel, in terms of energy content and potential to produce primary pollutants. The development and operation of pollution control devices can limit emissions. A difference in emissions can be made by electrical generation which meets the peaks and troughs of electrical demand by utilizing the most pollution-efficient generating stations first and the least efficient facilities last. Policy decisions that phase out pollution-inefficient plants as quickly as possible and replace them with more efficient ones can have an effect, as can the utilization of nonpolluting solar energy. Finally, increasing the efficiency with which we use energy will cut down on the demand for energy and the need to burn fuel in the first place (Loucks et al., 1978, Report of the New England Energy Congress, 1979).

Analyses of emission trends from 1970 to 1977 illustrate the interplay of regulatory, technological, and economic factors that determine emission trends (EPA, 1978). During this period sulfur dioxide emissions decreased slightly. Sulfur dioxide emissions are primarily due to combustion of coal and oil by electric utilities, and during this period the use of coal and oil increased 50 percent and 70 percent respectively. Emissions from utilities, however, increased only 10 percent, because of a shift from high-sulfur coal to low-sulfur coal. Major gains in emission control were also due to emission controls by nonferrous smelters and sulfuric acid manufacturing plants, in response to EPA regulation.

Nitrogen oxides increased by 18 percent from 1970 through 1977. This resulted from increases in the generation of electricity and the unavailability of technology to reduce nitrogen oxides in stack gases. Increased motor vehicle travel wiped out the gains realized by reduction of nitrogen oxide resulting from the production of cars with better mileage per gallon and mandated control devices that diminished emissions.

Hydrocarbon emissions decreased slightly during the period, despite an increase in industrial-process emissions of 17 percent. However, automotive emissions decreased 7 percent as a result of federally mandated emissions controls. Potentially the latter gain would have been much greater had not a substantial proportion of it been wiped out by a 30 percent increase in motor vehicle travel.

One unexpected result of EPA regulation was a shift from short to tall smokestacks. More than 425 tall stacks—higher than 61 meters—have been built since 1970. These stacks enable utility companies to meet NAAQ Standards by diluting effluents. Although high stacks improve local air quality, they promote long-range transport and thus contribute to primary and secondary pollution in distant areas (Speth et al., 1980). These data illustrate a central point. As energy use increases with economic growth, regulation of emissions must become more stringent just to maintain a constant level of total emissions.

Many attempts have been made to forecast future emissions, but it should be recognized that every model reflects the assumptions built into it. Two examples: the Strategic Environmental Assessment Systems model (SEAS) prepared for the Department of Energy by International Research and Technology and Mitre Corporation (Teknekron Research Inc.) forecasts 5 percent and 20 percent national increases in sulfur and nitrogen oxide emissions by 1990. This model, based on medium supply and demand of energy projections, *assumes* that sulfur dioxide emissions in the electric utility sector will not change because of a combination of controls that will bring existing sources into compliance, reducing their emissions and thereby offsetting the additional emissions from new facilities. Another model developed for electric generation in the Ohio River Basin presents a range of scenarios based on projected energy growth rates of 1.5 to 1.7 percent. It forecasts sulfur dioxide emissions in 1987 ranging from increases of 14 percent to decreases of 70 percent over 1977 emissions (Loucks et al., 1980). The range in results depends on whether existing facilities for the generation of power comply with state regulations (State Implementation Plans) and whether the states will increase the rigor of their regulations. It is assumed that all new facilities will meet New or Revised New Source Performance Standards.

It is clear that scenarios of future emissions prepared in the late 1970's contain a variety of potential outcomes ranging from substantial increases in emissions to substantial decreases. What the models do not reflect is the massive and mounting attack on the NAAQS and the NSPS (New Source Performance Standard) by industrialists and politicians, as well as by economists and scientists, many of whom are funded directly or indirectly by energy-based corporations.

The issue of National Ambient Air Quality Standards and related emission controls has extremely important economic implications. Cleaning the air is not cheap, and both costs and benefits are difficult to measure. John Frazer, Canada's Minister of Environment, estimates that to reduce sulfur emissions by 50 percent in eastern Canada and the northeastern United States would cost 4.5 billion dollars annually for twenty years. But, he warns, the cost of doing nothing is even higher (Dumanoski, 1979). On the other hand, My- rick Freeman estimates that the *benefit* to the United States of air pollution control in 1978 ranges between 5 and 51 billion dollars (Freeman, 1979); while the National Air Quality Commission (1981) estimates annual benefits accruing from control of particulates and sulfur are about 7 million dollars. Some benefits may be large and yet very subtle. Imagine how much further behind in world compe- tition for car sales United States manufacturers would be today if they had not been forced by mandated regulations to develop smaller, more fuel-efficient automobiles.

No one denies that using more expensive and less polluting fuels or modernizing old facilities to reduce emissions will be costly. One study of fifteen United States electric utilities, including most of the larger ones, found that those with relatively good emission records largely used low sulfur oil or natural gas, while those with the high- est emissions rely primarily on coal. TVA, the nation's largest utility, is least efficient in terms of emissions per unit of power output be- cause of relatively poor pollution-control equipment. The study es- timated that 9 to 19 billion dollars would be required to retrofit the major fossil fuel plants of the fifteen utilities, with 2.7 billion dollars as TVA's share (Carter, 1977). Another study estimates that the cost of electricity to the consumer in the Ohio River Basin would be about 20 percent lower in 1985 if fossil fuel generating plants cur- rently not in compliance with state emission-control regulations re- mained so (Loucks et al., 1980). In a study of coal-fired electrical generation, it was estimated that a 1988 coal plant would be 36 per- cent more expensive to construct but 76 percent less polluting than a 1978 plant. The same plant would be 129 percent costlier to con- struct but 91 percent better controlled than its 1971 counterpart. Antipollution equipment would be responsible for nine tenths of the increased costs (Komanoff, 1980).

Sulfur standards are not the only ones under debate. The Ameri- can Petroleum Institute claimed that the standard for ozone (0.08 ppm) was unduly protective and inflationary, with a projected na- tional cost of fourteen billion nationally to meet the standard. For this reason there was tremendous political pressure to push the standard as high as possible (Marshall, 1978). In 1979, the Ozone

Standard was raised to 0.12 ppm (King, 1979). Ironically, the intent of the law was weakened by the EPA. Originally the agency was charged with writing standards for photooxidants, but it chose to establish one standard for ozone in the belief that ozone was a reliable indicator of all other photooxidants. The standard was based on the presumed effects of ozone on human health, and industrial people have pointed out that there is very weak evidence for health effects at concentrations lower than 0.20 ppm. The EPA has created a Catch 22. What people breathe is not just ozone but a collection of photooxidants called smog. Yet because judgments on health effects are now based on ozone alone, people may have to settle for a still higher ozone standard and relatively high levels of pollution by the other photooxidants (Marshall, 1978). The implications of this for ecosystems is grave, since ozone even at the old standard can produce significant damage to ecosystems.

Air quality and emission standards are under attack not only because of added costs, which presumably raise the price of goods and services, but also because the 1970 Clean Air Act may bar industrial or energy growth in already polluted areas or in areas that already have clean air (R. J. Smith, 1981). For example, in some areas of the Ohio Valley, utilities are competing with one another heavily for the few remaining pollution rights (Carter, 1978).

An example of how political pressure works to circumvent standards is seen in the case of the Cleveland Electric Illuminating Company (New York Times, 1979). Two huge old utility plants on the shore of Lake Erie at Cleveland failed to meet NAAQ Standards for sulfur dioxide. To meet the standards, these plants could have installed expensive scrubbers to remove sulfur dioxide from the stack gases or converted to lower sulfur coal. Since the plants burn high-sulfur coal mined in Ohio, and a shift to low-sulfur coal could have caused a loss of about 70 percent of the coal mining jobs in Ohio, installation of scrubbers was judged inflationary by Carter administration economists. To meet the twin problems of potential inflation and loss of local jobs in a politically sensitive state, the EPA reclassified the plants as rural, which permits higher sulfur emissions because in rural areas sulfur is dispersed more quickly (New York Times, 1979). The EPA also allowed the height of smokestacks to be raised. Thus Ohio preserves jobs and has slightly cheaper energy, while downwind states lose on two counts: more sulfur pollution is permitted, and tall stacks assure its long range transport. In addition, because of the domino effect, loosening standards in one state inevitably leads utilities in other states to press for similar relaxation (Dumanoski, 1979).

The Clean Air Act, up for renewal in 1981, or early 1982, is the center of debate. Although the act enjoys widespread support and is thought by many to require only fine tuning, the clash of regional interests and heightened concern about industrial performance and energy production could result in extensive changes. Business groups, such as the National Coal Association, Chemical Manufacturers Association, Motor Vehicles Manufacturers Association, and Edison Electric Institute, claim that the act stifles industrial growth, constrains productivity, and bars the development of new energy sources by banning both new construction in polluted areas and expansion in areas that already have clean air (R. J. Smith, 1981). The new administration apparently accepts this position. Indications are that the Clean Air Act will be weakened allowing greater emissions and that energy conservation measures will receive less support in the federal budget promoting the use of more fossil fuel and consequently still more emissions.

David Stockman was quoted in *Science* (R. J. Smith, 1981) as saying of the Clean Air Act:

As many of you know, the National Commission (on Air Quality) consists largely of a choir of the faithful committed to issuing melodious harmonies to the tenets of orthodoxy regarding the Clean Air Act, and I'm somewhat of a self-avowed heretic in that regard so it's difficult for me to talk about it . . .

As I got into it and began to note anomalies . . . . I came to the conclusion that the Clean Air Act, like the Ptolemaic model of the solar system that began to develop more and more elaborations and exceptions and complications as the basic model proved to be wrong . . . has become increasingly unplugged from reality and that we are probably at a point today where the whole thing has gone off the deep end in terms of sheer bureaucratic fiction and in terms of what I would call institutionalized obscurantism . . .

In my view almost every one of those ambient standards are far too stringent relative to what both economic and public policy and the medical evidence would suggest. Clearly we know that in the case of ozone. There simply isn't any credible evidence to put the standard at 12 parts per billion. It could be substantially higher than that, but if it were, we would find, lo and behold, that 95 percent of the country is already in compliance and that you wouldn't need this witch hunt against hydrocarbon emission from paint shops and lawn mowers and so forth . . .

I don't know how closely any of you follow the national papers, but if you read the *Star*, the *Post*, and *The New York Times* you find that somebody's orchestrating a pretty careful strategy, because every other day there's a new article about the acid rain problem. And it's written by reporters who know not a damned thing, and you'll excuse my language, about pollution, the techniques of pollution, the chemistry of pollution. And they're writing such preposterous and absurd things that what it's doing is creating an intellectual climate, an attitudinal climate, that will probably cause the EPA or the Congress to lurch forward into an acid rain program that's based on nothing more substantial than the tail pipe standards were in 1970.

I kept reading these stories that there are 170 lakes dead in New York that will no longer carry any fish or aquatic life. And it occurred to me to ask the question . . . well how much are the fish worth in these 170 lakes that account for 4 percent of the lake area of New York? And does it make sense to spend billions of dollars controlling emission from sources in Ohio and elsewhere if you're talking about a very marginal volume of dollar value, either in recreational terms or in commercial terms?

Stockman went on to endorse relaxation of the air quality standard for sulfur dioxide. What are the prospects for reducing regional air pollution? Toxic waste disclosures have made us aware of the time-bomb effects ticking away in most environmental problems (Shabecoff, 1981). For this and many more positive reasons, there is much public support for a cleaner environment. We also have the technological knowledge to meet our energy needs and reduce pollution. On the other hand, there are powerful groups who view present air quality standards as a debilitating luxury stifling economic growth. Who will prevail in the current debate is uncertain.

Summary and Policy Considerations

Air pollution as a region-wide problem began four or five decades ago and since then has grown fairly steadily both in intensity and in extent. Pollutants are not simply acid rain or photooxidants but an array of substances often acting simultaneously whose interactive effects largely remain to be discovered. Recently it became apparent that much, perhaps the bulk, of the polluted air in New England comes from sources to our west both in the United States and Canada. Although the Clean Air Act and other policy decisions have slowed the increase in air pollution, today pollutants in the air of New England are intense enough to damage our landscape. This is occurring at a time when other stresses on the landscapes—such as more intensive forest harvesting, a rapidly increasing demand for fire wood, and rising recreational use—are rapidly escalating.

The measurement of damage to the landscape is difficult not only because of the complexity of natural systems, but also because we failed to establish baseline studies in prepollution times which could serve to evaluate modern changes. Nevertheless, a variety of evidence and inference indicates that the New England landscape may be endangered. Large-scale genetic, biological, and ecosystem changes are probably occurring under current levels of air pollution stress. Since the effects of air pollution on ecosystems are mostly indirect and cumulative—for example, reduction in the reproductive capacity of a key species or the progressive loss of soil fertility in forests or alkalinity in lakes—there is a legitimate concern that in a few decades vulnerable forest, lake, and stream ecosystems may simply fall apart. Already many lakes over an enormous area of northeastern North America have undergone severe deterioration and tens of thousands more are progressively moving toward that state.

The New England landscape uses solar energy to provide us with a multitude of material and psychological benefits, yet it may falter because of assumptions, made in ignorance, of how much mistreatment the landscape can accommodate. Without doubt, much more research is needed to clarify nature's capacity to absorb air pollution stress. Despite this uncertainty, spokesmen for both industry and the new administration in Washington present us with a choice between a revitalized economy or an "excessively" clean environment. The assumption, when it is given any thought at all, is that nature can somehow tolerate increased pollution with little or no loss of natural or human values. Or, perhaps, it is assumed that natural values simply are not very valuable. Whatever the reasoning, there is a massive campaign for the relaxation of air quality standards.

New England is doubly susceptible to the effects of weakened air quality standards. We are at the end of the pollution pipeline, in effect the garbage can of the United States, and we have a vulnerable landscape of great importance to us. It seems clear that our politicians should direct their best efforts toward the development and maintenance of a national energy policy that seeks a significant reduction in emissions of sulfur and nitrogen oxides and hydrocarbons. Within our region, it is particularly important to maintain strict ambient air quality standards and avoid the pitfall of granting local variances to burn dirtier fuels. Ultimately, to reduce air pollution over New England, we must convince states outside of New England to reduce emissions. Our arguments will not be very convincing if we are complacent about our own emissions.

If we consider the real values of our landscape and take linkage into account, the conflict between those concerned with the welfare of business and those worried about the welfare of the environment may be less real than it now seems. There can be energy and air pollution policies that properly value the energy contributions of nature and at the same time promote a healthy economy.

Although stricter air quality standards are required to reduce emissions, the best way to reduce them is not to burn the fuel in the first place. The best way to do this is to increase the efficiency with which we use energy: to reduce the amount of fossil energy consumed per unit of GNP produced. Our region should stand squarely behind President Reagan's proposal for reindustrialization. We could gain on several fronts by replacing old economically noncompetitive, energy-expensive, highly polluting industrial plants with modern, energy-efficient, highly competitive plants designed from the ground up to reduce emissions. Not only would our goods be more competitive on world markets while our solar-powered landscapes continued to pull their share of the load, but we would simultaneously reduce our rate of consumption of the world's shrinking energy supplies and reduce our contribution to the accumulation of carbon dioxide in the world's atmosphere.

There are many other actions that would contribute to the same end. Cogeneration and the manufacture of energy-efficient equipment should be encouraged. Insulation and weatherization of new and old buildings should continue to be fostered, as should energy-efficient mass transportation. Substitution of solar, water, wind, and tidal power for fossil power should be facilitated. Unfortunately, the linkage between these actions and a comprehensive energy and air-pollution policy has escaped the new policy-makers in Washington. Programs supporting these actions have had their budgets slashed.

If our politicians fail to create new policies of energy conservation, and the decision is made to produce cheaper energy by allowing more pollution to enter the atmosphere, New England can expect to pay a high price. Our landscape will lose its ambiance—first by drops and then perhaps in a cascade. We could become a northern Appalachia with the disadvantaged left behind, while those who can escape to the sunbelt, seeking more congenial surroundings.

REFERENCES

Abrahamson, G., K. Bjor, R. Horntvedt, and B. Tveite. 1976. Effects of acid precipitation on coniferous forest. In Finn H. Braekke, *Impact of Acid Precipitation on Forest and Freshwater Ecosystems in Norway.* Summary report on phase I (1972–75) of the SNSF-project.

Andresen, A. M., A. H. Johnson, and T. G. Siccama. 1980. Levels of lead, copper and zinc in the forest floor in the northeastern United States. *J. Environ. Qual.* 9:293–296.

Baldwin, H. I. 1977. Induced timberland of Mount Monadnock, N.H. *Bull. Torrey Botanical Club* 104:324–333.

Bell, J. N. B. and W. S. Clough. 1973. Depression of yield on rye grass exposed to sulphur dioxide. *Nature* 241:47–49.

Bormann, F. H. 1976. An inseparable linkage: Conservation of natural ecosystems and conservation of fossil energy. *Bio-Science* 26:754–760.

Bormann, F. H. and G. E. Likens. 1979. *Pattern and Process in a Forested Ecosystem.* New York, Springer-Verlag, 253 pp.

Brough, A., M. A. Parry, and C. P. Whittingham. 1978. The influence of aerial pollution on crop growth. *Chemistry and Industry* 3002:51–53.

Carter, L. J. 1977. More burning of coal offsets gains in air pollution control. *Science* 198:1233.

Carter, L. J. 1978. SO$_2$ emissions proposals pose growth issue. *Science* 202:30.

Cavender, J. H., D. S. Kircher, and A. J. Hoffman. 1973. *Nationwide Air Pollutant Emission Trends 1940–1970.* USEPA AP115. Research Triangle Park, N.C. 52 pp.

Cleveland, W. S. and T. E. Graedel. 1979. Photochemical air pollution in the northeastern United States. *Science* 204:1273–1277.

Cogbill, C. V. and G. E. Likens. 1974. Acid precipitation in the New York Metropolitan area: Its relationship to meteorological factors. *Environmental Science and Technology* 13:209–212.

Cronan, C. S. 1980. Solution chemistry of a New Hampshire subalpine ecosystem: A biogeochemical analysis. *Oikos* 34:272–281.

Davis, D. D. and R. G. Wilhour. 1976. *Susceptibility of Woody Plants to Sulfur Dioxide and Photochemical Oxidants: A Literature Review.* USEPA 600/3-76-102. Corvallis, Ore. 71 pp.

DeMarrais, G. A. 1979. *Association between Meteorological Conditions and High Ozone and Sulfate Concentrations: A 1974 Episode in the Eastern United States.* USEPA 600/4-79-009. Research Triangle Park, N.C. 65 pp.

Duchelle, S., J. M. Skelly, and L. W. Kress. 1980. The impact of photochemical oxidant air pollution on biomass development of native vegetation and symptom expression of *Asclepias*, spp. Abst. *Phytopathology* 70:689.

Dumanoski, D. 1979. The insidious killer called "acid rain." *Boston Globe*, November 19, 1979.

Eaton, J. S., G. E. Likens, and F. H. Bormann. 1978. The input of gaseous and particulate sulfur to a forest ecosystem. *Tellus* 30:546–551.

Emberlin, J. C. 1980. Smoke sulphur dioxide concentrations in relation to topography in a rural area of central southern England. *Atmospheric Environment* 14:1381–1390.

EPA. 1978. *National Air Quality, Monitoring, and Emissions Trend Report 1977.* USEPA 450/2-78-052. Research Triangle Park, N.C. 102 pp.

EPA. 1980. *Compilation of Air Pollutant Emission Factors.* Third Edition, Supplement 10. Research Triangle Park, N.C.

Falconer, R. E. and P. D. Falconer. 1980. Determination of cloud water acidity at a mountain observatory in the Adirondack Mountains of New York State. *Journal of Geophysical Research* 85:7465–7470.

Final Report of the New England Energy Congress: A Blueprint for Energy Action. 1979. Executive Summary, Vol. 2. Somerville, Mass.

Flamm, B. R. and G. E. Bangay, eds. 1981. *Memorandum of Intent on Transboundary Air Pollution United States—Canada Impact Assessment Interim Report.* February, 1981.

Freeman, F. M. 1979. *The Benefits of Air and Water Pollution Con-*

trol: A Review and Synthesis of Recent Estimates. Report prepared for the Council of Environmental Quality, G.P.O., Washington, D.C.

Galloway, J. N., E. B. Cowling, E. Gorham, and W. W. McFee. 1978. *A National Program for Assessing the Problem of Atmospheric Deposition (Acid Rain).* A Report to the Council of Environmental Quality. National Deposition Program NC-141.

Galloway, J. N. and G. E. Likens. 1979. Atmospheric enhancement of metal deposition in Adirondack lake sediments. *Limnology Oceanography* 24:427–433.

Galloway, J. N., J. D. Thornton, S. A. Norton, H. L. Volchok, and R. A. N. McLean. Trace Metals in Atmospheric Deposition: A Review and Assessment. *Atmospheric Environment* (in review).

Galloway, J. N. and D. M. Whelpdale. 1980. An atmosphere sulphur budget for eastern North America. *Atmospheric Environment* 14:409–417.

Geiger, P. 1965. *Climate Near the Ground.* Cambridge, Harvard University Press.

Gill, R. W. 1972. Effects of toxicity on ecosystems. In L. M. LeCam, J. Neyan, and E. L. Scoll, eds. *Proceedings of the Sixth Berkeley Symposium on Mathematical Statistics and Probability.* Berkeley, University of California Press, pp. 521–532.

Glass, N. R. 1979. Environmental effects of increased coal utilization: Ecological effects of gaseous emissions from coal combustion. *Environmental Health Perspectives* 33:249–272.

Gordon, A. G. and E. Gorham. 1963. Ecological aspects of air pollution from an iron-sintering plant at Wawa, Ontario. *Canadian Journal of Botany* 41:1063–1078.

Groet, S. S. 1976. Regional and local variations in heavy metal concentrations of bryophytes in the northeastern United States. *Oikos* 27:445–456.

Guderian, R. 1977. *Air Pollution.* Berlin, Springer-Verlag, 127 pp.

Havas, P. and S. Huttunen. 1980. Some special features of the ecophysical effects of air pollution on coniferous forests during the winter. In T. C. Hutchinson and M. Havas *Effects of Acid Precipitation on Terrestrial Ecosystems.* New York, Plenum Press, pp. 123–128.

Heggested, H. E. and J. T. Middleton. 1959. Ozone in high concentrations as cause of tobacco leaf injury. *Science* 129:208–210.

Hendrey, G. R. 1981. Acid rain and grey snow. *Natural History* 90:58–64.

Hendrey, G. R., J. N. Galloway, S. A. Norton, C. L. Schofield,

D. A. Burns, and P. W. Schaffer. 1980. Sensitivity of the eastern United States to acid precipitation impacts on surface waters. In D. Drablos and A. Tollan, eds. *Ecological Impact Acid Precipitation: Proceedings of an International Conference.* Standefjord, Norway, March 11–14, 1980. Oslo, As. pp. 216–217.

Hendrey, G. R. and F. W. Lipfert. 1980. *Acid Precipitation and the Aquatic Environment.* Report to the United States Senate Committee on Energy and Natural Resources, May 28, 1980. 23 pp.

Hultberg, H. and A. Wenblad. 1980. Acid groundwater in southwestern Sweden. In D. Drablos and A. Tollan, eds. *Ecological Impact of Acid Precipitation: Proceedings of an International Conference.* Standefjord, Norway, March 11–14, 1980. Oslo, As.

Hutchinson, T. C. and L. M. Whitby. 1976. The effects of acid rainfall and heavy metal particulates on a boreal forest ecosystem near the Sudbury smelting region of Canada. In L. S. Dochinger and T. A. Seliga, eds. *Proceedings of the First International Symposium on Acid Precipitation and the Forest Ecosystem.* U.S. Forest Service Center. Tech. Report NE-23. pp. 745–766.

Johnson, A. H., T. G. Siccama, D. Wang, R. S. Turner, and T. H. Barringer. Recent changes in patterns of tree growth in the New Jersey Pinelands: A possible effect of acid rain (manuscript).

Johnson, D. W., J. W. Hornbeck, J. M. Kelly, W. T. Swank, and D. E. Todd. 1979. Regional patterns of soil sulphate accumulation: Relevance to ecosystem sulphur budgets. In D. S. Shreiner, C. R. Richmond, and S. E. Lindberg, eds. *Atmospheric Sulphur Depositions: Environmental Impact and Health Effects.* Ann Arbor Science Pub. Ann Arbor, Mich. pp. 507–520.

Kadlecek, J. and V. Mohnen. Unpublished data from Atmospheric Science Research Center, Whiteface Mountain, N.Y. (manuscript).

Kelleher, T. J. and W. A. Feder. 1978. Phytotoxic concentrations of ozone on Nantucket Island: Long range transport from the middle Atlantic States over the open ocean confirmed by bioassay with ozone-sensitive tobacco plants. *Environmental Pollution* 7:187–194.

Kerr, R. A. 1979. Global pollution: Is the arctic haze actually industrial smog? *Science* 205:290–293.

Kerr, R. A. 1981. There is more to acid rain than acid. *Science* 211:692–693.

Kettlewell, H. B. D. 1961. The phenomenon of industrial melanism in *Lepidoptera. American Review of Entomology* 6:252–262.

King, S. 1979. Smog standard for cities is relaxed by EPA. *New York Times*, January 27, 1979.

136   F. H. BORMANN

Knabe, W. 1976. Effects of sulfur dioxide on terrestrial vegetation. *Ambio* 5:213–218.

Komanoff, C. 1980. Pollution control improvements in coal fired electric generating plants: What they accomplish, what they cost. *Journal of the Air Pollution Control Assoc.* 30:1051–1057.

Lazrus, A. L., E. Lorange, and J. P. Lodge, Jr. 1970. Lead and other metal ions in United States precipitation. *Environmental Science and Technology* 4:55–58.

Likens, G. E. 1976. Acid precipitation. *Chemical and Engineering News.* 54:29–44.

Likens, G. E. 1977. *Acid Rain: Causes and Consequences.* Institute of Water Resources. University of Connecticut, Storrs, Conn., 1976–77. Seminar Series Presentation. 17 pp. (mimeograph).

Likens, G. E. and F. H. Bormann. 1974. Acid rain: A serious regional environmental problem. *Science* 184:1176–1179.

Likens, G. E. and T. J. Butler. 1981. Recent acidification of precipitation in North America. *Atmospheric Environment* 14 (in press).

Likens, G. E., F. H. Bormann, R. S. Pierce, J. S. Eaton, and N. M. Johnson. 1979. *Biogeochemistry of a Forested Ecosystem.* Springer-Verlag, N.Y. 146 pp.

Lincoln, D. R. and E. S. Rubin. 1980. Air pollution emissions from increased industrial coal use in the northeastern United States. *Journal of the Air Pollution Control Association.* 30:1310–1315.

Lioy, P. J., P. J. Samson, R. L. Tanner, B. P. Leaderer, T. Minnich, and W. Lyons. 1980. The distribution and transport of sulfate "species" in the New York Metropolitan area during the 1977 Summer Aerosol Study. *Atmospheric Environment* 14:1391–1407.

Loucks, O., T. Armentano, R. W. Usher, W. T. Williams, R. W. Miller, and L. T. K. Wong. 1980. *Crop and Forest Losses due to Current and Projected Emissions from Coal-Fired Power Plants in the Ohio River Valley.* (ORBES). USEPA R-805588. 266 pp.

Loucks, O. and W. T. Williams. 1980. Estimating forest growth losses due to oxidants and pollutant-insect interactions. In O. Loucks, T. Armentano, R. W. Usher, W. T. Williams, R. W. Miller, and L. T. K. Wong. *Crop and Forest Losses due to Current and Projected Emissions from Coal-Fired Power Plants in the Ohio River Valley.* (ORBES). USEPA R-805588. pp. 217–236.

Ludwig, F. L. and E. Shelar, Jr. 1980. Empirical relationships between observed ozone concentrations and geographical areas with concentrations likely to be above 120ppb. *Journal of the Air Control Association* 30:894–897.

Manning, W. J. 1979. Air quality and plants. *Science* 203:834.

Marshall, E. 1979. EPA smog standard attacked by industry, science advisors. *Science* 201:949–950.

Miller, P. R. and M. J. Elderman, eds. 1976. *Photochemical Oxidant Air Pollutant Effects on a Mixed Conifer Forest Ecosystem: A Progress Report.* USEPA 600/3-77-104. Corvallis, Ore. 339 pp.

Mulder, J. 1980. *Neutralization of Acid Rain in the Hubbard Brook Experimental Forest* (master of science thesis). University of Wageningen, The Netherlands. 27 pp.

National Air Quality Commission. 1981. *To Breathe Clean Air. Report to Congress.* G.P.O., Washington, D.C.

Naegele, J. A., W. A. Feder, and C. J. Bryant. 1972. *Assessment of Air Pollution Damage to Vegetation in New England: July 1971 – July 1972.* USEPA 68-02-0084. Waltham, Mass. 18 pp.

New York Times. 1979. Ohio air pollution rules are relaxed to save jobs (June 7, 1979).

Nordo, J. 1976. Long range transport of air pollutants in Europe and acid precipitation in Norway. In L. C. Dochinger and T. A. Seliga, eds. *Proceedings of the First International Symposium on Acid Precipitation and the Forest Ecosystem.* U.S. Forest Service, Gen. Tech. Report NE-23. pp. 87–104.

Norton, S. A., D. W. Hansen, and R. J. Campana. 1980. The impact of acidic precipitation and heavy metals on soils in relation to forest ecosystems. In P. Miller, Coordinator. *International Symposium Effects of Air Pollutants on Mediterranean and Temperate Forest Ecosystem.* Pacific SW For. and Range Expt. Sta. Gen. Tech. Report PSW-43. pp. 152–157.

Overrein, L. N., H. M. Seip, and A. Tollan. 1980. *Acid Precipitation Effects on Forests and Fish.* Final Report of the SNSF Project, 1972–1980. Oslo, As., December 1980. 175 pp.

Pimentel, D. 1981. Pesticides and Ecosystems. 11 pp. (mimeograph).

Pratt, R. and P. Falconer. 1979. Atmospheric Science Research Center, Whiteface Mountain, N.Y.

Reiners, W. A., R. H. Marks, and P. M. Vitousek. 1975. Heavy metals in sub-alpine and alpine soils of New Hampshire. *Oikos* 26:264–265.

Reed, L. E. 1976. The long range transport of air pollutants. *Ambio* 5:202.

Rennie, P. J. 1979. *The Susceptibility of Eastern Canadian Terrestrial Ecosystems to Long-Range Pollution.* Prepared for Canada-United States Research Consultation Group on Long-range Transport of Air Pollutants. July 1979. 22 pp. (mimeograph).

Schindler, D. W. 1980. Implications of regional-scale lake acidification. In D. S. Schreiner, C. R. Richmond, and S. E. Lindberg. *Atmospheric Sulphur Deposition: Environmental Impact and Health Effects.* Ann Arbor Science, Ann Arbor, Mich. 568 pp.

Schlesinger, W. H. and W. A. Reiners. 1974. Deposition of water and cations on artificial foliar collectors in fir krumholtz of New England mountains. *Ecology* 55:278–386.

Schlesinger, W. H., W. A. Reiners, and D. S. Knopman. 1974. Heavy metal concentrations and deposition in bulk precipitation in montane ecosystems of New Hampshire, U.S.A. *Environmental Pollution* 6:39–47.

Shabecoff, R. 1981. Toxic chemicals loom as big threat to nation's supply of safe water. *New York Times.* August 13, 1981.

Shaw, R. W. 1979. Acid precipitation in Atlantic Canada. *Environmental Science and Technology* 13:406–411.

Shinn, J. H. and S. Lynn. 1979. Do man-made sources affect the sulphur cycle of northeastern United States? *Environmental Science and Technology* 13:1062–1067.

Siccama, T. G., M. Bliss, and H. Vogelmann. Decline of Red Spruce in the Green Mountains of Vermont (manuscript).

Siccama, T. G. and W. H. Smith. 1978. Lead accumulation in a northern hardwood forest. *Environmental Science and Technology* 14:54–56.

Siccama, T. G., W. H. Smith, and D. L. Madder. 1980. Changes in lead, zinc, copper, dry weight and organic matter content of the forest floor of white pine stands in central Massachusetts over sixteen years. *Environmental Science and Technology* 14:54–56.

Skelly, J. 1980. Photochemical oxidant impact on Mediterranean and Temperate forest ecosystems: Real and potential effects. In P. Miller, Coordinator. *Symposium on Effects of Air Pollution on Mediterranean and Temperate Forest Ecosystems: an International Symposium.* Pacific SW Forest and Range Expt. Sta., Gen. Tech. Report PSW-43. pp. 38–50.

Smith, R. J. 1981. The fight over clean air begins. *Science* 211: 1328–1330.

Smith, W. H. 1980. Air pollution—a 20th century allogenic influence on forest ecosystems. In P. Miller, Coordinator. *Symposium* on *Effects of Air Pollution on Mediterranean and Temperate Forest Ecosystems.* Pacific SW Forest and Range Expt. Sta., Gen. Tech. Report PSW-43. pp. 79–80.

Smith, W. H. 1981. *Air Pollution and Forests: Interactions between Air Contaminants and Forest Ecosystems*, Springer-Verlag, N.Y.

Smith, W. H. and T. G. Siccama. 1981. The Hubbard Brook Ecosystem Study: Biogeochemistry of lead in the northern hardwood forest. *Journal of Environmental Quality.* 10(3):323–333.

Speth, G., J. Yarn, and R. Harris. 1980. *Environmental Quality: The Eleventh Annual Report of the Council on Environmental Quality.* GPO, Washington, D.C. 497 pp.

Spicer, C. W., D. W. Joseph, and P. R. Stricksel. 1979. Ozone sources and transport in northeastern United States 1975. *American Chemical Society* 13:975–985.

Sprugel, D. G., J. E. Miller, R. N. Muller, H. J. Smith, and P. B. Xerikos. 1980. Sulfur dioxide effects on yield and seed quality in field-grown soy beans. *Phytopathology* 70:1129–1133.

Tomlinson, G. H., R. J. P. Brouzes, R. A. N. McLean, and J. Kadlecek. 1980. The role of clouds in atmospheric transport to mercury and other pollutants. In D. Drablos and A. Tollan, eds. *Ecological Impact of Acid Precipitation: Proceedings of an International Conference.* Standefjord, Norway, March 11–14, 1980. Oslo, As. pp. 134–137.

Treshow, M. and D. Stewart. 1973. Ozone sensitivity of plants in natural communities. *Biol. Conservation* 5:209–214.

Ulrich, B., R. Mayer, and P. K. Khanna. 1980. Chemical changes due to acid precipitation in a loess-derived soil in central Europe. *Soil Science* 130:193–199.

Usher, R. W. and W. T. Williams. 1980. Assessment of pollution injury to eastern white pine in Indiana. In O. Loucks, R. Armentano, R. W. Usher, W. T. Williams, R. W. Miller, and L. T. K. Wong, eds. *Crop and Forest Losses Due to Current and Projected Emissions from Coal-Fired Power Plants in the Ohio River Valley.* (ORBES). USEPA R-805588.

Vogelmann, H. W., T. G. Siccama, D. Leedy and D. C. Ovitt. 1968. Precipitation from fog moisture in the Green Mountains of Vermont. *Ecology* 49:1205–1207.

Whittaker, R. H., F. H. Bormann, G. E. Likens, and T. G. Siccama. 1974. The Hubbard Brook Ecosystem Study: Forest biomass and production. *Ecological Monographs* 44:233–254.

Wiersma, G. B. and K. W. Brown. 1980. Background levels of trace elements in forest ecosystems. In P. Miller, Coordinator. *Proceedings of the Symposium on Effects of Air Pollution on Mediterranean and Temperate Forest Ecosystems.* Pacific SW Forest and Range Expt. Sta., Gen. Tech. Report PSW-43. pp. 31–37.

Williams, W. T., M. Brady, and S. C. Willison. 1977. Air pollution damage to the forests of Sierra Nevada Mountains of California. *Journal of the Air Pollution Control Association.* 27:230–234.

Williams, W. T. and L. Wong. 1980. A review of mechanisms of action of ozone and sulfur dioxide pollutants on crops and forests. In O. Loucks, T. Armentano, T. W. Usher, W. T. Williams, R. W. Miller, and L. T. K. Wong, eds. *Crop and Forest Losses due to Current and Projected Emissions from Coal-Fired Power Plants in the Ohio River Valley.* (ORBES). USEPA R-805588.

Williamson, S. J. 1973. *Fundamentals of Air Pollution.* Addison-Wesley, Reading, Mass. 472 pp.

Wolff, G. T., P. J. Lioy, H. Golub, and J. S. Hawkins. 1979. Acid precipitation in the New York Metropolitan area: Its relationship to meteorological factors. *Environmental Science and Technology* 13, 2:209–212.

Woodwell, G. M. 1970. Effects of pollution on the structure and physiology of ecosystems. *Science* 4:29–33.

Wright, R. S. and E. T. Gjessing. 1976. Acid precipitation: Changes in the chemical composition of lakes. *Ambio* 5:219–223.

ENERGY:
THE CHALLENGE

Henry Lee

NEW ENGLAND'S use of energy emerges from an evolutionary process that began with the collection of firewood by the Pilgrims three hundred and fifty years ago. During these years many changes occurred in where the region obtained its energy and in the way energy was used. These changes came about not with any degree of suddenness, but from continual alterations in the structure of the region's economy.

The Past

People have speculated that if this country had been explored and developed from the West Coast to the East, New England would probably have been a sparsely populated region primarily administered by the National Park Service. A cold climate, poor farmland, high energy and labor costs, few indigenous natural resources, and long distances from national markets all have significantly affected New England's development and economic growth.

In the first two centuries these limitations were of no consequence. The nation was primarily divided between the industrial Northeast and the agricultural South. The nation's population was sparse, and the lack of transportation facilities acted as a barrier to interregional commerce. Goods manufactured in one area were either used within that area or exported by ship, primarily to Europe.

In 1634 the first hydropower project in the country was built in the Lower Falls of the Neponset River (near Milton, Massachusetts). These mill dams, through the production of mechanical power, were the focal point for development of many small towns throughout the region. At home, however, New Englanders relied on wood and wood charcoal as their primary energy fuel and remained dependent on these sources for the next two hundred and fifty years.

In 1793 the first textile mill was constructed in Pawtucket, Rhode Island, and triggered an expansion in the production of such nondurable goods as textiles, leather, and shoes. Factories sprang up near rivers that were used both for energy and as a means of transportation. Cities like Manchester, Nashua, Lowell, and Lawrence all developed as a result of the availability of water power. After the Civil War the development of new transportation systems and the dramatic growth in the national economy spelled the end of New England's manufacturing supremacy. Industries like iron and furniture moved to areas with more plentiful indigenous resources.[1] Farmers and manufacturers, no longer tied to local markets, could locate in areas with richer soil, warmer climate, and cheaper labor. Today the associated canals and abandoned dams are common sights in cities throughout southern New England.

Although the demand for wood and water as energy sources continued, the demand for additional energy production far exceeded that which could be supplied by these two sources. The railroad and iron industries alone doubled the demand for energy. New sources of fuel, such as coal and later oil, were needed in escalating quantities to meet this demand. By the final decade of the nineteenth century, the locus of the nation's manufacturing had shifted to states like Pennsylvania and Ohio and to places south. In New England coal replaced wood as the major fuel in both the industrial and residential sectors.

As the steam engine had freed factories from having to locate near water sites, so the advent of electric power allowed plants to locate at even greater distances from energy sources. Electricity was initially generated by factory-owned steam engines—which today are being rediscovered under the guise of co-generators. But by 1930 approximately 70 percent of the electricity generated in the region came from central stations using coal, with the remainder coming primarily from hydropower.

In the last fifty years several significant changes occurred in the region's use of energy. The automobile became the dominant mode of transportation and dramatically altered land-use patterns and the structure of our lives. In the late forties and early fifties, oil products replaced coal as the dominant fuel in the commercial and residential sectors, and in the 1960's coal was replaced by residual oil as the principal fuel for industry and electric utilities. By 1979 New Englanders consumed approximately 400 million barrels of oil annually, of which 130 million were barrels of residual oil.[2] This massive conversion from coal to residual oil was later locked in by the provisions of the Clean Air Act of 1970. Finally, in the early 1950's two major gas pipelines were extended from the Mid-Atlantic states into southern New England.[3] Today natural gas is a source of heating, hot water, and cooking for more than 30 percent of homes in the region.[4]

Implications of the Past.   In the last 130 years the region has twice restructured its mix of energy sources—first moving from reliance on wood to dependence on coal and, later, converting its coal-based economy to one based on oil. As a major factor in a dynamic regional economy, energy-use patterns have been continually changing as the region responded to new technologies and emerging market realities.

In our panoramic review of the region's energy past, four themes stand out. First, New England has consistently responded to change by taking those actions which were in its economic self-interest. Second, the manifestations of these responses were gradual and continual. Third, the region's economy and energy patterns were inextricably tied to those of the nation. Fourth, energy crises were common, short-term phenomena whose effects in the longer run were proportional to their relationship to the fundamental evolution of the region's economy.

It is worth examining these four themes, since they will be significant factors in shaping the region's future.

(1) *Acting in the Region's Self-Interest.*   It is often argued that New England's energy policies have been destructive to its self-interest. Its predominant dependence on imported oil is held up as evidence of this regional economic masochism.

In fact, the opposite is true. In the late 1960's, Venezuelan residual oil was priced at about $1.85 a barrel or one third the price of delivered coal from Appalachia. If the utilities had insisted on buying a fuel three times more expensive than that of a readily available substitute fuel, the consumer outrage would have been overwhelming. The economic signals in the 1960's demanded that the region shift to oil.

Only recently has the cost of oil begun to exceed the prices of delivered coal plus the amortized cost of necessary new pollution abatement equipment. As a result, many utilities and industries are now actively trying to reconvert to coal, at least to the extent that the Clean Air Act and State Public Utility Commission will allow them.

During the first part of the 1970's, the Nixon Administration, after opposing the Machiasport refinery in Maine, turned around and berated the region for its failure to build an oil refinery. With hindsight one can argue that if the region had then followed this advice and built a refinery, a combination of recently promulgated federal regulations, a substantial surplus of existing domestic refinery capacity, and uncertainties in the world oil market would have made the benefits of such a refinery minimal.

Finally, given the present 40 percent reserve of electrical generating capacity and a host of financially tottering utilities, the region's decisions in the mid-1970's to slow down the construction of additional nuclear plants may have been to its advantage.

Whether advertently or inadvertently, New England responded to the influences and pressures of self-interest.

(2) *Gradual and Consistent Nature of the Response*.   The implications of dynamic exogenous pressures, such as significant changes in price or availability of supplies, historically tend to manifest themselves gradually. Although it was evident soon after the Civil War that heavy-manufacturing firms in New England would have difficulties competing with similar firms in the South and Midwest, New England's economy is still adjusting to this change one hundred years later. The move from wood to coal took fifty years, and the move to oil from coal has taken a similar length of time.

Adjustments to higher energy prices and greater insecurity of supply occur slowly. Homes, machines, and existing transportation systems cannot be discarded and replaced overnight with modern, more efficient models. Furthermore, energy is only one cost factor among many. Often, labor, transportation, insurance, and capital costs may override any consideration of energy costs. The influence of any one cost category is directly related to its size compared to other categories and to the relative ability of each of those categories to adjust to higher prices.

Earlier changes in energy occurred at times when the amount of embedded capital stock was far less than it is today. Thus, although the incentives for change resulting from the tenfold increase in oil prices during the 1970's may provide stronger incentives than earlier signals, the infrastructure to be changed is much larger and the absolute cost of the changes much greater. Today there is simply more embedded capital in every sector of our economy, and the cost of restructuring that capital will be high.

The forms in which New England uses energy and the type of energy fuel it uses have been gradually changing throughout the past two hundred years. It is clear that the process of change will continue. The key question, though, is how much the shocks of the 1970's and possibly the 1980's will accelerate that process.

(3) *No Region Stands Alone.* Two paradoxical themes that have dominated the energy rhetoric of the past ten years have been (a) the demand for a homogeneous national energy policy and (b) the simultaneous need for such a policy to fulfill the heterogeneous needs of the different regions. The balance between the two is difficult to achieve. Yet their interaction has been evident throughout our history.

In the 1960's a series of federal policy decisions, such as the removal of the import quota for residual oil and the passage of the Air Quality Act of 1967, provided irresistible incentives to convert from coal to oil. When domestic petroleum production began to decline and domestic demand increased to such an extent that more oil had to be imported, the logic of logistics directed the imported oil to the Northeast. Several major oil companies have refineries both in the New York-Philadelphia areas and in Texas. The former rely almost entirely on imported oil, while the latter utilizes nearby domestic oil. It would be foolish to ship North African crude oil to Texas while shipping Texas crude oil to New York just so that each region would get its fair share of imported oil.

It has always been irksome to listen to federal officials berate New England on its excessive use of imported oil, when such dependence was derived from a combination of national economic distribution patterns and past federal government policies.

All regions benefit from interregional commerce that exploits the diversity of this country for the benefit of all. As the nation's economy and energy policy evolves in response to higher oil prices, New England's economy will also respond, not only to the higher oil prices but also the emerging federal policies and programs. For example, recently the federal government has been artificially subsidizing natural gas through price controls while decontrolling oil. The result has been significant shifts by homeowners in southern New England away from oil to gas.

Decisions made in Washington on pricing and allocation issues have historically affected the way energy is used in any single region. There is no reason to expect this tendency to change.

(4) *Energy Crisis.* We often think that the crises of the moment will profoundly affect our lives; yet when we look back, we find effects of that crisis, in isolation from other factors, to be small.

In the 1970's New England went through a series of energy crises. In 1971 the region experienced an asphalt shortage during the road-building season; in 1972 breakdowns in Caribbean oil refineries resulted in a shortage of low sulfur oil; in 1973–74 we had the Arab oil embargo and the quadrupling of oil prices; in 1977 we had the natural gas crisis in the Midwest; in 1978, the coal strike; in 1979–80, the Iranian cut-offs and another dramatic increase in oil prices; and in 1981 eastern Massachusetts suffered through a shortage of supplemental peak-shaving gas. If the pattern continues, we will undoubtedly confront an equal number of energy crises in the 1980's, each emerging in an unexpected manner and each quite different in form and substance from the crisis that preceded it.

When we look back on the decade of the 1970's, none of these crises seem as dire as when we were going through them. Instead, what lingers are dramatically higher prices and a sense of uncertainty about the energy future. It is these two factors, more than the crisis of the moment, that will influence the shape of that future.

Summation. These four themes have influenced New England's present uses of energy and will significantly affect its future use. To this future we now direct our attention. In the following sections of this chapter, I will examine four ways in which the region uses energy: (1) to fuel industries; (2) to heat buildings; (3) to transport people and products; and (4) to produce electricity.

There is an old saying: "to prophesy is extremely difficult, especially with respect to the future." Thus the following pages attempt not to predict the future but rather to isolate the factors that will shape it.

Energy to Fuel Industry

In the aftermath of the 1973–74 embargo, officials in New England tended to depict the region's economy as an entity strangled in the noose of skyrocketing energy prices. Five years later many of these same officials were applauding the health of that same economy and praising the region's foresight in adjusting to the new energy reality. Although some politicians might claim that their election was the catalyst for this new prognosis, the reasons are probably more attributable to fundamental trends underlying the region's economy.

Move away from Energy Intensive Industries.   New England has been moving away from energy intensive manufacturing for one hundred years. Today the industrial sector accounts for only 16 percent of the region's consumption of energy compared to a national level of 38 percent.[5] New England manufacturers use less than half the energy per dollar value added than their national counterparts.[6] This trend continued to be evident during the past two decades. For example, in the fifteen-year period, 1960–75, industrial energy used in New England declined 7 percent, a rate of decline twice that of any other sector of its economy. In fact, in Massachusetts total energy use by the industrial sector is lower today than in 1964.[7] (The one exception to this trend is Maine; it relies heavily on the pulp and paper industry, which is very energy intensive. The implications of this intensity, though, are minimized by the industry's use of wood and wood by-products for a portion of its energy.)

This direction is reaffirmed in the region's industrial mix. In 1955, 42 percent of the region's labor force was employed in manufacturing; by 1975 this figure had fallen to 28 percent, of which 47 percent were working in industries that produced high technology products, such as electronic and communications equipment.[8]

Regional Price Differential. The fundamental reason for the low energy intensity of the region's industrial base is that energy is more expensive in New England and has always been so. Prior to the first oil embargo the differential between New England's energy prices and those in the United States as a whole was 27.7 percent. This figure rose to 38.9 percent directly after the embargo and declined to 22 percent in 1977, rising again to 40 percent after the Iranian crisis of 1979.[9]

Part of the reason for this differential is the distance from New England to the energy production centers of the United States. An equally significant reason has been New England's inability to acquire cheap, price-controlled natural gas and its subsequent reliance on nonregulated oil products. New England manufacturing firms use natural gas for only 11.3 percent of their energy needs, compared with a figure of 48.9 percent for all U.S. manufacturing firms.[10]

The energy price increases of the 1970's were primarily in oil. Products such as natural gas and coal increased at a much slower rate. Today regulated gas prices are as much as 40 percent below those for oil. This differential will narrow as gas prices are gradually deregulated, but the process will take time. Meanwhile, parts of the country with unlimited access to gas will have an advantage over those with limited access.

Decoupling Energy from Economic Growth. Two effects of the rapid escalation in energy prices deserve special attention. First, New England made major strides in decoupling energy from economic growth. During the period 1940–72 a close linkage existed between domestic economic growth and energy consumption. This linkage led many people to argue that we could not have one without the other. Recently the linkage has been questioned, and although it is clear that there is some relationship, it certainly is not the one-to-one relationship previously forecast.

Energy is only one of several factors in the production of goods and services. As energy prices increase relative to the other factors, business will use more labor and capital and less energy. There is obviously a limit to the ability to make these substitutions, and there are constraints on the rate at which the changes can be made. This is why a link remains between the level of production and the level of energy use; but it is a reasonably flexible link.

Following a period of increasing energy prices and decreasing consumption, New England's economy entered the 1980's in relatively good shape. Over the preceding thirty years real personal income in the region almost quadrupled, and gross regional production continued at a steady annual rate of growth. Although there remains a disagreement on the exact ratio between regional energy consumption and economic growth, a figure of 0.5 seems to be easily supported by available data.[11] Translated, this means that for every one-percent increase in Gross Regional Production per capita, energy demand increases by 0.5 percent.

Declining Birth Rate of New Industries.   The second effect has been the accelerated decline in the birth rate of new manufacturing firms. In any region a number of new firms go out of business every year, but at the same time, many new firms start up. In New England the former category has been approximately 1.8 times larger than the latter.[12] Contrary to popular belief, however, there has been little out-migration of industry. In the period 1969–75 firms moving into the region exceeded firms moving out by a 2.5:1 margin.[13] New England's industries have tended to stay in the region, but the cost of doing business in a rapidly inflating economy have forced many to close their doors.

During the 1970's it was customary to place the responsibility for this decline in the birth of new industries on energy prices; but energy is only one of several factors contributing to either the health of an individual firm or its decision to locate in one area rather than another. Factors such as labor force availability and skills, state and local taxes on income and property, wage levels, access to supplies of raw materials, and proximity to markets all contribute. It is true that over the long term energy and labor have had a very significant effect in shaping the structure of the region's industry mix. As the region moves to less energy-intensive industries, however, the importance of energy price increases as compared to increases in other factors declines. In fact, with the exception of the paper and pulp industry, the low energy intensity of New England firms should result in a greater emphasis on factors other than energy prices. Even in the paper and pulp industry, access to raw materials and transportation to markets are becoming as important as energy. In a recent study of two regional industries, wood furniture and metal-working machinery, labor costs were twenty times higher than those for energy per dollar of shipped value.[14] On average, energy costs are now only between 4 and 5 percent of a New England firm's cost of production.

Future Trends in Industrial Energy Use.   The move toward less dependence on manufacturing, especially of nondurable goods, will continue regardless of the energy situation. Competition from imports, declines in demand for certain products, and the aging of the existing capital stock will have a negative effect on such industries as textiles, apparel, lumber, and leather goods. However, existing low energy-intensive industries, like service industries and high technology firms, will be less susceptible to increasing energy prices. Thus, as New England continues to move toward a service-based economy, the region as a whole will be less hostage to the energy problem than the economies of other regions. This is not to imply that the effect will be insignificant. If industry in the Midwest suffers severely because of rapidly escalating energy prices, and industry in New England suffers 10 percent less, neither region will flourish.

There are four key variables that will directly influence energy's impact on the future of the region's economy: (1) the world price of oil; (2) the willingness of the federal government to price fuels (or allow them to be priced) on a relatively equal basis; (3) the ability of the region to accelerate the adoption of indigenous sources, such as renewables and conservation; and (4) the capability to develop strategic reserves of energy as well as contingency plans that can be used during future shortages. Each of these variables complements the others, and should not be considered in isolation from the others.

Absent from this list are the willingness of the public sector to facilitate transitions to a new energy regime, and its success in doing so. This absence does not imply that the public sector has no role; quite the contrary, the public sector can have an enormous impact on the rate at which the transition proceeds and the level of pain and suffering inherent in that transition. If one is exploring the question of what this region will look like twenty years hence, however, the effect of public sector subsidies and incentives lessens. In summary, government through a variety of programs can assist firms and business to adjust to higher prices or it can ignore the problem and allow some to go out of business. In either case the use of energy in the industrial sector will not be dramatically different in the year 2000. Yet there is a vast difference in the overall implications of the two alternatives to the health of the economy in the intervening years.

World Price of Oil. Most differences of opinion on the future course of energy policy can be traced to differences of opinion about the future price of oil. If one believes oil prices will reach $50.00 (1980 dollar) per barrel by the year 2000, one will be inclined to predict relatively minimal changes in the present way we use energy and to espouse a go-slow approach on high priced production options—such as synthetic fuels. On the other hand, if one predicts a future world oil price of $100 (1980 dollar), one would foresee more severe changes in our economy and life styles and would be inclined to advocate the acceleration of more expensive production and efficiency projects with less regard to price than optimistic colleagues might forecast.

One-hundred-dollar oil would be triple the 1980 price. Since it is unlikely that the price of other factors will increase at a similar rate, the weight of energy as a cost factor in industrial location and investment decisions will increase. The cost of operating facilities and machinery will escalate, causing marginal firms to reevaluate their use of those facilities and machines. Investment decisions would shift to more capital and labor intensive facilities and away from energy intensive plants.

Furthermore, at $100 the incentive to substitute other sources of energy for oil will increase substantially. The use of coal, either burned in a new efficient combustion process or converted into synthetic gas, will expand, as will the use of electricity generated by fuels other than oil. Energy-efficiency investments that do not currently meet corporate criteria for a satisfactory rate of return will suddenly become profitable. Machines, boilers, and furnaces, on average, turn over at least every thirty years, but oil at $100 per barrel would significantly increase the turnover rate in order to improve the energy efficiency of plants and factories.

However, every 10 percent increase in the cost of energy moves one billion dollars out of New England.[15] In 1979 the region paid approximately $17 billion for energy—an expenditure equal to 20 percent of New England's total annual personal income. Since most of this money leaves the region to pay energy producers from other parts of the country (or other parts of the world), it represents a drain on the region's economy. A tripling of oil prices will accelerate this drain and could cause a decline in regional economic activity. For although the region's economic base is better prepared for higher energy prices than that of other regions, increases of this magnitude will have severe effects on any consuming region and will have equally beneficial effects on any producing region. Recent trends toward rapid gains in real personal income in producing areas, and equal decreases in personal income in consuming regions, will accelerate under the high-price scenario.

Government Pricing.   As noted earlier, it has been the comparative increase in competing fuels rather than their absolute increases which has worked to the competitive disadvantage of New England. Throughout the 1970's natural gas, which is the primary fuel for 48.9 percent of the nation's industrial production, was kept at controlled prices substantially below the price of fuel oil. Even in New England, where natural gas prices are 30 percent higher than the national average, gas fuels are currently priced cheaper than oil. Unfortunately, most New England industries do not use gas, and many of those fortunate enough to obtain gas contracts have them on an interruptible basis and must provide for backup energy supplies.

A metals fabrication plant in Providence using fuel oil which in January 1981 was priced at $6.00 per MMBTU (million British thermal units) is at a disadvantage in relation to a similar plant in Illinois or North Carolina which has access to regulated natural gas at $2.50–3.00 per MMBTU.[16] If this differential came about because of market forces, one could argue that it reflects real costs of doing business in different parts of the nation. The differential, though, does not occur solely because of markets, but rather stems from government price controls on the production of domestic gas, controls which serve as a subsidy paid by producers of gas to consumers of gas, and benefits regions that have historically enjoyed a strong reliance on that fuel.

This section is not intended to be an argument for or against price controls per se, but rather points out that controlling one fuel used by certain regions of that country and not controlling a competing fuel used in other regions of the country has an adverse discriminatory impact on the latter in a period of rapid energy-price increases.

Natural gas prices are currently being decontrolled on a phased basis, but there are many problems with the phasing formula which will make it difficult for Congress to allow the decontrol of gas, as now structured, to go into effect. In the interim period oil-fueled industries will find their costs higher than those for gas-fueled industries. If one believes the $100-per-barrel oil price scenario and is pessimistic about the willingness of Congress either to deregulate natural gas or to control oil prices, one must conclude that New England's competitive position vis-à-vis gas-intensive regions will decline. Industries that produce nondurable goods will be especially disadvantaged. If one believes in the $50-per-barrel scenario and believes Congress will find a mechanism to allow oil and gas to compete, then one should be more optimistic about the future.

It is important to remember that we are not talking about literal price equality, but rather about returning to historical differentials. New England is energy poor, and very likely it will always pay higher prices for energy than the national average.

Use of Indigenous Energy Supplies.   Since the turn of the century, New England has had to rely on fuels produced and processed outside the region. As energy prices have escalated, the flow of dollars to pay for those fuels has increased accordingly. In 1979 the energy bill for the region was $17 billion. This flow of energy into the region and flow of dollars out is not necessarily bad. Economists refer to this phenomenon as trade that can work to the advantage of both trading partners. When the rate of outflow of dollars increases rapidly, however, it is incumbent upon the region to explore ways to limit the growth in that rate.

This reduction can be achieved by producing more indigenous energy resources or by substituting energy-efficient plant equipment for older, less efficient capital stock. Admittedly, New England is not well endowed with indigenous energy supplies. It does, however, possess access to sunlight, wind, and water and it produces liquid and solid waste materials. It also possesses significant supplies of wood. All of these sources can be converted into usable energy forms through different energy technologies. These technologies are not inexpensive, but neither is the cost of conventional fuels. As the prices of oil, gas, and electricity increase, it will behoove the region to find ways to increase its use of these indigenous fuels.

It is worth noting that not only are many renewable sources of energy cost competitive with conventional sources of fuel, but they are also significantly more labor intensive. Incremental investments in renewables will make some contribution to regional employment; whether this contribution will be large or small depends on the scale of the investment. Furthermore, most of these sources can be used at a community-scale level. To many people the decentralization of energy production is an attractive feature, since it provides a sense that one is gaining greater control over one's economic destiny.

A more inexpensive option to ease the regional dependence on external sources of energy is investment in more energy-efficient capital stock. As with renewable energy sources, there are two benefits from such investments. First, a percentage of the material and equipment is manufactured in the region, and most of the construction and installation will be done by regional firms. Secondly, energy saved by using such plants and equipment will result in a decrease in the amount of dollars that must be shipped out of the region to pay for energy. A portion of these dollars can be reinvested in the region, creating greater economic activity and more jobs. A study by the Massachusetts Energy Office claims that such investments in all sectors could increase regional output by $2 billion (1977) and reduce energy costs by $1.4 billion (1977).[17]

The need for increased energy efficiency is more important in New England than in other regions—not only because of its dependence on outside energy sources, but also because the region has a disproportionate number of old industrial plants. Private industry will be more willing to invest its own funds in promoting energy efficiency in plants that are expected to be in operation for many years. Otherwise, the full benefits of the investment could not be captured. Older plants, many of which are located in cities of New England, are less likely to be the sites of private energy-efficiency investments. Therefore, as energy prices increase, companies will be more inclined to shut down their older facilities and lay off workers.

Programs to assist investment in retrofitting these plants and purchasing more efficient equipment become more important to the region as energy prices continue to rise.

Although investment in energy efficiency and renewable resources will ease the growth in the outflow of dollars to pay for conventional fuels, such investments will not be inexpensive. Energy from solar collectors costs approximately $16–20 per MMBTU or twice that of natural gas and substantially higher than oil.[18] Photovoltaic solar systems are currently five to seven times more expensive than conventional electricity. Instead, the future marketability of these systems is directly proportional to the inflationary change in their costs as compared with the inflationary changes in the costs of oil and gas.

Wood fuels could be an attractive source of energy for industry, but lack of a reliable network of regional supply, an inability to capture economies of scale, and a concern over quality control will, in the short term, limit wood use to industries that use it as a feedstock in their production process (that is, pulp, paper, lumber, furniture, etc.). If conventional energy prices continue to rise rapidly, this situation will change, and investments will be made to develop the supply network and increase the use of wood, probably in the form of chips and pellets. Finally, as the value of wood increases, competition between uses of wood will increase. Investors in energy systems will find themselves bidding against investors in lumber, housing, and other wood products. The end result is sure to be higher prices for wood and for the products made from wood.

Solid waste is yet another source of fuel if used as feedstock to produce process steam. The RESCO facility in Saugus, Massachusetts, which has been in operation for several years, has already demonstrated the economic feasibility of this option. However, again it is expensive and is heavily dependent on the ability to aggregate significant volumes of solid waste. (Smaller-scale operations, however, have been very successful in Europe.) As with other options, the rate at which investments in these renewable resources are made will reflect the price of conventional fuels and the perceptions of the future price of those fuels. The individual who believes oil will hit $100 (1980 dollars) by the year 2000 will be inclined to invest substantially more money in these alternatives than the person who believes in the lower oil-price scenario. Government programs to remove institutional barriers, enhance technology transfer, and provide financial assistance can also affect the rate of investment in these technologies. For New England, with its large negative energy balance of trade, the social benefits of such programs may be substantial.

Strategic Reserve.   Although short-term energy crises do not significantly alter the long-run trends, they can exact a short-term, high cost on the economy. Most crises involve a shortage of one fuel or another for a limited period. If the shortage is severe customers who desire that fuel either will not be able to obtain it or will be forced to pay a very large premium. If the customer cannot obtain the fuel, he must shut down his facilities, thereby losing significant sums of money. If by chance he can get this fuel, he must still pay a very high premium, which substantially increases his costs, decreases his profit, and puts pressure on his plant managers to consider operating his facilities at a lower rate of utilization.

Energy shortages can be extremely costly to individuals, businesses, and the economy in general. Since New England relies intensively on oil, and since oil is our most vulnerable fuel, the ability to develop surge capacity to minimize the dangers of future shortages is important to the region.

Surge capacity is the capacity to bring additional sources of energy quickly into the market in cases of shortage. For example, if the region reduced its consumption of oil by 20 percent and there were a 20 percent shortfall, regional energy officials would have to reduce oil consumption still further (another 16 percent). On the other hand, if the region reduced its consumption by 20 percent and half of that 20 percent was stored in either a strategic regional reserve or in private stockpiles, those reserves could act as surge capacity which could be used to bridge a temporary gap in supply.

Given continuing turmoil in the Middle East, it is very likely that over the next twenty years this country will confront future cut-offs of oil. Unless strategic programs like private and public storage of supplies, contingency planning, and investment in dual fuel capacity are adopted, the cost of these shortages will be very high for oil-dependent regions. No region stands to gain more than New England from the development of a national strategic oil stockpile and perhaps a regional product stockpile. Even if one is optimistic about future oil-price trends, one cannot dismiss the high probability of politically motivated cut-offs of imported oil and the need to be prepared for this eventuality.

Energy to Heat Our Buildings

Although energy is used for a number of functions in New England, residential and commercial energy use connotes space heating. In a climate significantly colder than the national average,[19] heat is not a luxury, it is an essential prerequisite for health and, in some instances, survival.

National statistics have historically lumped the commercial and residential sectors together. In the case of New England, aggregating these two sectors is more difficult to justify. With a relatively low industrial demand for energy, the commercial sector plays a more influential role in the region's energy future. Approximately 21 percent of the region's energy is used commercially, and 26 percent is consumed in the residential sector.[20] Much of the growth in energy consumption in the commercial sector, however, is for air conditioning, not space heating, and stems from increased use of electricity, not heating oil. Since this section focuses primarily on heating, the commercial sector will not receive the attention it deserves. Nevertheless, many of the critical factors that shape future energy use in the residential or utility sectors will also shape energy use in the commercial sector.

Energy in the Residential Sector. There are 4.6 million households in New England—of which a significant proportion heat with oil (almost 70 percent of the homes). Of the approximately 17 million households nationally which rely on fuel oil for heat, almost 16 percent are in New England, which has less than 6 percent of the nation's population.[21] In southern New England natural gas also plays a significant role. In some areas, such as Greater Boston, as many as 35 percent of the houses are heated with this fuel; but in the northern three states natural gas is almost nonexistent; competition with oil is limited to propane, electricity, and, more recently, wood.

The price shocks of 1973–74 and 1979–80 dramatically increased the cost of heating a home in New England. Home heating oil prior to the 1972 embargo were in the range of 20 cents a gallon. By 1981 they were rapidly approaching $1.40. In 1981 it costs about $1500 to heat a house, while nine years earlier that same house could have been heated for $300 or the present cost of one delivery of oil.

The effect of these price hikes is magnified by the age of New England's housing stock, which is disproportionately older than the national average. Over 56 percent of the houses in New England are more than forty years old.[22] If one factors out Connecticut, which has recently benefited from the population exodus from New York City, the percentage of houses built prior to 1940 increases to 62. Since in 1940 builders usually installed no more than two inches of insulation in the attic and no insulation in the wall, much of this housing is poorly insulated.[23] Furthermore, many of these homes suffer air infiltration from cracks and holes in walls, window casings, and doorways that will require actual repairs.

As one would expect, the rapid escalation in oil prices has caused significant conservation and, where feasible, fuel switching. All the New England states show a decrease in the demand for heating oil since 1973. For example, prior to the first embargo the average New England home used between 1450 to 1600 gallons annually. In 1981 oil retailers claimed that their annual deliveries dropped below 1000 gallons.[24] Furthermore, there has been significant fuel switching. In southern New England over 100,000 homes have converted from oil to gas, while in the northern states more than half of the owner-occupied homes provide at least some of their heat with wood.

Yet investing in conservation improvements or purchasing alternative heating fuels are options precluded to a proportion of the New England population—specifically the poor and near poor. These individuals, who are primarily located in the older cities, make up about 14 percent of the households in the region. (For the sake of simplicity, we will define poor and near poor as the people whose income is below 125 percent of the poverty level.) About 142,000 of the poor are elderly individuals on fixed incomes, living alone.[25] A disproportionate percentage of the poor rent their homes and thus have neither the incentive nor the ability to invest in energy-efficiency improvements. Finally, though only a small percentage of low-income people in the United States heat with oil; in New England a vast majority depend on this unregulated source of fuel.

The effect of the price increases on this segment of our society has been severe. Low-income peoples confront energy costs during the winter months equal to 35 percent of their annual income.[26] It is only through the availability of the federal low-income energy-assistance program that these people have been able to purchase heating fuels.

Factors Shaping the Future. As in the case of the industrial sector, the single most significant factor shaping energy use in this sector will be the price of oil. If one believes in a world of $100 a barrel oil, accelerated rates of investment in energy-efficiency improvements and substitute fuels, including renewables, will not only be justified but expected. If one is more optimistic about fuel prices, then levels of investment will be lower and the rate of change in this sector will be less.

What these changes might look like, and their implications, will depend on four additional factors: (1) the availability of economical substitute fuels; (2) technological breakthroughs; (3) the availability of subsidized financing; and (4) the willingness of government to address the plight of lower-income people.

Availability of Substitute Fuels. Many energy experts believe that the future competition for the privilege of heating one's home will take place between the electric and natural gas utilities, with the heating-oil industry pricing itself out of the competition. This belief is dependent on the premise that natural gas supplies will increase over the next twenty years while oil supplies will rapidly decrease. Presently the United States produces about 20 trillion cubic feet of gas per year; projections of the supply in the year 2000 range from a low of 18 trillion cubic feet to a high of over 30 trillion cubic feet.[27] These projections also differ from how much of the new gas supplies will be imported from Canada, Mexico, or elsewhere and how much will come from new domestic sources. What they do agree on is the continuing decline in conventional domestic gas supplies. If one believes in a high oil-price scenario and the optimistic domestic gas-supply scenario, one should expect conversions from oil to gas to continue, with gas meeting 40 to 50 percent of the residential space heating demands in southern New England by the year 2000.[28] If one believes that gas supplies are not as plentiful as the industry claims or that most of the incremental gas will be supplied through expensive imports or unconventional gas production, then one would expect a much slower rate of conversion away from oil. Under this scenario, the relative price of oil and gas would be identical, thus eliminating the major incentive to convert.

Technological Breakthrough.   With the possible exception of solar photovoltaic cells and fuel cells, the technological breakthroughs that will make a difference in how New Englanders heat their homes will be in areas of energy utilization, not energy production. If the electric industry can develop a heat pump that will work in the middle of New England's winter, or a method to store energy during off-peak periods (when electricity is less expensive), so that it can be used as a source of heat during on-peak periods, it might be able to improve its competitive position dramatically. The same is true of the gas industry for devices like the gas mechanical heat pump, which produces heat much more efficiently than conventional systems. But even if such technologies as photovoltaics arrive on the scene in the 1990's, their effect on the region's energy situation by the year 2000 will be minimal, since their commercialization will still be in its infancy. On the other hand, new technologies for utilization of energy could have a dramatic effect over the next twenty years, since most homeowners would be in the replacement market for new space-conditioning equipment during this period.

The Availability of Financing.   Numerous studies have documented the enormous potential for energy savings in the building sector. Although New England is ahead of most regions in its reduction of energy consumption, a significant potential for further reduction remains. In a report from the Center for Energy and Environmental Studies at Princeton, reductions in energy use as high as 75 percent were found to be technically feasible, given reasonable, technical criteria.[29] Also, as mentioned in earlier sections, energy efficiency and renewable energy options are indigenous sources of energy. Revenue derived from such investments will have a more advantageous effect on the region's economy than similar investments in conventional fuels.

Although the relative costs of efficiency investments as compared with most conventional production options are low, they're not inexpensive. The cost of weatherizing an average single-family home is approximately $3000. If you add the purchase of a new energy-efficient heating system, the cost could easily reach $5000. Finally, using more sophisticated equipment, such as used in the Princeton studies, there is even more cost-effective savings which could be realized, but at a cost of still $1500 more. The cost of making a poorly insulated house totally energy efficient is about $6500 (1980 dollars). For larger buildings these costs are greater. Cost-effective renewable energy options are even more expensive, and many of the more economical alternatives, such as passive solar systems, are incorporated mostly into new housing construction.

Decisions on whether to make these investments will be made by thousands of individual decision-makers—like homeowners, landlords, store owners, and office building managers. Over the short term, factors such as access to information and the presence of institutional barriers will affect these decisions, but over the longer term, two factors will predominate: (1) alternative investment opportunities and (2) the ability of the investor to obtain financing. If interest rates are at 16 percent, there will be a number of alternative uses of a homeowner's money which on a discounted cash-flow basis will be superior to many energy investments. Furthermore, at 16 percent many people will be reluctant to borrow large sums of money unless they believe that inflation rates will continue at a double digit level of annual growth. Instead, they will make improvements that are low cost or no cost and with the highest pay-offs, leaving the more substantial improvements for a later date.

If a family earns $12,000 or less after taxes, investments of $2,000 to $3,000 are difficult. A three-year loan for $3000 at 15 percent compounded annually will require monthly payments of over $140, or more than 14 percent of the individual's monthly paycheck. Since $12,000 (1980 dollars) after taxes is above the median for families living within the Boston metropolitan area, many people fall into this category.

Unless the present inflation rates are lowered and unless subsidized financing is accessible to the vast majority of New England homeowners, many investments in energy efficiency improvements will not be made. There are a number of federal government programs such as the Residential Conservation Service and the Conservation and Solar Bank which could provide low-interest loans. However, there is uncertainty as to whether these programs will over the long run be adequately funded and effectively administered.

The Plight of the Poor.   As oil prices continue to increase, low-income people will find it more and more difficult to afford heating fuels. Even under our moderate price scenario of $50 per barrel of crude oil, in the year 2000 the cost of heating fuel will be in the vicinity of $1.80 per gallon (1980 dollars), and the cost of heating an average home will increase to approximately $1700 per year. Gasoline prices and electricity will also increase, and the total annual energy bill for a low-income household will be about $2500. Both of these price estimates are extremely conservative and assume substantial conservation. If our $100 per barrel scenario is used, these prices will double; in that case, people whose income is about $7500 per year would need $5000 to pay for their basic energy needs.

Obviously this situation is untenable. One of three events will have to occur. The government will have to provide ever-increasing levels of assistance to ever-increasing numbers of people to offset the oil price increases. Secondly, if for political or fiscal reasons these transfer payments are not forthcoming, poor families will either migrate to areas with warmer climates or simply be unable to afford heat. The effect of depriving the poor of their ability to heat their homes will be serious health problems, especially among the elderly, and most likely increased social unrest. The third possibility will be a coordinated government program to weatherize low-income houses while continuing transfer payments at a lower level. Such an effort would necessitate a more comprehensive commitment on the part of government than has heretofore been manifested.

The ability of low-income people to afford heat will be one of the most pressing social-equity issues confronting the region in the 1980's and 90's.

Energy for Transportation

More than one half the oil consumed in the United States is consumed in the transportation sector. This sector bore the brunt of both the 1973–74 embargo and the Iranian cut-off of oil in 1979, as evidenced by the long gas lines; and in all likelihood it will be asked to bear a similar burden in future crises.

Our societal and economic structure is closely tied to the automobile. Shopping centers, restaurants, and office complexes are sited so as to be accessible by car. For example, the economic boom in Nashua and southeastern New Hampshire is, at least in part, dependent on access to Boston. The rule of thumb is that a company must be able to deliver its goods to Logan International Airport in one hour to justify the selection of a distant location.

New England's use of energy in the transportation sector is similar in many respects to those in other regions of the country. Gasoline prices in Maine are not much different from prices in Texas, Illinois, or California. Regional population densities are greater, so New Englanders tend to drive less. On the other hand, they own more cars than the national average (1.6 per household versus 1.4).[30]

Consumption of transportation fuels seems to be less affected by price increases than are other fuels. During 1973–78 gasoline consumption in all six New England states continued to climb while the use of distillate and industrial fuels declined; the three northern states increased their use of gasoline during this period by 14 percent.

The most accurate measure of automobile use is not how much gasoline one consumes, but the cost per passenger mile. An efficient car allows one to travel the same distance at a lower cost. If one looks at the experience in Europe, where gasoline prices are $2.00 to $3.00 per gallon, one sees a continuing increase in vehicle miles traveled. But those miles are traveled in progressively more efficient cars.

In the United States gasoline prices are only one of several factors that enter into personal transportation decisions. The largest factor must be the cost of the automobile itself, which in 1980 ran between $5000 and $10,000 for a new model. Using a median figure of $7,500, and amortizing the car over five years at reasonable interest rates one calculates that a new car will cost about $2000 per year. Let us assume that the cost of auto insurance is about $500 per car and excise taxes are about $100 (an average over the five-year period). The cost of parts and service, new tires, etc. adds another $500 per year to the bill. In total our hypothetical car owner faces annual capital

costs of $2000 and operating costs of about $1100. Now let us assume that the cost of gasoline rises to $2.00 and that our car aver-
ages 25 miles per gallon and the owner drives 15,000 miles per year.
Six hundred gallons of gasoline will cost $1200, or about 50 percent
of the total operating costs or 30 percent of the total annual cost of
owning the car.

Now let's assume that our car owner buys a car that gets 30 miles
per gallon. This more efficient vehicle will save him only $200 per
year, or about a 9 percent reduction in his operating costs. On the
other hand, the car owner can respond to the high energy prices by
moving his family from the suburbs to the city, where he can take
mass transit to work. (In modern America, of course, many jobs are
located in the suburbs.) Now he only drives 8,000 miles per year.
The gasoline bill shrinks to $640. He saves $560 per year in gasoline
bills, but he takes on new expenses, like moving, mass transit fares,
and higher insurance and property tax payments, which in most
cases will exceed this figure.

Most of these hypothetical figures are conservative, but the point
is that gasoline prices per se may have a significant influence on the
type of passenger automobile purchased but are not going to provide sufficient incentive for people to change their driving habits
dramatically, at least not until prices reach a level of $4.00 or $5.00
per gallon. Despite popular rhetoric, you will not see a massive in-
flux of suburbanites into the cities because of energy prices. Furthermore, in New England, where the cost of oil to heat a home for
a winter will be almost double that of fueling one's car for a year,
gasoline prices will not be the number one energy problem. In fact,
New England is the one region that should be supportive of programs to subsidize heating costs through increased gasoline prices.

An alternative to the automobile is mass transit. Given our present dispersed land use patterns, however, and the high cost of new
rail systems, investments in new transit systems will be limited.
Furthermore, even under the best of circumstances, mass transit is
no great energy saver. A fully loaded bus uses only a little less fuel
per passenger mile than a car that uses 40 to 50 miles per gallon and
carries two people.[31] The energy costs of building both the intracity
rail systems and the rail vehicles, as well as the energy expended in
getting the passengers to and from the transit stop, can make some

transit systems net energy losers, at least over the first ten to fifteen years of operation.

Mass transportation does serve important societal needs. It is a source of mobility for large portions of an urban population, a means to reduce pollution and congestion, an incentive for community development, and an important factor in enhancing the quality of urban life. But mass transit is not an energy-saving alternative, and its future will not be tied to energy considerations.

Intercity rail, especially in the Northeast Corridor, may, however, be justified on energy grounds, given the existing infrastructure and the escalating cost of aviation fuel and diesel fuel for trucks. There will be increased utilization of new freight-haul concepts, such as piggybacking, a procedure in which trucks are driven to a major rail line, placed on a train, and hauled to a point from which they can be driven to their ultimate destination.

Another alternative is the electric car. In some respects New England, with its high population densities, might be an ideal location for such vehicles, although further developments to increase the performance and range of these vehicles are needed.

One last concept which will receive an increasing amount of scrutiny is that of purchasing transportation. Given that the type of vehicle one needs to drive to the supermarket is not the same vehicle one needs to drive five hundred miles to the ski resort, leasing transportation services rather than owning a car may become a valid alternative. Under this arrangement an individual would, for a fee, lease whatever type of vehicle he/she needed at any specific time. For example, while driving in the city, one would lease a small urban car; when driving significant distances, one would turn in the smaller car and get a larger one.

In the year 2000, New Englanders will still be predominantly dependent on their cars for transportation. That car will certainly be more efficient—how much more efficient depending on the price of gasoline rather than on any technical limitations. The use of rail for freight will increase as well as the development of more efficient trucks, planes, and ships. Energy costs as a subcategory of transportation will not be the overriding factor in shaping regional land-use patterns but will influence the development of new concepts in transportation, such as piggybacking and options to car ownership.

Energy to Produce Electricity

The inclusion of the electric utility sector in my four general categories may seem inconsistent, since utilities are usually perceived as producers of energy. Yet they are also consumers of fuel. Approximately 52 percent of the region's electricity is produced by oil-fired generating facilities which consume between 60 and 70 million barrels of residual oil annually. Furthermore, during the last twenty years the utility industry has undergone significant changes, and it is likely that the next twenty years will be even more tumultuous. Any assessment of New England's energy future must include this sector.

Setting the Stage.   Prior to the 1960's the utility industry enjoyed a relatively calm, stable existence. As franchised monopolies regulated by government, they enjoyed a guaranteed rate of return and a relatively risk-free business environment.

In the 1960's four factors altered this stability: (1) the conversion from coal to oil; (2) the emergence of nuclear power; (3) the 1965 blackout; and (4) a dramatic increase in the demand for electricity.

(1) *Conversion from Coal to Oil.*   In 1965 President Johnson agreed to exclude residual oil from the oil-import quota system, thus making Venezuelan residual oil a more economical boiler fuel than Appalachian coal. The effect of this decision was dramatic. In 1966, 24 utilities plants in New England burned coal.[32] Seven years later, only one plant remained on this fuel. Until very recently, the strict sulfur and particulate standards contained in the Clean Air Act of 1970 made a return to coal uneconomic.

(2) *The Emergence of Nuclear Power.*   With the construction of the Oyster Creek Plant in New Jersey in the mid 1960's, many utilities in New England jumped on the nuclear bandwagon. The promise of cheap reliable energy from safe and clean facilities was alluring, not simply to the utility industry but to all segments of society. The nuclear skeptics during the 1960's were a quiet and small minority. Furthermore, nuclear power was a natural investment for utilities who were confronted with economies of scale and a regulatory

framework that provided strong incentives to maximize the level of capital investment.

(3) *The 1965 Blackout.* In the fall of 1965 a series of system malfunctions blacked out most of the northeastern United States for several hours. As a result, utility executives were hauled over the coals of public outrage. Committees, commissions, and agencies at all levels of government castigated the industry for not building sufficient power capacity. The presidents of most of today's utilities in the region were young executive officers during this period and were directly influenced by the experience. The public was demanding that the utilities increase their investments in new generating stations—an action that admittedly was in the financial interest of the utilities to make. However, this single event had a significant effect on industry's perspective on the need for future power.

(4) *Increase in Demand.* The period of the 1960's also saw energy prices of all fuels declining and demand rising. Electricity was no exception. Fueled by the dramatic increase in economic growth stemming from the Vietnam War era, the demand for electricity in New England grew at 7.6 percent during 1960–72. In fact, during 1960–75 the utility industry increased its consumption of energy faster than any other sector of the New England economy, until by 1975 it was consuming 18 percent of all the energy used in the region.[33]

To most observers, New England's utilities entered the 1970's poised to reap the obvious benefits from the actions they had taken in the 1960's. However, as events unfolded their strategies and plans came unglued. The 1973–74 embargo resulted in a quadrupling of the price of residual oil, the very fuel the region's utilities had just converted to. Therefore, as oil prices rose, so did electricity prices. The 7 percent annual growth in demand for elecricity shrank to 1.6 percent per year for 1972–75.

At first, the industry refused to admit that their world had been turned upside down, and their executives argued that the lower demand was an anomaly that would soon be reversed. But the reversal never came. The construction boom of the 1960's left the region with large surpluses of generating capacity, at a time in which industry was in the midst of planning and financing ten additional large nuclear plants. To complicate matters, the antinuclear movement was gathering momentum while the consensus behind nuclear power was falling apart. All of these factors were enough to give a utility executive nightmares, but the worse was yet to come. By the latter part of the 1970's, escalating inflation set in. The cost of new capital construction skyrocketed, and the utilities saw their bond ratings decline and their interest payments on debt climb. Their stock prices mirrored their bond ratings, forcing them to pay higher dividends to attract stockholders. The era of declining economies of scale had ended and the regulatory rules, which were so favorable to the industry in the 1960's, made it very difficult to finance any capital construction.

Finally, the Three Mile Island accident unalterably changed the public perspective on nuclear power. The bright hopes and ambitions of the 1960's had disappeared, to be replaced by doubt and uncertainty. Several utilities are still trying to complete nuclear plants, but they are primarily trying to avoid losing vast amounts of sunk capital. Most are approaching the 1980's with great uncertainty, realizing that the next twenty years could easily be more tumultuous than the last.

The Future

The key questions regarding the future of electricity are (1) What will be the mix of fuels and facilities used to generate electrical power in the 1990's and beyond? (2) What will be the role of the present electrical utility industry in providing that mix?

The Mix of Fuels.   The need-for-power issue that dominated debate in the 1970's is today almost extinct in this region. With the completion of two of the several nuclear plants now under construction, the base-load power needs for the region will be met for the foreseeable future. (The only exception would be if electricity prices dropped dramatically, inducing the substitution of electricity for liquid fuels.) Furthermore, if one returns to our $50 and $100 oil-price scenarios and examines their implications on the price of New England's electricity, one arrives at a price between 15 and 25 cents per kilowatt hour. It is unlikely that the region will experience a dramatic increase in the demand for electricity at those prices, especially if the prices tend toward the high side of the range. At those prices, however, the region may not be able to afford its present mix of generating plants. As oil prices continue to increase, New England will pay a heavy cost in the 1990's unless the industry begins now to replace these older oil-fired facilities.

In developing replacement options, it is important to consider the present uses of these plants. All of the major power facilities in New England are hooked up to a regional grid, and each separate facility is brought into operation at a rate reflective of the region's need for power at any specific time. Obviously less power is needed at 4:00 A.M. than at 4:00 P.M. or during a cool spring day rather than a hot, muggy, summer day. The order in which these facilities are hooked into the grid system is related to their cost of operation; thus the capital-intensive, low-operating-cost facilities like nuclear plants are brought on first, and the smaller oil-fired facilities last. Utility planners refer to the former facilities as base-load plants and to the latter as peaking units. Plants which fit in between are called intermediate units. It is these peaking and intermediate units which primarily rely on oil and which will be the target of any replacement strategies.

Until nuclear power can remedy its financial problems and its public image, only three options will be available to replace oil: (1) coal, (2) decentralized community-based options, and (3) hydroelectric power imported from Canada.

(1) *Coal*. It is ironic that twenty years after they divorced themselves from dependency on coal, New England's utilities are looking toward return of this fuel. Already work has been almost completed on converting the region's largest oil-firing facility at Brayton Point, Massachusetts, and several other plants are being targeted for future conversion. Converting many of the existing plants back to coal will be difficult, since they are now old and were built to burn coal of significantly higher pollutant content than would be permissible today. If coal is to make a substantial contribution, new and more efficient coal facilities will have to be built.

There are a number of new coal technologies which would meet federal air-pollution standards and are feasible options for New England. These include the oil/coal slurry that produces a mixture of

50 percent residual and 50 percent pulverized coal. The mixture is then fed into a utility boiler. A number of such slurries are now in existence, and at current prices slurries may be able to compete favorably with residual oil.

A second technology is converting coal into a low or mid-BTU gas which is then fed directly into the generating plant. The conversion process is not complicated and is substantially cleaner than burning coal directly. A major project in southeast Massachusetts which would use this technology is currently being studied.

A final set of coal-burning technologies involves burning coal directly but more efficiently and with less pollution. Examples of these technologies range from new processes for burning coal, such as fluidized bed combustion to more effective pollution abatement equipment that could be incorporated into new, conventional, coal-generating stations.

As this country invests more resources in synthetic fuels, more options may be developed, but these three offer the potential for meeting both our energy and environmental goals. As oil prices increase, the economic pressures to use more coal will force the region to seize more and more of this potential. The difficulty is that the region may have to make those investment decisions before those prices increase in order to escape the potentially high economic costs of dependence on oil.

(2) *Decentralized Community-Sized Options.* These options include renewables, such as wind systems, wood-fired generators, solar photovoltaics, and small-scale hydro and nonrenewables, such as solid waste to energy facilities, fuel cells, and cogenerators. Some of these options are still in the developmental stage; others are currently economical only under certain circumstances. They all produce electricity, and with limited exceptions all are smaller than conventional generating systems; but each must either feed its electricity into a grid system or find ways of storing it on site.

A future that includes community-sized options will require significant changes in the structure of the existing utility systems. Currently, electricity flows from a central power station to the consumer. In the future, though, electricity could flow both ways. For example, a community housing development could set up a small wind farm which on a windy day would produce more electricity than demanded by the development. The excess power would be fed into the grid system and the development would receive credit from the utility company. On days with no wind the development would purchase backup electricity from the utility. Obviously, the price at which the utility purchases the electricity and the price at which it sells the backup power are essential factors in determining the economics of these systems. Also, the development of a system in which hundreds of small decentralized electric generators feed into a grid system represents a dramatic departure from the present system, which depends on a small number of large, central, generating stations all directly owned and controlled by a franchised utility company. The role of the electric utility companies would be changed to a provider of power rather than a producer of it. They would not only buy and sell power produced by small producers but also serve as a major source of financing for an array of energy services, including energy-efficiency improvements.

As with all the options discussed in this chapter, the rate of development will be determined by the price of oil. At 15–25 cents per kilowatt hour many of these systems will become economically attractive, but since they also represent a departure from the traditional, institutional structure of producing and distributing elecricity, major regulatory reforms will be needed in order to realize the full benefits.

(3) *Imported Hydroelectric Power from Canada.* In recent years, New England utilities have evidenced a significant interest in purchasing excess hydroelectric power from Quebec and, to a lesser extent, from New Brunswick and Newfoundland. The interest has been stimulated by several factors. First, Quebec is undertaking a mammoth hydro-construction program in the area of James Bay (located just south of Hudson Bay), which is the point of confluence for several large rivers. The total potential power from James Bay could be as much as 35,000 megawatts or about one and a half times the present demand in New England on the hottest day of the summer.

Quebec would like to prebuild as much of this capacity as is financially feasible and to export a percentage of the power to the Northeast until their internal demand increases to absorb the on-line capacity. Also, by selling the electricity, Quebec can obtain income to continue financing the remaining James Bay projects without having to increase the domestic rates.

New England utilities, faced with higher interest rates, significant investor skepticism, and escalating fuel costs, are eager to pursue options that would allow them to use less oil without further eroding their fragile financial condition. Quebec hydroelectric power has the potential to provide such an option. Whether this potential is realized depends on the proposed contractual arrangements. For example, any contract to purchase electricity would have to include a guarantee that Quebec would supply firm power for a length of time, sufficient to allow the cost of the necessary transmission systems to be amortized. Furthermore, unless there are assurances of a continued relationship, New England utilities must begin to build redundant capacity to replace the hydropower when the contract with Quebec expires. This necessity puts a ceiling on the amount of money the region will be willing to pay for imported power.

Therefore, although there are difficulties to be worked out, there are advantages to both Quebec and New England in pursuing a long-term energy relationship.

The Future Role of Utilities.   The electrical utility industry enters the 1980's in poor financial health, constrained by a regulatory structure that provides limited incentives for investment in an inflationary economy and with an almost negligible need for incremental power. Given these conditions, utilities will be increasingly reluctant to make new investments. Ironically, the situation in the 1980's and 1990's will likely be the reverse of the situation in the 1970's. In the past decade, the utilities clamored to build more capacity; in the 1980's they will resist building more unless reforms in the regulatory structure are forthcoming.

Given this economic environment, changes in the structure of our electricity utility system must occur. These changes could occur in three forms.

The first would emphasize massive reforms in the existing regulatory structure and could include allowing the utilities wide latitude in charging customers the cost of construction prior to its completion, offering special tax breaks for utilities and utility investors, or providing incentives for utilities to merge their resources in the planning, design, and construction of new facilities. In the latter case, all the regional utilities might join together to form a single entity for the purposes of financing and constructing new plants. Once the plant is built, the individual companies could either buy portions of the plant itself or purchase the electricity directly in the same way Exxon used to buy oil from Aramco. (Exxon owns 30 percent of Aramco, which, up to a few years ago, owned the Saudi Arabian oil concessions.)

Under the second set of options, the public sector would establish their own public power corporations. These corporations would finance new facilities through tax-exempt bonds, construct the facilities, and wholesale the electricity to the private utilities.

Such corporations would be set up not to compete with the private utilities but to build facilities which the private companies, under the present regulatory system, are either unable to finance or unwilling to build. The New York Public Power Authority (PASNY) is an example of such an entity. PASNY played an important role in building the plants that Consolidated Edison could not finance after their financial problems of the mid-1970's.

The third option would be to deregulate gradually the wholesaling of electricity. Under such a system, electricity wholesalers would compete to sell power to distribution companies which in turn would purchase the cheapest and most reliable power available. To an extent, the emergence of decentralized sources and the passage of legislation at both the state and federal level, preventing discrimination against these sources, has signaled the beginning of the deregulation process. If a private power producer can produce electricity at a rate equal to or below the replacement cost of power, the utility companies must buy it.

It is difficult to determine how far this trend toward fostering competition at the wholesaling level will go. Currently it is focused on small producers, but as the cost of conventional power increases and the plight of the existing utility structure worsens, pressure may grow to exempt larger and larger producers from regulation.

This third option would be complementary to a strategy that fostered greater reliance on decentralized community alternatives, while the first and second would tend to be more supportive of centralized alternatives. Neither decentralized or centralized power options will be successful, however, unless the financial health of the utilities improves.

Although each of these options for changing the structure of the industry has been considered separately, it is likely that forms of all three will adopted. In all cases though, the present set of circumstances confronting New England's private utility companies will force change. Probably the structure of the electric utility industry in the year 2000 will look very different from that of today.

Conclusion

To those who seek drastic change, the assessments of the following pages will be disappointing. Gradualism is never as exciting or as self-fulfilling as revolution. Although governments come and go, the economic fabric of a society adjusts more slowly. To an extent the oil-price shocks of 1973 and 1979 are among the most severe exogenous economic pressures ever to confront New England. Adjustment to them will take time and will occur within the context of the dynamics of the region's economy, the ingredients of which were mixed together over one hundred years ago. Energy prices may accelerate the ongoing move away from manufacturing, but one would be hard pressed to argue that energy is the sole factor in that move.

For most of this chapter, I have tried to describe the factors that will influence the region's energy future. However, the region's use of energy in the year 2000 is not predetermined. The influence of people acting through the various institutions of our society cannot be precisely forecast. Nevertheless, the people must focus on problems that are unique to New England. In the course of this chapter, four problems stand out.

The first and foremost is the price of oil. New England is an oil-intensive region, and as oil prices increase, the need to lessen that intensity increases. As mentioned above, every 10 percent increase in the price of oil and gas moves one billion dollars out of the region. This drain of monies from the region places New England's economy in an extemely vulnerable position to future oil shortages and price hikes.

The second problem is the high cost of heating a home. Annual heating bills of $1500 affect all but the very rich, but it is the poor, and especially the elderly poor, who are most affected. Although the growth in household heating costs may slow, New England's climate will ensure that heat for the poor and the elderly will remain a major social concern.

The third problem is the competitive disadvantage facing New England's industries as a result of federal pricing policies which through price regulation subsidize natural gas consumption. The result is that New England industries that use unregulated oil are forced to pay substantially more for energy than industries in other regions with access to regulated natural gas.

The fourth problem is that the region must solve the first three in a period of financial austerity, an unhealthy utility industry, and continuing difficulties in meeting federal air-pollution standards. All these limitations will hamper the region's ability to adjust to higher energy prices.

However, New England does have resources which can be brought to bear on these problems. It has some of the most highly competent technological industries in the world, and many of them have already begun to invest substantial sums of money into developing new ways to produce and use energy. The region is also blessed with indigenous resources. Wood, hydro, wind and waste products will all provide assistance over the next twenty years. Finally, the region's move to less energy-intensive industries and its strong efforts to reduce its consumption of energy will make it less vulnerable than it would otherwise be to future price shocks.

In the next few years, New England will have to not only depend more heavily on these resources but also act effectively on four fronts:

(1) It must significantly reduce its use of oil in the utility sector and to a lesser extent the industrial sector. To achieve this end, it must increase its ability to use coal and indigenous resources as well as develop more energy-efficient means of using energy, specifically electricity.

(2) It must support actions at the federal level which could have disproportionately large benefits to an oil-intensive region like New England. These actions should include measures to end pricing policies which discriminate between oil and gas and to establish strategic petroleum stockpiles and national contingency plans, in order to ease the effects of future oil shortages.

(3) It must provide effective relief to enable the poor and elderly to heat their homes.

(4) It must be willing to explore and where feasible adopt institutional reforms that will ensure a utility industry that is not only healthy but sufficiently flexible to meet the demands of a rapidly changing energy marketplace.

Throughout its three-hundred-and-sixty-year history, New England has responded effectively to each challenge confronting it. There is no reason to believe that over the next twenty years it will not do the same. The ever-increasing price of oil is not only the problem of this quarter century, but also its challenge and inspiration—the challenge to change and the inspiration to make those changes happen.

New England has historically been a self-reliant region in that it has had the capacity to reach within itself and produce men and women of vision whose imagination and entrepreneurial leadership struck a path for all to follow. In the end, the ability to tap this resource once again will probably be the essential factor in shaping New England's response to the events of the past decade and those of the future.

NOTES

1. New England farmers made no conscious efforts to reforest their lands until the early twentieth century. Thus mass-produced furniture industries moved to the Great Lakes region during the last half of the eighteenth century in order to be closer to major sources of timber.

2. New England Energy Congress, *Final Report* (May 1979), p. 24.

3. The Algonquin pipeline was completed in October 1951 and the Tennessee line in October 1953.

4. American Gas Association, *Gas Facts* (1979), p. 74.

5. Department of Energy, *Federal Energy Data System* (February 1978).

6. New England used 11.20 thousand BTU per dollar value added. The nation used 25.47. See New England Regional Commission, *Analyses of Energy Use in the Manufacturing Sector* (March 1979), p. 46.

7. Energy Information Administration, Department of Energy, *State Data Report* (1979).

8. New England Regional Commission, *Analysis of Energy Use in the Manufacturing Sector* (March 1979), p. 6.

9. Department of Energy, Region One Office. Information obtained by telephone interview.

10. New England Regional Commission, p. 34.

11. Massachusetts Energy Office, *New England Energy Policy Alternatives Study* (October 1978), p. 6.

12. Carol Jusenius and Larry Ledebur, *Where Have All the Firms Gone?: An Analysis of the New England Economy* (U.S. Department of Commerce, Economic Development Administration, 1977).

13. Most of the in-migration came from firms moving to Connecticut from locations in New York City.

14. Harbridge House, *The Economic Impact of Energy Policies on the Wood Furniture and Metal Working Equipment Industries in New England* (Boston, December 1977), p. 15.

15. New England Regional Commission, *The New England Regional Plan: An Economic Development Strategy* (September 1980), p. 85.

16. Department of Energy, *Monthly Energy Review* (December 1980).

17. Massachusetts Energy Office, p. 6.

18. New England Energy Congress, *Final Report of the New England Energy Congress* (1979), p. 160.

19. New England's climate is 36 percent colder than the national average.

20. That is, .65 quads in the commercial sector and .79 quads in the residential sector. These statistics were obtained from the New England Energy Congress (note 2, above).

21. New England Energy Congress, p. 248.

22. Ibid., p. 253.

23. Ibid., p. 372.

24. Based on interviews with selected oil retail companies and officials of the New England Fuel Institute.

25. New England Energy Congress, p. 248.

26. Fuel Oil Marketing Advisory Committee of the Department of Energy, *Low Income Assistance Programs*, DOE/RG 0039 (July 1980), p. 9.

27. The low number reflects the low estimates made by the Department of Energy; the high number is taken from studies by the American Gas Association.

28. The price of gas will have a dominant effect on the rate of conversion. If gas is only plentiful because of the availability of high-priced alternatives, this rate of conversions will be much slower.

29. M. H. Ross and R. H. Williams, *Drilling for Oil and Gas in Our Buildings*, Center for Energy and Environmental Studies, Princeton University (1979).

30. Oak Ridge National Laboratory, *The Regional Transportation Energy Conservation Date Book* (1978).

31. Aspen Institute, *Options for Fueling America's Transportation* (1980).

32. New England Energy Congress, p. 43.

33. Ibid., p. 269.

REFORMULATION
OF THE CITIES

Kenneth Geiser

THERE IS an urban renaissance taking place in Lowell, Massachusetts. A decade ago this city was a deteriorated and depressed mill town: the most significant New England relic of the flight of the traditional textile industries to the South, characterized by vacant mill buildings, high unemployment, poorly maintained residential neighborhoods, and an aging business district losing market to outlying shopping centers. Today the "Spindle City" mills are being renovated and reopened as museums, the industrial canals are being redeveloped as recreational waterways, and the downtown is being renewed with new sidewalks and parks. Downtown merchants are reinvesting with commercial renovations, a new hotel is planned, and central residential neighborhoods are witnessing an in-migration of young middle-class professionals. Wang Laboratories has recently completed a corporate office complex outside the downtown. The rate of unemployment in Lowell has declined significantly over the past three years, and last year over a quarter of a million tourists visited Lowell Historical Park. Urban planners attending the World Cities Conference recently toured Lowell, a shining example of the newest form of city renewal.

Ninety miles west of Lowell lies Chicopee, Massachusetts. Chicopee is not witnessing a renaissance. Chicopee is an old textile and tool manufacturing city developed along the flats of the Chicopee and Connecticut rivers. It is neither pleasant to look at nor economically vital. In July of 1980 Chicopee Uniroyal, the city's largest industrial plant, closed—leaving some 1600 workers with no readily available job opportunities. This economic blow only added to the depressive character of a city where already one out of fourteen was on AFDC welfare. Not surprisingly Chicopee is increasingly the home of an aging population with an overrepresentation of low income black and Hispanic residents.

The increasing decline of cities like Chicopee and the remarkable resurgence of cities like Lowell mark the enormous variability of urban dynamics in New England. For every city like Waterbury, Pittsfield, or Lawrence that struggles with plant closings, diminishing tax base, obsolete infrastructure, and little private investment, there exists a Boston, Hartford, or Stamford where significant public and private investments are producing gleaming downtowns and gentrified neighborhoods or a Newburyport, Portsmouth, or New Bedford where a combination of historic restoration and summer tourism is creating livable, culturally rich, historical jewels. Life in one New England city and the potential for its future quality can be as radically different from another New England city as it can from a city in the far West. Yet through an intricate and carefully tied knot, the future of all New England cities and towns is bound together. Urban life in New England has a particular character, a particular harshness and richness, as well as a particular set of future options, which leaves no room for the improvement of one city without serious consequences for all.

Prophecies about the future abound. The industrial development boosters promise renewed cities built on high technology and service industries bolstered by rich recreation and cultural institutions. Others foresee a depleted garrison economy made up of only those people and services needed to maintain the infrastructure of New England for the yearly flood of vacation-seeking tourists who come for sport, relaxation, and a dip in the national heritage. The quaint New England village, the historic markets and fishing ports, the rejuvenated mills filled seasonally with artisans and craftspeople come to resemble a natural-based Disneyland, marketed more than really functioning, and dependent to the utmost on the whims of the leisure dollar. Somewhere between these extremes the future lies.

This paper explores the current conditions of cities and city life in New England, examines probable changes in the future, and suggests choices that could favorably or adversely affect that future. The paper is constructed on a model of urban development that portrays the quality of life as a result of formal aspects of urban organization. These formal aspects are both horizontal—that is, the spatial and physical distribution of people, resources, services, and amenities—and vertical—that is, the social, political, and cultural integration of institutions, practices, and traditions. In turn, this formal organization is based on more fundamental economic and value-directed conditions. The paper begins with the more fundamental conditions, follows with changes in the formal organization, and leads to suggestions for affecting favorably the future quality of New England urban life.

The Given Form of New England Cities

New England in this last half of the twentieth century is largely an urbanized society. Seventy-six percent of the population lives in urban areas, and though city and country can still be differentiated spatially, the quality of rural life for most New Englanders resembles the quality of urban life more than it differs from it. Except in the far northern reaches of the region, most rural New Englanders move in and out of city life, using city services and enjoying city resources as easily as do their urban kin. Thus in a discourse on the future quality of urban life in New England, particularly in considering nonspatial aspects, what is written of city life is true of life throughout the region.

New England is noted for its rich settlement pattern of quiet rural hamlets, industrial river mill towns, and bustling seaport cities. This settlement pattern is more a result of New England's past development than its current functioning, and a quick review of that past will help build a base for thoughts about its future.

The urban organization of New England is actually the result of three or four waves of economic development, each fixing and constraining those which followed. The location and hierarchy of New England cities and towns arose during the early colonial agrarian and mercantile developmental period. The spotty distribution of settlements is a result of agrarian determinants regarding the sufficiency of soil and topography and the proximity of market centers and religious institutions for servicing and shepherding the farm-based population. The hierarchy of settlements where some grew dense and central and others lagged as hamlets arises largely from the trade routes and differential transportation opportunities capitalized on by early commercial entrepreneurs and later institutionalized by public investments and commitments. The river valleys, frequent seaports, canals, and turnpikes drew investments into select communities like Boston, Newburyport, New London, and Springfield, and the growth that followed differentiated these communities and augmented their functions and identity.

The rise of industrial capitalism during the nineteenth century built upon this settlement framework and transformed the visual and social character of the region's cities. For it is really the Industrial Revolution with its mechanization, its mill wheels, its turbines, its railroads, its trolleys, its ability to recruit and deploy labor, and its resultant concentration of capital and talent that shapes the physical plant and ethnic diversity of today's New England cities. The mill towns, the port cities, the row houses, tenements and triple deckers, the libraries, churches, municipal edifices and schoolhouses, the sewer lines, water works and transit lines, the parks, boulevards and promenades—all set the visual style of New England cities and clearly set them aside from the quaint common-focused villages of the earlier period. Industrial capitalism both built cities and ravaged them. It not only produced the complexity, permanence, and density of New England cities, but eventually all but abandoned them, leaving behind the patina of deterioration and decline that distinguishes their urban ambience. The mobility of developmental capital which characterizes capitalist development has a long history of threatening the quality of New England city life.

The most recent wave of urban development followed the closing of World War II. The corporate developmental wave has united financial and service institutions with governmental agencies to alter both the fringes and centers of cities. The fringe results are evident in the single-family household suburbs, the freeways and airports, the commercial strips and shopping centers, and the industrial parks and belts—all dependent on automobiles and cheap energy. In the deteriorated heart of the industrial cities the state and developer met to clear the artifacts of earlier development phases and renew and redevelop with new glass office towers, brick plazas, concrete parking garages, and covered pedestrian malls.

The form of the region's cities today is a result of these past waves of development. Cities located in the seventeenth century, differentiated in the eighteenth century, and constructed in the nineteenth century rested in aging neglect until the latter half of this century. With much that is fixed and given, built and determined, we are now passing through a period of reordering, redeveloping, and rehabilitating. In terms of geography, the built environment, and our social and political institutions, we work within the constraints and opportunities of this legacy of the past. New England cities bear an unforgiving rigidness—a solidity that drags at change and makes for rearrangements only with great cost. Yet for those immersed in the daily life of these matured settlements, we are pointedly aware of the significant changes just completed, in process, or soon anticipated. The quality of life is anything but stale or tranquil. There is a vitality, a turgidity, a lunging forward that suggests that this developmental period is anything but over. Ahead lies yet a different quality of urban life in New England and current changes suggest the outlines of its emergent structure.

Current Developmental Conditions

Urban development is a complex process. Structural elements of social organization fuel processes that open opportunities for development, but the specific directions and forms are the product of individual and collective choices. Projections on the future of urban life in New England must consider both structural and willful factors. The quality of city life in New England is based on formal aspects of urban organization, both spatial and sociopolitical, and these in turn are based on four fundamental conditions: (a) demographic trends, (b) resource availability, (c) private investment decisions, and (d) public policy changes. These four conditions set both the environmental context and the behavorial possibilities of urban growth and change. We will consider each in turn.

Demographics.   Since the late nineteenth century there has been a continuous movement of people out of New England, first to the Midwest and, more recently, to the South and far West. This outmigration picked up relative speed following World War II as the availability of jobs, cheap land, and resources and a fluid social climate attracted New Englanders to the warm Sun Belt regions. Between 1970 and 1977 the New England region experienced a net in-migration of only 0.4 percent, compared to 5.8 percent for the South during this same period. General population growth further skewed the results of this disequilibrium. The total population of New England grew by 12.5 percent between 1960 and 1970—less than the national average of 13 percent—while the total population of the far West region was growing by 18.7 percent.

The cities of New England have been further affected by the nation-wide changes in metropolitan and non-metropolitan population dynamics. During the 1970's the national rate of metropolitan population growth fell below the rate for non-metropolitan areas, reversing a decades-long trend of increasing metropolitanization of the population. Between 1970 and 1974 the twenty largest metropolitan areas in the country experienced a net out-migration of 1.2 million people, while non-metropolitan areas witnessed a net in-migration of 1.5 million. Although significant in New England, this reversal has been less marked here, where the urbanized percentage of population has been constant since 1930, than elsewhere. Yet the effects are evident. Lewiston, Maine, which ten years ago accounted for half of the state's metropolitan population, in 1980 accounted for 42 percent, and Portland now accounts for 36 percent of its metropolitan population, compared with 54 percent in 1950.

These population shifts can be seen dramatically in the continuing exodus from the center cities of metropolitan areas. The long-term suburbanization of urban populations is notably draining inner city areas. The Boston area serves as a useful example. In 1950 the Boston proper population stood at 801,000. By 1975 that population had fallen to 638,000, a decrease of 20 percent over the twenty-five year period. Somerville and Chelsea, both inner Boston suburbs, experienced even more dramatic population decreases during this period. The overall picture for the metropolitan area inside the Route 128 beltway for these twenty-five years was one of decline—4.4 percent. Yet even inside Route 128 the population decrease was not ubiquitous. During this period Woburn experienced a 72 percent population increase and Lexington's population grew by 87 percent. But the major areas of growth lay outside of Route 128, particularly to the west, along the South Shore, and in singular communities like Topsfield, with a population increase over twenty-five years of 319 percent, and Sudbury, where the population doubled with each decade. What is new in this population dynamic is that smaller non-metropolitan areas, particularly towns, are reversing their role as exporters of people. New Englanders appear to be re-attracted to the smaller non-metropolitan towns, like Brattleboro, Lebanon, Athol, and Barre.

These two dynamics—out-migration from New England and out-migration from cities—have resulted in slow growth and actual population decline for New England cities. While the Boston metropolitan area experienced a 13 percent increase in population between 1950 and 1970, during the past ten years the metropolitan population declined by 4.7 percent. Metropolitan Portland lost 5.4 percent of its population during the most recent decade. Compare these figures with those for Phoenix, where the metropolitan population grew 192 percent between 1950 and 1970 and 31 percent between 1970 and 1980.

Within this declining population other demographic dynamics set the stage for urban transformations. The population of New England as a whole is aging. Increases in life expectancy coupled with a declining birth rate and an out-migration of younger families and single youths has produced a population noticeably large in older and elderly people. This is particularly true in the cities and towns of the upland areas, which are more distant from major employment centers. For instance, 18.6 percent of the 1970 population of Augusta and 19.4 percent of the 1970 population of Barre was over 60 years of age. Of the younger population there is an exaggerated cohort of people now in their late twenties and mid-thirties. This is a major period of family formation and child-birth. But it is almost as much a period of family dissolution as formation, and the result is that in aggregate there is a sizable population of single parent families and divorced or separated individuals, both among middle-income and low-income households. The consequence is that household size is decreasing and the number of households is increasing.

Resource Availability.   The material resources for maintaining a high quality of urban life in New England are increasingly costly and less available. Because New England is precariously dependent on supplies from outside the region, substitutions of local resources for imports is not easy. In some cases—for example, construction—wood and concrete can be substituted for steel and plastic, which are less indigenous, but this requires changes in marketing and distribution. Difficult as such changes are, rapidly rising costs are forcing increased resource conservation and in some cases direct substitutions. In the case of food, substitutions are already in process. There is a renewed interest in New England farm produce and the maintenance of productive agricultural areas in all of the states. Each year the number of family gardens increases. Within the last several years direct farmer markets have sprung up in most of of the region's cities, where local produce is provided more cheaply than that trucked in to supermarkets from outside the region. Last year supermarket chains in Maine and Vermont greatly increased their seasonal purchase of local produce both as a support to local rural economies and as a means of competing with the direct farmer markets.

In other cases this substitution of local resources for imports is more constrained. Consider water. During 1980 serious spot water supply emergencies were declared in thirty Massachusetts communities, with severe conditions reported in Brockton, Pittsfield, Acton, Lee, Attleboro, Rockport, and Gloucester. In Brockton all outdoor water uses were banned, pumps were lowered in Silver Lake reservoir, and old abandoned wells were reactivated to stave off a major crisis. A moderate precipitation deficit of five to ten inches as experienced during that year reveals how precarious urban water supplies are. Although the large regional systems of Hartford, Providence, Bridgeport, and the Boston Metropolitan District can probably withstand one or two years of dry weather, most cities are critically dependent on high annual precipitation. This is particularly true where chemical contamination has forced the closing of source aquifers. Nearly one third of the communities in Massachusetts have experienced serious water-supply contamination problems. In the past year major losses have occurred in Acton, Massachusetts, where 40 percent of the water supply was lost; Bedford, Massachusetts, where 80 percent was lost; and Lincoln, Rhode Island, where 45 percent was lost. These losses, coupled with low precipitation, place serious constraints on once profligate water use in New England industries and residences.

Furthermore, the future of energy resources places serious constraints on urban development and the quality of life. Currently in New England 63 percent of all regional energy sources is imported oil. This compares most unfavorably with 18 percent for the nation as a whole. Also, energy costs in New England are 26 percent higher than the national average. The region lacks large resources of fossil fuels and is remote from the nation's coal and oil fields. Nuclear power, which has operated in New England since 1961 and currently supplies 32 percent of the region's electricity (compared to 12 percent for the nation) has served to protect New England from an even greater dependence on energy imports; yet rising construction costs, environmental and safety concerns, and political controversy have all but stopped further development of the nuclear contribution. Increasingly, conservation programs and small local efforts at renewable energy substitutions are developing, but such contributions are still relatively small.

Projections for the immediate future point to increased constraint and rising costs. In summary:

—Oil costs will continue to rise. Although availability will most likely continue, the consistency of supply will be uneven and costs will continue upward.

—Nuclear power, which currently supplies 9 percent of the region's total energy supply will not continue its recent rate of increase, because new plant construction will be slow, limited, and costly.

—Gasoline will follow oil costs, with some unevenness of supply and increasing costs due to both increases in market costs and taxes.

—Natural gas which currently supplies 8 percent of the regional supply will become increasingly scarce and costly, rising to the level of oil.

—Alternative new-technology energy and coal will provide some substitution for more expensive sources. Alternative solar, wind, and hydro sources will also increase, though at a fairly low rate.

—Conservation and inflation will continue to decrease demand, but the margin between demand reduction and supply increase will occasionally provide hardships, especially for those on low or fixed incomes.

What this means is that energy will be an increasingly costly part of the equation that determines the quality of life and its acceptability in New England. Hard winters set on home owners who remain unprepared will encourage the long-term exodus from the region of those not otherwise bound to New England by job specialization, kinship, friendship, or particular affection for the area's unique amenities.

Private Investment Decisions. Such resource costs seriously affect private investment decisions. There is perhaps no more sensitive barometer to the rise and fall of confidence in New England than the subtle fluctuations in private market-investment decisions. An historical examination of private investment behavior reveals a re-formulation of economic activities in New England—much of which has been in evidence for decades. Although the many abandoned mills that characterize the downtown areas of New England cities testify to the long trend of disinvestment in textiles, clothing, and footwear, New England cities still retain a surprising vitality in specialized and custom clothing production. Maine still claims more shoe companies than any other state in the Union, though increasingly these firms are abandoning downtowns for nearby suburbs.

Nevertheless, new industrial development in New England over the past decade has been relatively slow. There is widespread concern over the effects of plant closings, but the actual number of closings has been small. Instead, the current slow growth of industrial activity is due more to reductions in the number of new enterprises, the reluctance of existing firms to expand existing New England plants, and the failure of New England to attract branch plants of major national corporations.

Construction activity has also slowed over the past decade. New housing starts began to fall off in 1972, and not since then have they regained the level common in the previous decade. Commercial construction contracts and public work projects have shown a marked decrease since 1970. Tighter credit and less federal investment in New England during this past decade has meant that major construction projects like highways, airports, office complexes, and shopping malls have been less frequent.

Yet not all private enterprise has been slowed. While the dollar volume on rail freight continues a long decline, truck transport volumes are increasing. The geographic dispersion of production facilities and retail operations has proved beneficial to truck trans-

188   KENNETH GEISER

port. With increasing reliance on foreign sources for energy and for goods like cars and appliances, ocean cargo transport has also shown growth. Containerization facilities like those at Boston and Portland have made the truck-boat transhipment system a vital new locus of investment.

Military contracts continue to spur Massachusetts and Connecticut economies, particularly in the aircraft industries. The instrument and light electronic industry around Boston has grown at rapid rates, even during the recessionary period of 1974–75. The apparel and leather industries around Providence appear to have done better than the national average during the past decade, and Rhode Island is also developing a strong instrument-manufacturing base. The computer, micro-communication, aircraft, and defense-production industries have all experienced renewed investment. The major production areas around Boston, Springfield, New London, Bridgeport, and New Haven have witnessed a resurgence, with promise of vitality that matches that of the 1960s. Employment opportunities for skilled engineers is high, and lesser skilled technicians are easily finding work. Massachusetts currently exhibits the second highest employment rate in the country. Much of this mini-boom is determined by increased defense spending and a slow-down in high-technology production areas in Florida and California. Moderate growth continues in the services and in professional, managerial, and proprietor jobs as well. White collar jobs in insurance, banking, law, health care, and government have increased over the past decade. As New England continues to grow as a finance, education, and health-care area, upper middle-class professionals continue to find Boston, New Haven, Hanover, Providence, and Hartford attractive places to live.

Employment possibilities have been increasing in New England, although not as rapidly as elsewhere. Between 1970 and 1977 non-agricultural employment increased by 8.4 percent in New England, compared to 16.2 percent for the nation as a whole and 25.9 percent for the South alone. This in part explains the regional exodus of the New England population. Between 1970 and 1976 some 20,000 New England workers left the region.

Although the regional economy has slowly expanded, New England wage earners have not fared nearly as well during the past decade. Relative to the nation as a whole and the rising cost of living, they have lost their once high status. Not only have wages not kept pace, but overtime and working hours have also decreased. Along with these losses has come an aversion to unions. The once heavily union-organized Massachusetts labor force is now only 24.6 percent unionized. Union strength at the bargaining table as well as politically has been increasingly eroded.

Unemployment also has hit New England workers hard. Between 1970 and 1975 the unemployment rate was between 6.1 and 10.3 percent. During this same period the national rate lay between 4.9 and 8.5 percent. Boston alone counted 60,200 persons unemployed in recessionary 1975, a number that represented a 12.8 percent unemployment rate. Unemployment has been worst in central cities, especially among young and minority persons.

Public Policy Choices.   Public policy is the fourth major determinant of urban development. Many observers note how federal policy has discouraged private investment in New England and, particularly, New England cities. Increases in federal aid to depressed New England cities through revenue sharing, Community Development Block Grants, Urban Development Action Grants, and Section 8 housing subsidies of the U.S. Housing Act have not made up for the loss of defense contracts, the virtual completion of the Interstate Highway system, the depletion allowances and deregulation on energy supplies, and the rapid inflation of the past decade. New England has suffered under federal administrations more committed to Western and Southern regional interests, and the current administration only exaggerates this trend.

Locally, government services and expenditures have continued to rise even though the rate of growth of tax revenues has consistently declined since 1975. The fiscal squeeze which seriously threatened Boston, Springfield, and Bridgeport in the mid 1970's is now more ubiquitous and serious, as Massachusetts municipalities face the consequences of the so-called "Proposition 2½" tax-limitation referendum. Service cutbacks and threats of default, once only a big city problem, have now spread throughout the Commonwealth. At this writing it is far too early to guess at the results, but it is clear that public services, including school systems and fire companies, may be fighting for their very existence. Throughout New England, credit, bond capacity, and public subsidies have been tightened.

Anxiety over fiscal collapse has meant a much more conservative approach to expanding urban debt, and both capital and revenue bonds have been more cautiously advocated.

Over the past decade few cities have embarked on major capital investments. Pollution control facilities, heavily underwritten by federal programs, were an exception. Instead, capital campaigns primarily targeted the upgrading and "rounding-out" of physical infrastructure. Water systems and sewer systems were replaced, public buildings refurbished, municipal lighting plants upgraded, and transit systems, such as Boston's, extended and modernized.

A more cautious approach to program development has also developed. Existing services have been expanded more slowly and new services postponed. Administrative streamlining in government structure, budgeting, and monitoring has paralleled efforts to increase efficiency and productivity and decrease graft and malfeasance. There has recently been an increasing effort by both services and planning to contract with private vendors rather than to increase public overhead. This, plus an increasing fee-for-service approach to certain previously free services like concerts, parks, and libraries, has resulted in a growing network of private firms whose primary contracts are with local or state governments.

Increasingly the public sector is viewed with skepticism. The recent tax caps, bond rejections, and demand for deregulation reveal a bitter popular sense that the promise of public-sector intervention has been broken. Governments that were intended as mechanisms for expressing the people's will increasingly have become the instruments for serving the people's needs, and in so doing they have proven incapable of keeping pace. The personal tax outlay for funding what appears to be a doomed effort now breeds resentment. The public sector is increasingly operating from an austere and defensive position.

Trends in Urban Form

Demographics, resource availability, private investment decisions, public policy choices—these are the conditions of urban development. Together they provide the genesis of many different spatial and social futures. The exact configurations of these mixes—the horizontal and vertical consequences—are already perceptible.

Horizontal Form. During the past two decades there have been on-going horizontal shifts that are gradually redistributing the location of various economic activities and residential groups. Much of this redistribution is composed of movements between city centers and their peripheries. This center-periphery reformulation is affecting where people go to work, go to shop, go to play or receive services, and where they will and will not be able to purchase or rent housing. Several of these trends are worthy of note.

The de-industrialization of the center cities. Old mills stand vacant at the heart of many of New England's cities. Urban renewal has demolished innumerable vacant industrial blocks, and often the land has remained equally vacant. The industrial centers of New London, Merrimack, and Haverhill are dominated by parking lots and vacant land. Private investment decisions have favored outlying suburban and rural locations over inner city areas, where crime, parking, congestion, and difficult real estate configurations have discouraged consideration. The result has been not only abandonment of downtown locations but, with the encouragement and inducement of public policy investment, the development of suburban-ring industrial developments, first evidenced by Boston's famed Route 128 beltway. While Boston expands its second such industrial beltway on the Interstate 495 corridor, other cities, like Hartford, Springfield, and Portland, develop similar rings. Many medium-sized cities, like Norwich, Taunton, Fitchburg, and Nashua, have opened outlying industrial parks that have also helped to deplete their central areas of traditional firms. Not only has new industrial development spurned the city in favor of suburban parks and beltway rings—an increasing amount of new industrial-plant development is occurring in the distinctly rural areas of New England. A boom in new production plants has occurred in York County, Maine, Rockingham County, New Hampshire, and Chittenden County, Vermont. Rural locations like these are attractive to industrial developers because of lower wage expectations among rural workers, a more consistent supply of nonunionized labor, low property taxes, and easily available tracts of land at attractive prices.

The decommercialization of the center cities. As industry flees the older urban cores, commercial activities follow suit. Vast new shopping centers have been constructed along the beltways around Boston and along the arterial highways extending out from cities like

Worcester, Burlington, Portland, Waterbury, and Bridgeport. Enclosed malls, magnet department stores and discount marts, free
parking, and easy proximity to the suburban shoppers have made
shopping centers heavy competitors to downtown retail areas. Commercial investments in suburban areas have surpassed investments
in inner-city centers, further eroded downtown attractiveness, and
increased shopper preference for outlying centers. Decisions by retail giants like Filene's and Jordan Marsh in Boston, discount marts
like Zayre's, King's, Caldor, and K-Mart, and smaller chains like The
Gap, Waldenbooks, Thom McAn, and C.V.S. have favored outlying
centers for new investments. The result is that commuting to shop,
which historically drew shoppers in town on Thursday nights and
Saturdays, now draws shoppers out to the suburbs. The central cities are left with older, smaller, often locally owned stores with a depleted clientele and a disrupted image. Only in major office centers
like Boston, Portland, Hartford, and Providence have large retail investments kept pace with their outlying siblings.

   The service segregation of the center city. As industrial and commercial activities leave the central urban areas or fail to reinvest
there, the inner-city centers become more segregated in function.
It is not so much that financial, banking, and professional activities
have been drawn downtown—they always were downtown. Rather,
they have remained as the residual activities and in the absence of
growth in other activities have tended increasingly to dominate the
downtown area. Office buildings, often tall and glass-skinned, have
become the twentieth-century symbol of a city's core. Government
and entertainment have become the other functions of downtown
life. As government services have grown and developed their own
bureaus and departments, professional administrators have replaced
politicians as the chief employees of city and state governments.
Downtowns in Concord, Montpelier, Augusta, and Hartford are
filled with government workers who, like their sibling professionals
in the financial and legal services, come downtown only to work.
The daytime life of such cities is dominated by the coffee breaks and
lunchtime activities of employees seeking food and drink. By six or
seven o'clock the din of activity is gone, and the streets take on a
vacant, occasionally threatening ambience. Only nighttime entertainment remains vital in small city downtowns—bars, clubs, restaurants, and theaters provide the bright lights and economic vi-

tality of the post-work-day urban core. Larger cities recently have experienced a boon to downtown night life. As public auditoriums like Springfield's or Portland's Convention Centers add to newly revived entertainment districts like Portland's Old Port Exchange or Boston's Quincy Market, and the new Symphony Hall of Worcester and Opera House of Boston add to the rise of legitimate theaters in the downtowns, the center city has become a segregated enclave for the daytime office worker and a nighttime enclave for entertainment with only vestiges of older functions.

The revaluation of historical artifacts and cultural uniqueness. The emergence of a new downtown catering to the occupations and tastes of middle-income professionals has spurred a rediscovery of the rich heritage of the older areas of New England cities. Increasingly older buildings have become more valuable, nineteenth-century architecture and districts have become worthy of protection, and rehabilitation and local ethnic customs and institutions have become economic attractions. The waterfronts of Newburyport, New Bedford, New London, and Newport have become national landmarks and regional assets. Affluent families—particularly young and childless families—have increasingly been reattracted to these older districts, often bidding up housing values and displacing lower-income families. In smaller cities such "gentrification" is encouraged, while in larger cities the displacement is much bemoaned but seldom halted, except where those displaced provide ethnic uniqueness to the area. Thus efforts are made to protect and encourage ethnic neighborhoods like Boston's Italian North End, Boston's Chinatown, or Lewiston's French Cathedral Hill. Festivals, fairs, and art and cultural shows are used to call attention to ethnic diversity and exhibit the unmixed character of New England's urban neighborhoods. Ethnic quaintness has a marketable quality, and city boosters and neighborhood residents alike feel there is benefit in some commercialization.

The redistribution of persons of nonconventional life styles. The central cities of New England have long been the location of the vagrant, the widowed elderly, the drug abuser, the prostitute, and the immigrant. Where once the marginal members of society were pushed from the colony's tiny hamlets, there has been a long history, particularly in port cities, of driving the nonconventional into the grey areas of lowest housing value. The central cities today still serve as the home of those most marginal and deviant. Along with poorer families exist those who cross legal boundaries in pursuit of property, money, or drugs. Today as central institutional care for the mentally abnormal, the delinquent, the criminal, and the handicapped has fallen into disrepute, the central cities have become the home of the deinstitutionalized. Halfway houses, out-patient clinics, and congregate living centers have been established in most downtown locations to serve those who otherwise are attempting conventional life styles. The transitional neighborhoods that have long been the home of immigrants adjusting to new social expectations have become the socialization site for many who might otherwise be separated and confined.

Vertical Form. Along with these horizontal shifts have come vertical dynamics which are altering family structure, religious and political institutions, and the means of government. Whereas the spatial dynamic is characterized by center-periphery redistribution, the vertical dynamic is characterized by fragmentive-integrative reformulations. While family, community, and political integration is eroding, media, corporate, and associational affiliation is increasing. The most significant of these trends are easy to note.

The reorganization of the family. Although the large nuclear and extended family as the norm of the past is overromanticized (even in the nineteenth century it was common only in rural and lower-class immigrant life), there is clear demographic evidence of increasing numbers of previously married adults with children and never-married single adults in the urban population. Divorce, separation, single-parent families and childless couples have all shown significant increases. The two-parent family is less likely to endure intact through the trials of marriage. Urban New England's housing stock typically designed for nuclear family households is undergoing major transformations as group resident, single person, and single parent households attempt to modify legally and physically the structures from previous eras. In some inner-city cases whole neighborhoods, such as Boston's South End, Portland's Munjoy Hill, and New Haven's East Side, are emerging as locations of single, single-parent, and childless households.

A second factor in the transformation of kinship patterns has been the automobile and the concomitant ease of transportation. First, ease of transportation has meant that relatives are more comfortable about moving farther from each other without jeopardizing family bonds and, second, relatives that must for employment or other reasons move far from relatives can retain close relations through frequency of visits. The first factor tends to draw families apart and the second factor compensates for the apartness. This has been particularly noticeable in relation to New England's rural to city migration when youths seeking employment or schooling move relatively long distances without jeopardizing family bonds. The automobile has also altered the integrity of urban ethnic neighborhoods. Thus oriental residents of Boston's Chinatown can move to Sharon and other suburbs without loss of family or shopping continuity, and North Enders move to Reading and beyond without loss of close Boston family ties.

The rationalization and depolitization of the governmental sector. Planning, budgeting, data processing, and professional management increasingly turn state and local governments into effective but inaccessible vehicles for the administration of public services. The advancement of managerial professionals into agencies with programs that rationalize decision-making and distributional issues decreases the dominance of parochial and immediate interests over public policy and increases the concerns for long-term economic viability in maintaining the public sector. The consequence is that only major policy decisions raised to the level of media issues are open to electoral or civic debate. Personal accountability is diminished by bureaucratic procedures, and decision making is increasingly insulated from public review. This process with both its efficiency benefits and accessibility limits is not likely to reverse as the public sector is further constrained by rising costs and diminishing revenues. Productivity and planning are becoming central watchwords of effective public administration.

The mass culturization of leisure-time activities. New England cities long noted for superior, high-culture institutions are witnessing a renewed popularity of cultural, recreational, and entertainment activities. Local symphonies and art museums have opened or been expanded in Worcester, Springfield, Burlington, and other mid-size cities. Several local sports teams, particularly in soccer and hockey, have been formed outside Boston, and the civic auditoriums in Portland, Worcester, Springfield, and Providence have become attractive stops for large-audience touring performers reaching beyond Boston. Museums, craft shows, legitimate theaters, and movie houses have all noted expanded markets. Activities which once catered more to elite communities increasingly have mass appeal. Nor is all this popularity merely a big-city phenomenon. Traditional rural sports like hiking, skiing, and boating are also noting high popularity. Health clubs, tennis clubs, handball, and pool clubs are proving to be profitable ventures in Bangor, Fitchburg, Concord, and Waterbury.

Each of these cultural and recreational enterprises alters, commercializes, but reinforces associational and socializing bonds among family and friends. Beyond the reach of any of these enterprises remains the phenomenal integrative impact of the electronic media. Radio and television reach into almost every home in urban New England. The effects on childhood development, responses to humor and tragedy, and political attitudes is the subject of countless research efforts. Whatever the range and depth of these effects at integrating and homogenizing, the future will not diminish their roles.

The re-energization of spiritual and moral enterprises. The significant growth in church and revival attendance particularly among fundamentalist sects is only the tip of a broad sweep of traditionalism in values. The renewed concern over family values, abortion, capital punishment, deviance, and nonconventional life styles is part of a national response to the rapid social upheavals of recent decades. Such responses signal an attempt to reintegrate a fragmented value code and find moral stability in an increasingly amoral and secularized world. While legal and popular behavior codes have been increasingly liberalized, New Englanders have held on to several morally based traditions, like Sunday commercial bans, public liquor stores, local option on liquor permits, sexual conduct laws, and restriction on gambling, pornography, and drug use, though often as much for economic as for moral reasons. The future of these trends is hard to predict. History suggests that they are cyclical but offers no particular time schedule.

The disenchantment with public services. New England cities introduced the nation to the public school, and for a long time it held sway as the primary public service. The common school, the school for americanization of the immigrant and socialization of the child, has come increasingly under skepticism during the past decade. Particularly in the larger cities, where race and class differences are extreme and volatile, those who can afford to are enrolling their young in parochial or private schools. Old private academies are experiencing a renaissance even as their tuitions escalate, and throughout the suburbs small, new private schools have been founded and are flourishing. The case is most apparent in Massachusetts, where recent waves of school bond rejections have been exacerbated by a serious tax cap and the removal of school board budget autonomy. There the die has been cast for a serious deterioration in the public schools. As deteriorated schools fail to retain good teaching staffs, they begin a self-destructive spiral where further erosion of public confidence leads to deeper revenue cuts. Institutions long considered sacred may soon become institutions for the disadvantaged and uninstructed. Again history provides little insight, and the future is vague. But trends that are now apparent in schools may be harbingers of the fate of such other common-use public services as libraries, parks, and hospitals. Increasingly we may be developing a two-class service system—high quality private services for those of means and poorly financed public services for those without.

Summary of Trends

In summary we can expect that the major metropolitan areas will not significantly expand through urban dispersion. The rising costs of commuting and the even more significant costs of new residential development in the outer suburbs will be major factors in constraining expansion and intensifying the densification of center city areas. The neighborhoods of central cities in metropolitan areas will see an increase in housing units through new construction and conversions of older larger units to more and smaller units. Smaller units will follow the needs of smaller, often single-person, childless, or single-parent households. Thus while housing units may increase in older central cities, populations will grow quite slowly. This same pattern will also be noticeable in smaller metropolitan areas. Yet in these urban areas there will also be modest but continual growth through suburban expansion as new construction and land costs become lower and commuting costs become less constraining.

The commercial reformulation of the central-city downtowns will continue. Particularly in smaller metropolitan areas only modest production and distribution enterprises will remain downtown. There and in larger central business districts the white-collar professional, financial, and governmental enterprises will come to dominate along with the service activities that support these functions. Tourism and entertainment will also become a major downtown activity in cities where heritage, geography, or entrepreneurship provide the kind of activities that attract the leisure-time market.

Major industry will continue to abandon center-city locations in favor of outlying sites around smaller metropolitan areas where downtowns cannot compete with the land values, tax advantages, infrastructure, and lower-wage labor availability of suburban and rural locations. In contrast, some central areas of the major metropolitan areas may see significant industrial reinvestment precisely because in those areas central cities can compete through tax abatements, infrastructure investments, real estate packaging, and the availability of low-skilled, low-wage workers.

Capital investment in the construction of new infrastructure will remain modest by recent standards. Investments in transit, parks, utilities, civic facilities, and roads will be focused on improving and "rounding out" existing capital stock. Fixed-rail passenger transit around Boston and between major metropolitan centers will be expanded and improved while highway construction will focus more on upgrading and maintaining existing facilities. Bus, van, and other highway-dependent public transit will expand as private transportation costs show significant increases.

Inequality will endure in New England. Class bias in terms of educational resources, employment opportunities, the enjoyment of public and private services, and opportunities to achieve wealth will continue to be the norm. How broad a range exists between those who have plenty and those who have little will be greatly affected by private investment decisions and public policy choices.

Although class relations will remain reasonably stable in the foreseeable future, race and ethnic relations may show more marked changes. As new immigrants arrive in city labor structures, they tend to push upward previous immigrants. Those whose skin color and cultural habits—Armenians, Greeks, Portugese, Chinese, and Franco-Americans—differ least from the norm will find easier class ascendency than blacks. Yet except in racially charged cities like

Boston, blacks will slowly and gradually move socially and geo-graphically into previously white strata and communities. The sharp rise of Hispanic, Near Eastern, and Caribbean populations indicates that in time they will occupy the lowest rungs of the economic ladder. Yet these trends will not affect all New England cities equally. Some will benefit more, and some will pay out more.

The hierarchy of cities established early on in the region's first wave of economic development and augmented by successive waves of development thereafter provides a dominance framework that sets some cities at a greater advantage than others to attract and maintain capital investment. Competition among cities for resources will mean that cities that serve as the region's financial and administrative capitals, like Portland, Hartford, Providence, and, particularly, Boston, have more potential to prosper than the Chicopees and Waterburys of the region. Life in certain sections and suburbs of Boston will continue to be stunningly affluent even as life in many other parts of the city and region may be a testy struggle for survival.

Options for the Future

Where then does this lead? Observing trends is not the only means of prediction. Extrapolations tell nothing of surprises or willful efforts to alter courses of events. New Englanders are shaped by the quality of their life, but they also have the capacity to take hold of that quality and shape its development. For this they require a good sense of history and a willingness to explore and embrace options.

The legacy of New England's past is rich. The form, both vertical and horizontal, is well developed and fixed in heavy investments and traditions. This is not a developing region, it is a mature region, and, well adapted or not, its formal structure is largely in place. This means that New England cities have major advantages over cities in more rapidly developing regions because the infrastructure and traditional technique is largely in place. New and costly investments are required less here than in regions where basic infrastructure and traditions lag behind the requirements of rapid development. This heavy investment in capital structure and social and political tradition also means that changes—even changes that are immediately required—are and will be slow and cumbersome in coming. In this instance New England cities serve as models for the future of newer, more rapidly developing cities that will some day slow their growth and deepen their tradition.

The horizontal and to a large degree the vertical form of New England cities brings to the future a heavy legacy of eighteenth-century water-based commercial capitalism and, to an even greater degree, nineteenth-century industrial capitalism. Such forms are set and dare not be overlooked in projecting the future. Better yet, such forms provide a solid base for developing the future.

The current conditions of demographics and resource availability are also generally determined. Both will certainly change in the next fifty years, but the basic patterns are predictable and changes in them will occur slowly. The activity of private investment and public policy is far less predictable and far more open to willful intervention. If there are options for changing the future quality of life in urban New England, they are locked in the decisions of private investors and public-policy makers.

What options are there? To what degree can private and public choices create different futures for urban New England? Such questions clearly invoke issues of ideology. The values that New England has long stood for—independence, productive labor, democratic localism, private entrepreneurship, religious tolerance, and social liberty—still provide guidance for the future. It is possible in weaving divergent events to identify strands of ideology that remain emergent. For the sake of clarity three such perspectives can be identified, although as such they are purely abstractions. Here they are defined as the Competitive Market Approach, the Corporate Planning Approach, and the Community Self-Sufficiency Approach.

The Competitive Market Approach.   This perspective seeks to advance individual initiative and reduce social regulation. The call is to roll back public budgets, deregulate industrial and commercial enterprises, permit energy prices to rise to true market rates, rely on market scarcity to encourage limitation and conservation in the consumption of energy and goods, and cushion social inequities only where basic life sustenance is endangered. The massive support for the tax-limitation referendum in Massachusetts, the many school bond defeats, the conservative turnout in gubernatorial elections in New Hampshire, and the editorial commitment of the *Man-*

chester Union Leader all provide strong evidence for the range and acceptance of this approach.

The vision here is of cities with small housekeeping governments which do not conduct major social programs or try to correct tensions in social structure. Land would be developed more intensively with fewer controls. Some neighborhoods of the most disadvantaged would deteriorate to barely livable conditions, encouraging their residents to acquire jobs, work hard, and save enough so that eventually they might flee such miserable conditions. Critics of this approach fear that urban development will be disorganized, disharmonious, and without respect for the environment. Disadvantaged residents of inner-city neighborhoods, because of social, racial, and economic barriers, will become trapped in increasingly volatile reservations of violence and desperation. Effective control of such smoldering colonies will require enormous public effort by a garrison-style government that will eventually lead to municipal bankruptcy.

The Corporate Planning Approach. This perspective draws its adherents from the elites of the financial and advanced technology industrial communities. The thrust here is to deepen and broaden government involvement in economic and environmental management, but only through highly rationalized administrative planning. Tripartite public-private-union development strategies focused on sophisticated technology, tourism, health care, education, and other highly professional services would spur development. The disadvantaged would benefit from the "trickle down" and "spin off" residuals of a tertiary economy. For those most in jeopardy a welfare floor at a modest level would be maintained that would do least to interfere with the incentive to work. This form of corporate liberalism is found in the recommendations of the New England Regional Commission, the rhetoric of the Massachusetts High Technology Council, the prophecies of the First National Bank of Boston and the Federal Reserve Bank, and the editorial musings of the *Boston Globe*.

The vision is of a systematically integrated city where most decision-making is centralized in sophisticated government-industrial policy bodies. Neighborhoods are recycled in a well planned fashion that allows for both careful relocation of poorer households with minor upgrading and a sizable return on private investment. Inner cities would become pleasurable residential and cultural districts, and reasonable bargains would be struck between economic development, environmental regulation, and social control. The limits to this approach are found in the enormous amounts of capital that must be made available for simultaneous urban redevelopment and economic expansion and the unprecedented degree of consensus that must be achieved among parties that have traditionally and structurally been divided. Without massive federal interventions, the revenue and consensus must come from a coalition of the suburban middle class and the inner-city working class at a time when both groups have serious skepticism about expanded government and are resisting higher taxation.

The Community Self-Sufficiency Approach.   This view seeks in the resources of an organized community of residents and workers the means of achieving locally controlled, self-sufficient forms of community development. It calls for a smaller scale, more decentralized production, and a distribution system in which more goods and services are produced at the community level. Government is valued as a means of coordination, integration, and redistribution but not as a vehicle for special-interest protection. The market is preserved as a means of maintaining consumer choice and lowered costs, but cooperatives, neighborhood development corporations, and small private firms are encouraged wherever feasible. The support for this perspective grows from the cooperative networks, the small-town progressives, and the cultural and academic institutions distributed throughout the region. Media commitment to this vision is found in small alternative newspapers like the *Maine Times* and Amherst's *Valley Advocate*, and in local monthly magazines like *New Roots* and *Country Journal*. The goal is cities of decentralized but cooperative social units affirmatively addressing their own needs wherever possible with their own resources. Lower-income residents are provided training and resources but are expected to initiate and maintain their own self-development enterprises. Municipal and community ownership is expanded in order to capture and return the wealth that is needed to provide for new venture development and revenue redistribution. The limit here is the significant change in values and commitments that is required. It is not generally in the interests of those corporations and persons that currently hold power and affect private and public policy to turn over otherwise wealth-creating activities to local units. Furthermore, after decades of more centralized, corporate policy making, it is not easy to find or develop the capacity at the local level for effective economic development and enterprise maintenance.

Clearly each of these visions holds keys to determining the future. Proponents of each will continue to vie for their own agenda. The current antigovernment, antitax movement in many cities lays the groundwork for those who argue for competitive market policies, while the recent resurgence of economic vitality in Massachusetts, largely spurred by investments in new, advanced technology, encourages those who seek government-industry planning policies. The rapid creation of community development corporations in Massachusetts and the success of the food cooperatives throughout New England strengthens the political base of those who profess local self-reliance. From the mix of these ideological streams will emerge the guidance for shaping the future of New England cities. That future is irrevocably locked up in the only elements of formal determination we can really control: public and private policy. Whether New England's cities are to prosper as vital, lively self-generating centers or are to become simply outposts of a seasonal tourist economy, a colder version of the Caribbean Islands, should be the basis for political debate.

That debate would be best clarified if it could grapple with the issue of the expected quality of life in terms of regional social control and ownership. The history of New England's urban development outlined above is a history of boom and bust dependent upon the availability and commitment of capital—either public or private. Where capital has been available, urban structures have been developed and maintained to support a rich and varied quality of life. Where capital has not been available, the quality of life has suffered. But decisions over the availability and placement of capital have seldom been based on the expected quality of life. Instead investments have been primarily determined by private interests seeking to maximize private gain. Urban form has thus been an artifact of a process that held other private goals as more salient than the social result. Where the state has acted as developer or regulator, it has typically done so in order to benefit, not alter, this private-oriented process. Until we in New England are to claim that decisions about the availability and placement of capital and, in turn, the quality of our lives should be a locally determined, region-regarding, social process, we will maintain a life setting that is residual, vulnerable, and coldly dependent.

Implications for the Quality of Urban Life

What, then, can we say about the quality of urban life in the next fifty years? First, it will be like the last fifty years, tumultuous, varied, and filled with social and political activism. Second, it will be more socially directed. The public sector and the community-owned sectors will gradually expand and private actors, both citizens and firms, will increasingly look to the public institutions for guaranteeing their safety and well being. Third, it will be more constrained in its affluence and more conscious of its fragile base. Although there will continue to be a strong conservative, hesitant bent to approaching change, there will be an increasing focus on improving the local and immediate community. New England is a mature region. The future of its development lies in details and adjustment. Its cities will maintain and improve the quality of their residents' lives only by paying close attention to small-scale and immediate concerns. The boom of urban growth is well past not only because the population has stabilized and the frontiers of new urban expansion are elsewhere, but also because the hard, cold facts of energy and resource availability will not be reversed. To live in urban New England requires valuing its heritage, its varied environments, and its intimate community and family orientation more than the highest wage standards or easiest creature comforts. It will remain a fragile attraction, for many a national birthplace and vacation haven, but not a home. We who do choose to make New England our home may learn more of the inherent interconnectedness of all of us to one another and to the environment that sustains and pleases us.

CONTRIBUTORS

CARL REIDEL is the Daniel Clarke Sanders Professor of Environmental Studies and Director of the Environmental Program, University of Vermont. He is past president of the American Forestry Association, a forest resource policy consultant to a variety of government agencies, and frequent contributor to *American Forests* on resource policy issues.

THOMAS JORLING is Professor of Environmental Studies and Director of the Center for Environmental Studies, Williams College. He is former member of the President's Commission on the Agenda for the 8os, and was Assistant Administrator of the Environmental Protection Agency during the Carter Administration. He has served as counsel and policy analyst to the United States Senate and to other national and regional environmental agencies.

BENJAMIN LABAREE is Director of the Williams College–Mystic Seaport Program in American Maritime Studies, and former Ephraim Williams Professor of History at Williams College. Among his several books are *Colonial Massachusetts: A History* (Kraus-Thomson, 1979) and *Boston Tea Party* (Oxford, 1964).

MARK LAPPING is Professor and Director of the School of Rural Planning and Development, University of Guelph, in Canada. He was Associate Director of the University of Vermont Environmental Program and has been a consultant to the National Agricultural Lands Study and New England River Basin Commission. He recently contributed a chapter to *Farm and City* and is a frequent contributor to planning and resource journals.

F. HERBERT BORMANN is the Oastler Professor of Forest Ecology, School of Forestry and Environmental Studies, and Co-Director of the Hubbard Brook Ecosystems Study. He is senior research scientist in forest ecosystems, a member of the National Academy of Sciences, author of many research publications, and co-author with Gene Likens of *Pattern and Process in Forest Ecosystems*.

HENRY LEE is Executive Director of the Energy and Environmental Policy Center, Harvard University. He is the former Director of Energy and Special Assistant to the governor of Massachusetts. His most recent publications include "Role of Local Government in Promoting Energy Efficiency" in *Annual Review of Energy* (1981) and "Oil Shale Development," a paper of the Harvard center he now directs.

KENNETH GEISER is Assistant Professor, Department of Urban and Environmental Policy, Tufts University, and Director of the Center for the Study of Public Policy in Cambridge, Massachusetts. He has served as a social policy research consultant for the Institute for Judicial Administration and regional private and public agencies.

Library of Congress Cataloging in Publication Data
Main entry under title:

New England prospects.

(A Futures of New England book)
Contents: Alternatives in a time of change / Thomas Jorling—An historical
perspective / Benjamin W. Labaree—Toward a working rural landscape / Mark B.
Lapping—[etc.]
   1. Environmental policy—New England—Addresses, essays, lectures.
2. Natural resources—New England—Addresses, essays, lectures.   3. New
England—Economic conditions—Addresses, essays, lectures.   4. Quality of
life—New England—Addresses, essays, lectures.   I. Reidel, Carl H., 1937–
II. Series.
HC107.A11N3446   333.73'17'0974   81-51604
ISBN 0-87451-213-1   AACR2
ISBN 0-87451-220-4 (pbk.)